THE NEW ICONS?

To
Maggie O.,
who abhors commercials

PAUL RUTHERFORD

The New Icons?
The Art of
Television
Advertising

UNIVERSITY OF TORONTO PRESS
Toronto Buffalo London

© University of Toronto Press Incorporated 1994
Toronto Buffalo London
Printed in Canada

ISBN 0-8020-2928-0 (cloth)
ISBN 0-8020-7428-6 (paper)

Printed on acid-free paper

Canadian Cataloguing in Publication Data

Rutherford, Paul, 1944–
   The New Icons?

   Includes bibliographical references and index.
   ISBN 0-8020-2928-0 (bound) ISBN 0-8020-7428-6 (pbk.)

   1. Television advertising. I. Title.

HF6146.T42R8 1994   659.14'3   C93-094882-3

This book has been published with assistance from the Canada Council and the
Ontario Arts Council under their block grant programs.

Contents

List of Photographs

Acknowledgments

This project took shape only after Ernie Dick, then at the Public Archives of Canada, told me of the existence of the Bessie Collection of Television Commercials at the Cartographic and Audiovisual Archives in Ottawa. I was able to expand the project to include commercials from around the world because of a research grant from the Social Sciences and Humanities Research Council of Canada, supplemented by research funds from the Research Board of the University of Toronto and the Ontario Arts Council. This funding allowed me to purchase tapes of television ads and to visit depositories in North America, Britain, and France.

My research task was made easier by the goodwill and assistance of people in these depositories. Loretta de Sousa, the member services coordinator of the Television Bureau of Canada, arranged my purchase of the entire Bessie Collection at a reduced rate. The efforts of archives manager Philip F. Mooney at the Coca-Cola Company in Atlanta ensured my trip there would be productive; Phil also informed me of the existence of the Center of Advertising History in Washington. Maggie Shrubshall, the librarian of the Independent Television Association Film Library in London, gave me generous access to the library's extensive collection of British commercials and arranged a reduced charge for my viewing privileges. Mimi Minnick, the collections manager, prepared the way for my visit to the Center for Advertising History at the National Museum of American History, Smithsonian Institution.

There are a number of people I would also like to thank for their assorted kindnesses during the course of research: Caroline Forcier (Cartographic and Audiovisual Archives, National Archives of Canada), Professor Richard Pollay (History of Advertising Archives, University of British Columbia), Fred Stinson (AdFilms, Toronto), Laura Jester (Coca-Cola Archives), Joan Hafey (Young & Rubicam), Philip Messina (Television Centre, Brooklyn College of the City

University of New York), and Robert Scott (The Museum of Broadcasting).

I received permission to use photographs from commercials owned by a range of companies in Canada, the United States, Great Britain, and France. Some of these firms sent me tapes and stills, or instructed their advertising agencies to forward material. I acknowledge, with thanks, their willingness to allow the publication of this material:

Canada: Bell Canada; Campbell Soup Co. Ltd.; Chesebrough-Pond's Canada; Dairy Bureau of Canada; Kraft General Foods Canada Inc.; Labatt Brewing Company Ltd.; Levi Strauss & Co. (Canada) Inc.; London Life; Molson Breweries; Robin Hood Multifoods Inc.; Speedy Muffler King Inc.; Thomas J. Lipton Co.

United States: Apple Computer, Inc.; Bristol-Myers Squibb Co., Inc.; Chevron Corporation; Coca-Cola Company.; General Motors; Pepsi-Cola Co.; Pet Incorporated; Procter & Gamble Co.; S.C. Johnson & Son Inc.; Volkswagen United States, Inc.; Westinghouse Electric Corporation; Young & Rubicam, Inc.

Great Britain and France: Bass Brewers Ltd.; British Airways; C. & J. Clark Ltd.; Source Perrier; Volkswagen (United Kingdom) Ltd.; Whitbread Beer Co.

I received the generous help of people in advertising agencies when I went in search of photographs: Kevin Tedesco (Young & Rubicam, New York), Gary Croke and Guy Gostling (J. Walter Thompson, Toronto), Will Harris (Lowe Howard-Spink, London), and Karen Wiederer (McKim, Baker Lovick/BBDO, Toronto).

In many cases, however, it proved impossible to locate actual photographs or slides from the commercials. Even in the case of the famous 'Marlboro Country' campaign, for example, all that the Leo Burnett agency could supply were photographs used in a magazine campaign of the early 1970s. Consequently, I have captured black and white images from videotapes of the advertisements and reproduced these using a computer. That explains why the quality of these photographs is not always the best.

Once more I am fortunate to have had Virgil Duff as my editor at the University of Toronto Press. He and I have now collaborated on three books for the Press. It has been a happy and profitable association.

PAUL RUTHERFORD
March 1993

THE NEW ICONS?

Introduction: Ads as Art

We never forget that commercials have become icons for part of the American culture. We are a consumer-oriented society. Network TV is in the business of selling products, attracting the largest audiences to consume products. And because several generations have grown up with commercials an integral part of their lives, the TV commercial has become our folklore.
  – Scott Garen (Doylestown *Intelligencer*, 22 November 1983), co-producer of a historical compilation of TV ads intended to entertain Americans

Consider these three incidents:

Barcelona, May 1988: I was lying on the bed in my hotel room watching local television, much of which struck me as bland by comparison with all the flash and glitz of the North American product. Then on came a commercial for Panrico, a brand of sliced white bread, the name of which translates roughly as 'tasty bread.' What seemed so startling was just how familiar were the images, the announcer's enthusiasm, the air of frenzy. Though my understanding of Spanish was rudimentary, it was easy to decipher the meaning of this commercial: buy convenience, buy taste, buy modernity. The ad could have run in Canada, with the addition of an English or French voice-over. That started me thinking. Were commercials a global form of expression? Did they speak a language of consumption common everywhere, or at least everywhere the consumer society had established a foothold? Here was the seed from which the book grew a few years later.

New York, July 1990: I was in line just inside the lobby of the Museum of Broadcasting (now the Museum of Television and Radio), waiting to enter the library to view the Young & Rubicam collection of TV ads. I struck up a conversation with a fellow visitor. As we slowly moved forward, she glanced at a collection of museum leaflets announcing special evening showings, one of which was for a retrospective of American commercials. She was incredulous: why would anyone choose to watch commercials? When I wryly admitted my purpose, she hastily apologized for any insult – but I'm sure she remained convinced that I was a bit strange. I could sympathize, since years ago I too was amazed when a dinner guest baldly announced that what she really enjoyed on television was the commercials, not the programs. The point is that commercials do provoke a response from viewers, whether or not they are interested in the goods that are advertised.

Paris, February 1991: I was travelling up the escalator inside the peculiar snake-like passageway of the Centre Georges Pompidou to an exhibition entitled Art et Publicité, 1890–1990, which filled the whole of the fifth floor. How fitting that venue seemed: the Centre is an example of postmodern excess, reminiscent of an unfinished factory full of steel and glass, walkways and levels, and pipes all over – yet dedicated to the enjoyment of Culture. Where better to view a display that celebrated the liaison between two supposedly distinct, if not antagonistic, forms of expression?

Even though this was the last week of the exhibition, which had opened back in November, interest remained high. Just outside the actual entrance, crowds of young people had gathered around three separate sets of raised television monitors, two in each kiosk, to watch a selection of international commercials, many of them winners in the Cannes advertising festivals during the 1980s. Inside was a series of discrete sections devoted to the art and advertising of a particular period, explained by a text, via a voice-over, or through a film – a cornucopia of delights for the eye and the mind. Here were examples of the poster art of Toulouse-Lautrec and his contemporaries of the 1890s; Cubist collages of Picasso and Braque; evidence of how both Futurism and Dada were turned to the advertiser's purposes (including Fortunato Depero's extraordinarily imaginative campaign for Campari); an extensive survey of the ads and the paintings of the Surrealist René Magritte, creator of the Sabena 'bird' (who once declared he hated *la publicité*, even if it gave him a living); samples of commercial architecture, neon art, and the paintings of Andy Warhol and other Pop artists; and, finally, a jumble of TV ads (some, ironically, bereft of sound), tattered collages of posters or *affiches lacérées*, subversive ads like Hans Haache's *A Breed Apart* (1978), and bitterly ironic commentaries, such as Barbara Kruger's untitled *I Shop Therefore I Am* (1987), a favourite of mine.

An exhibition so rich in insight and so popular could only be counted a success – and further proof of success was the fact that it received a lengthy write-up in *Time* (17 December 1990). Still, I couldn't help feeling that the curators were playing coy with the public. For all the evidence of the linkages between painting and ads, the way artistic movements had penetrated the ad world and the way commerce had affected aesthetic conventions, the exhibition rested on the presumption that art and advertising constituted two quite separate domains. It embodied a long-held conceit of the apologists of High Culture that paintings, photographs, sculpture, collages, and the like must stand outside and above other, more common modes of expression if they are to be counted *as art*.

My book treats television commercials as though they were art, indeed 'the art of our times.' I recognize that this is like waving a red flag in front of some people, especially those for whom the word 'art' translates into 'treasure' or 'truth.' Art criticism and art history appear, at least to this novice, full of contention over just what art is, never mind whether something as lowly as advertising could fit within the definition. I have found particularly interesting one attempt to explain art, by an anthropologist: Ellen Dissanayake in *What Is Art For?* argues that art is a means of 'making special,' turning the ordinary into the extraordinary – which, by the way, is much like a slogan for Hellmann's, a brand of mayonnaise marketed in Canada. That notion of 'making special' fits my own approach. In the other camp are generations of hard-nosed ad-makers, as far back as the 1900s, who have been vehement in their claims that advertising is not, and should not be, a form of art, often preferring instead the appellation 'science.' I am not about to engage in any argument with such industry types: clearly they believe 'art' means 'frill,' something antithetical to business, and this is one accepted meaning of the word. Here I will follow in the footsteps of Marshall McLuhan, who declared, according to the *Time* story on the Paris exhibition, that advertising was 'the greatest art form of the 20th century.'

Let me break down that grand claim. Ads are an accidental art, born of necessity. Usually advertisers set out to finance the creation of a marketing tool, not a work of art. But ads bridge the gap between the world of symbols and the world of goods: they try to turn commodities into brands by bestowing special meanings (or an 'added value') upon a product. Advertising works its magic by using the tools of both spectacle and rhetoric to create pleasing images. The need to condense messages soon fostered a reliance on stereotype and metaphor, drawn from the wider realms of ordinary life and popular culture. Hence the old charge that ad-makers sell back to us our dreams – or is it our fears? – about status, sex, individuality, whatever. Many ads fashion a promise of transformation, taking the consumer from some state of grievance or inadequacy to a state of satisfaction, if not happiness. What I've found most striking about commercials is their penchant for contrasts. Ads strive to communicate through a form of binary logic. Now this logic doesn't operate in the same fashion as a digital computer, meaning you rarely find such contrasts as yes/no or human/ not human. Rather they employ antonyms such as ugly and beautiful, masculine and feminine, high and low, and so on. But the result is a simplified and compelling portrait of life that evokes an aesthetic response from consumers.

One Canadian survey of opinion in the late 1960s, the Martin Goldfarb report, discovered that seven out of ten respondents believed advertising was a kind of art. Exactly what kind of art depends upon who you ask. To the ad-makers and advertisers, advertising must be above all a *useful* form of art: the successful ad has to motivate consumers to do something, usually to make a purchase. A retired ad-maker told me recently how disgusted he was with all the bizarre and artsy flourishes, which he found much too prevalent in present-day commercials. To the critics, advertising is really an *evil* art: the advertisement works to instill a false understanding of life in its victims. Much of the academic literature on advertising, for example, reflects a distaste for hype, materialism, and capitalism that verges on the hysterical. To the public, advertising is the most *common* form of art: it is almost impossible in North America to escape advertising, whether at home, on the street, in the car or on the subway, at the doctor's office, at the movies, or anywhere else.

TV ads have become the most expensive and pervasive type of advertising in North America and western Europe since the end of the Second World War. Commercials can employ an extraordinary range of stimuli by using pictures, words, sounds, body language, gestures, and motion to speed their messages. Right from the beginning, they have utilized the most advanced methods of conveying visual information, whether animation in the 1950s or computer-generated graphics in the 1980s. At least since the mid-1960s, television advertising has proved an exceptionally flexible tool of communication, drawing upon a wide range of social and cultural resources to present messages in a pleasing fashion. You can find a commercial somewhere, sometime that serves as a spotlight upon an aspect of ordinary life, be it the tax audit, marriage, homecoming, partying, showing off, sexual display, or fast driving – although only recently have TV commercials begun to explore the dark side of life and death. Since 1980 a new wave of commercials has pioneered a kind of expression that is laden with fragmented images and touches of irony especially suited to the postmodern moment. In short, commercials have offered both realistic and crazed reflections of daily existence, of common fantasies, of accepted stereotypes, all of which make them the richest source of commentary on contemporary civilization.

I look upon commercials as akin to the icons of medieval Europe. The element of propaganda is inherent in both art forms: like the icon, the commercial is an instrument of cultural power, in this case of commerce rather than of a formal church, as well as an expression of a popular passion, consumption instead of Christianity. Commercials enjoy a privileged place in one of the most important institutions of contemporary life, namely, television, just as icons graced the walls of the cathedral. The making of commercials uses up much artistic time and talent, though only rarely do their creators become famous; similarly, the artisans who painted the icons usually remained anonymous. Commercials are highly stylized and cosmopolitan, and thus cut across boundaries of language and class, though, as with icons, it is possible to show how commercials express the particular styles or myths of a national culture. Icons display pictures of saints, acts of devotion, tales of martyrdom, all to exalt things spiritual; commercials display pictures of celebrities, acts of consumption, tales of satisfaction, all to exalt things material. The analogy can be carried too far: the icons were objects of worship, commercials are more often objects of disdain. Even so, it is a useful way of approaching the history of the art form.

This is a story of one kind of cultural power: how it was generated and stored, articulated and exercised, resisted as well as maintained. It encompasses findings on the production, distribution, consumption, and above all the form and content of television advertisements. The book concentrates on 'commercials of distinction,' meaning ads that have been singled out for some special merit. Some readers may think this approach is cheating because it focuses only on the best exemplars of television advertising. Here I conform more to the traditions of art history than social history or sociology: look at the most celebrated pieces of work to understand what was so creative, so significant about this art. I have surveyed roughly six thousand commercials, spanning the years between 1948 and 1992 and covering much of the globe, from Sweden to Hong Kong, Canada to Ecuador, France to South Africa. Many of my sample have won an award at an advertising festival (Canada's Bessies), others have been preserved by an archive (the 'Marlboro Country' campaign) or a museum (the Young & Rubicam exhibit) because they were deemed particularly significant, and still others, because a company (Coca-Cola) or a knowledgeable individual (Lincoln Diamant) considered them worthwhile. Most of the book is arranged into separate studies of the form and content of these collections: the resulting five chapters outline the history of the commercial, and of its cultural significance, as it moved from being an American to a global form of art. The last chapter explores the way people handle commercials; there I am especially intrigued by the aesthetic response to television advertising. An afterword amounts to a sort of 'reality check,' taking the reader through a quick trip to three cities in Europe to see how (and what) ads actually appear on the little screen. My technique of analysis is outlined in a special appendix, which has the further, subversive purpose of showing how readers can learn to enjoy ads of all kinds.

By now it should be obvious that this book is in no sense an exposé of some master conspiracy to buttress capitalism or to debauch the public mind. At times I too have the feeling that ad talk is everywhere: we're all followers and victims of 'the philosophy of Pierre Cardin,' in the words of a friend of mine. My argument in this book does contain a touch of irony. I repeat: *The New Icons?* employs the hypothesis that ads are 'the art of our times.' Accepting this hypothesis can easily lead to gloom and doom: it suggests a society so smitten with materialism that it will never escape the obsession with consumption, whatever the cost to the well-being of humanity or the planet. Proving this hypothesis, though, would require a very different and a much longer argument, which explored other forms of art common throughout the late twentieth century. It would also demand an extensive treatment of just what art is in our world, a question that cannot really be answered because 'art' is a term of approbation, whatever else it may be. Art is in the eye of the beholder: we give a special meaning to the assorted representations of beauty, life, and experience that we encounter each day. My task is to explore a largely neglected realm of artistic expression.

Consequently, I am more interested in what commercials *are* than what they *do*. I have become an aficionado of fine commercials: I take what might be considered a perverse delight in the artistry, the variety, and the splendour of these little works of imagination. That's why I record America's annual Super Bowl extravaganza, not because I relish the football game, which bores me, but because its huge audience makes it a vehicle for some of the best ads then current. (The highlight of the 1993 Super Bowl was a minute-and-a-half-long spoof of advertising in which Michael Jordan and Bugs Bunny save the earth's Air Jordans from thieving Martians – afterwards Nike promised to replay *Bugs & Michael* in the postgame show 'for those of you just watching this [game] for the commercials.') I think that people often 'read' these ads in ways that resist or undo the preferred meanings and the purposes of their makers, and even contradict the expectations of worried critics of advertising. Like many Americans, I enjoyed the wit, the cleverness, the intelligence, the special effects of the 'New Generation' campaign mounted by Pepsi-Cola in the United States from the mid-1980s into the early 1990s – but that has never shaken my addiction to its grand rival, Coke. I believe that commercials encourage the attributes of what is sometimes called a postmodern sensibility: cynicism and fascination, a taste for paradox and juxtaposition, for the play of images, a short-term perspective on life, as well as an acceptance of what has been called commodification. So even those readers who don't share my fascination, who lament that gospel of consumption sung so lustily by television advertising, might heed an old maxim: Know Thy Enemy.

I have dispensed with the footnotes common in most histories. Instead there are two final sections entitled 'Listing of Commercials' and 'Sources.' You will find in the 'Sources' a discussion of the chief primary and secondary sources used in my account, plus a briefer listing of supplementary references from which I have occasionally drawn material. Throughout the five chapters on the collections, there are coded references to specific commercials: a letter or letters to indicate the source, then a figure that identifies the year of the award (or sometimes the initial year of broadcast), and finally a number giving the location of the ad on the tape. For example, you would decode C90004 in this fashion: the 'C' indicates that the ad is part of the Cannes collection, '90' the award year, and '004' indicates the ad's position in the sequence of commercials on the tape. Other abbreviations are 'D' (the Diamant Collection of Classic Clios), 'Y' (the Young & Rubicam exhibit), 'B' (the Bessie tapes), and 'IS' (the International Showcase tapes).

1

The First Clios (1948–58)

In the late '40's and early 2'50's, as commercials came to golden flower, American life began to balance on a fulcrum of things. Things that could be bought, used, swallowed or puffed – all sold at a frantic pace day and night by the most accomplished practitioners of the huckster's art.
– Lincoln Diamant, *Television's Classic Commercials: The Golden Years*
1948–1958

Black and white pictures. A homely, fake-wood stage setting. Square-dance music. A loud caller telling the couples to 'circle,' 'allemand,' and 'promenade.' Is this a scene from an old-time country music show in the golden age of vaudeo? No, the couples are actually sixteen dancing cigarettes, photographed using the stop-motion technique. They swing through the steps of the square dance in neat formation, under the command of another cigarette, the caller, standing on a box of Lucky Strikes. Aired in 1948, *Barn Dance* (D4801) was a bouncy little ad for one of the leading brands of cigarettes of the day – 'Smoke'em, smoke'em; then you'll see: LS, LS, MFT! (Lucky Strike … Means Fine Tobacco).' (Forty-eight, the first figure in the code, represents the first year the commercial was broadcast.)

That is the first ad featured on the tape of the Celia Nachatovitz Diamant Memorial Library of Classic Television Commercials. The collection of sixty-eight ads came about because in 1959 or 1960, Wallace Ross, the founder of the Clios, called together a group of thirty-four ad-makers and clients to select the best commercials over the previous decade. Later the veteran 'adman' Lincoln Diamant wrote up the collection in a 1971 book that reproduced the video and audio script of each of the winners.

What possible meanings could *Barn Dance* have, other than a hokey celebration of good times? Even this attack of cute, though, is an entry into a 'world we have lost,' a time of innocence in the history of the consumer society when people en masse seemingly shared in the joys and pleasures of the postwar economy of abundance. This was a time when Vice-President Richard Nixon, visiting an American exhibition in Moscow in 1959, could point reporters from around the world (in the words of historian Lary May) 'to a well-stocked ranch-style home, complete with kitchen appliances, as proof of capitalism's superiority to communism.'

In the Beginning

Like so much else in the twentieth century, commercials were born in the U.S.A. New York's WEAF broadcast the first sponsored message on radio in 1922, and New York's WNBT carried the first TV spot in 1941. The commercial was widely seen as a surrogate for the salesman, so prominent a figure in American mythology, which was why it excited the imagination and greed of advertisers. Initially the commercial amounted to little more than a radio message with pictures, featuring talking heads and lots of words. But that soon changed. Much time and attention was lavished on improving the new art form, especially after the early 1950s, when TV surpassed radio as an advertising medium. The live spot gave way to the filmed ad, animation briefly enjoyed a lot of favour, and after 1956 came experiments with videotape. One expert stood out: Horace Schwerin, who ran a theatre on New York's Sixth Avenue, where he tested commercials. Schwerin waged war against what he saw as bad commercials: he insisted on clarity and simplicity, a unified impression, logic or emotion (but not both), an emphasis on video (show not tell), involvement of the viewer (highlight the benefits), and a definite sell (don't hide the message). Agencies listened because commercials had become the most expensive item on TV. By 1960 the cost of producing a filmed ad was reaching $10,000 to $20,000 a minute, whereas the budget for a telefilm was around $2,000 a minute.

Americans soon exported their know-how to other lands, notably via international agencies like J. Walter Thompson and Young & Rubicam. Schwerin's maxims and his tests proved popular in both Canada and Great Britain – Canada's *Marketing* magazine was forever publishing his lists of do's and don'ts for its readers. New York remained the chief production centre for filmed and animated commercials made for Canadian audiences throughout the 1950s. The first British TV commercial, *Ice Mountain* for Gibbs toothpaste, created by Young & Rubicam and aired in September 1955, was indistinguishable in style from American ads. According to the American Burton Paulu, writing in 1961, however different an American visitor might find British television, he or she would have little difficulty understanding British ads. As late as 1971, Lincoln Diamant could still observe that German commercials were 'stodgy carbon copies of U.S. work.' The American form had gone international, though the Americans remained its masters.

The reason for American mastery was fundamentally economic. No country had moved so fast to develop mass television as had the United States: by 1960 three nationwide networks plus 515 stations offered a huge variety of programming to 45,750,000 households (or 87.1 per cent of all homes). Canada ran a close second as a land conquered by TV: according to the Census of 1961, there were 3,750,000 TV households (82.5 per cent of the total) – more households had a set than their own baths or showers, flush toilets, furnace heating, or cars. In contrast, outside of North America, there were many more stations (1,488) but slightly fewer TV sets (42,950,000), and over half of these were located in western Europe.

Like radio before, television in America was controlled by private, commercial networks and their affiliates, which exploited the airwaves to generate what became super profits by satisfying the taste for escapism and selling the resulting audiences to major advertisers. At the end of the decade, the industry was earning over $1.5 billion a year in ad revenues, making TV the leading medium in national advertising. According to the annual report of the Federal Communications Commission, pretax profits in 1960 for the networks (including their owned and operated stations) stood at $95.2 million and $148.9 million for all other stations. Success had its costs, though. In 1961 Newton Minow, the newly appointed chair of the Federal Communications Commission, shocked his audience of broadcasters and excited the imagination of journalists by calling television 'a vast wasteland.' Why? Because American TV offered only a dreary display of trivia, vulgarity, violence, boredom, 'and, endlessly, commercials – many screaming, cajoling and offending.' Mammon ruled the airwaves.

The American example became both a promise and a warning to decision-makers outside the United States. Few countries allowed such unfettered commercial exploitation of the new medium. True, early in the 1950s private interests introduced TV to Mexico, Brazil, Cuba, Argentina, and Venezuela, relying heavily upon American expertise, investment, and sometimes programming to win audiences. And business did pioneer TV in the Philippines in 1953, Luxembourg in 1955 (where commercial broadcasting had a long history), Iran (1958), Nigeria (1959), and Lebanon (1959). In Third World countries, only local entrepreneurs and foreign businessmen were willing to invest the monies and time to build television.

Elsewhere the state tried to avoid the perils of commercialism. At first the

British Broadcasting Corporation (BBC) was granted a monopoly, funded by licence fees, to create a kind of television that would embody the rival notion of public service. Public, noncommercial systems were also launched in France (1948), Switzerland and Belgium (1953), Holland and Scandinavia (mid-1950s), and of course in the communist world. But other governments decided that they could not afford to follow so pure a course. In 1949 the Canadian government gave the Canadian Broadcasting Corporation (CBC) authorization to introduce television (begun in 1952), though it was compelled to supplement public monies with ad revenues and to work with privately owned affiliates. Variations of such a mixed system were launched in Italy and West Germany (1953), Spain (1956), Finland (1958), and Austria (1959) after an initial experiment using licence fees only. Italy consigned most ads to a nightly segment called 'Carosello,' while West Germany jammed commercials into a single twenty-minute period. A third group of countries established competing public and private TV. Japan started such a dual system in 1953, and that same year Australia authorized a similar partnership. A year later, Britain's Conservative government ended the BBC monopoly and established a closely regulated commercial ITV – the result of much lobbying and agitation by a coalition in which J. Walter Thompson and other agencies played a key role. Similarly in 1960 Canadian Conservatives allowed the establishment of an independent, wholly commercial service, the so-called second stations and the CTV network, to satisfy the consumer demand for choice.

Overall the cause of public broadcasting had clearly lost ground. Public funds just weren't sufficient to generate rapid growth: in France, for example, TV was a very slow starter (as late as 1965 France had only 6.5 million sets to Britain's 13.5 million). Those public broadcasters using advertising soon discovered that they must tailor programming to suit the mass taste: this proved a special problem for CBC programmers in English Canada, who were compelled by popular demand and fiscal need to turn over much of primetime to American imports. One Canadian nationalist, Graham Spry, writing in the *Queen's Quarterly* (Winter 1960–1), concluded that Canadian television was 'essentially an imitation or replica of the American system,' especially at night when it was used 'to sell goods, most of them American goods.' Where competition reigned, the public broadcaster found that audiences preferred the offerings of the private rival, commercials and all: as early as 1956, ITV secured a commanding lead over the BBC in the ratings, often as much as two to one. Little wonder that the television program companies were soon able to produce super profits, Associated-Rediffusion earning in 1960 a pretax profit (£7,850,000) that was itself more than 100 per cent of issued share capital.

So Minow's charges could apply, with some licence, to commercial TV around the globe. The priority of profit meant that producers had to submit to the will of the advertisers. Sometimes that resulted in censorship, as Eric Barnouw has recalled: the noted American playwright Rod Serling changed his story about the lynching of a black boy so as not to offend Southern viewers, a 'Playhouse 90' script on the Nuremberg trials was stripped of references to the use of gas in death chambers to avoid upsetting the sponsor (the natural gas industry), a manufacturer of filter cigarettes insisted villains on its sponsored series must smoke nonfilter cigarettes, and so on. The agency handling the General Motors account objected to so many scripts that the CBC's play anthology 'General Motors Presents' earned the nickname 'General Motors Prevents.' More important, programs were built around commercials – even the famed teleplays, according to the historian Kenneth Hey – to ensure that viewers were in the right frame of mind to receive the commercials. Not only did the presence of commercials interrupt the enjoyment of a program, the clusters themselves shaped the episode and the series by breaking the programs into discrete segments. The priority of profit meant that commercial interests preferred shows which secured the largest ratings, not shows which pleased highbrows or offered much stimulation. Advertising was as much the master as the servant of mass TV.

Hard Sell/Soft Sell

The Diamant Collection is not typical of the thousands and thousands of American commercials aired during the 1950s. The judges were given a list of criteria (believability, tastefulness, longevity, influence, etc.) to apply to select the best examples of television selling. One must surmise that the mysteries of individual taste as well as committee compromise determined what ads finally appeared in the winners' circle. There isn't a single ad from the largest agency, J. Walter Thompson, and just one commercial from the powerful Ted Bates agency. That agency was guided by Rosser Reeves, the chief theoretician of advertising in the 1950s, who touted the virtues of hard-hitting ads that emphasized the Unique Selling Proposition (USP) of a brand. Indeed only about half of the ads suit the designation 'hard sell,' where the commercial tries to confront and coerce a viewer, the other half falling into the 'soft sell' camp, where the commercial tries to seduce the viewer. That finding doesn't bear out the prevailing assumption that the fifties was the grand era of the hard sell.

The Diamant Collection is not eccentric, however. The sixty-eight ads cover such leading product groups as alcoholic and nonalcoholic beverages, food, automobiles and automobile accessories, tobacco, household products and appliances, health and beauty, even consumer services. Match this list with the top six in terms of advertising expenditures on TV in 1958: health and beauty ($258 million), food ($234.5 million), household products ($132.5 million), tobacco ($93 million), automotive ($81.5 million), and beverages ($69.5 million). There are samples from such major agencies as Young & Rubicam (nine ads), McCann-Erickson (six), Foote, Cone & Belding (five), Benton & Bowles (three), and Leo Burnett (two), as well as from lesser-known agencies like General Motors' Campbell-Ewald (five) or Gillette's Maxon Inc. (three). And these Clios are similar to other American and Canadian commercials I have found randomly preserved in the programming of the 1950s. So the collection does strike me as indicative of the range of techniques and approaches employed in those first heady years of television advertising.

The contemporary eye will find these Clios quaint and at times unintentionally funny – the students I've shown samples to often laugh at the blatant hype of these pioneers. One obvious difference is that the ads are in black and white, which drastically limited their ability to appear realistic or convey sensuality: Clairol's marvellous *Does She … Or Doesn't She?* (D5724), for example, could use only shading to suggest the transformation of a woman's lifeless hair into lustrous hair. Another difference is the length of some of these ads: the live *Chicken Zoop* (D5426), delivered by Arthur Godfrey for Lipton Soup, is almost a skit because it lasts for over four minutes. Most of the ads ran sixty seconds or more, which allowed ad-makers the time to explain or portray a brand's virtues in a leisurely fashion. Their creations lack the economy of means that became so characteristic after 1960. A third distinction is the wordiness of so many ads, hard or soft sell, a legacy from radio: sometimes it was a loud-mouthed announcer, sometimes a lusty singer who went on and on to ensure the viewer got the message. They can't resist telling us what's new, what's happening. All in all, these Clios are much less sophisticated and visual, much more didactic and blunt, and a good deal more intrusive than their successors.

One of the major shifts of the era was from the live to the filmed ad, a move that actually increased costs since a live ad was usually much cheaper. At its best the live commercial could seem spontaneous and immediate, and offered the sponsor the services of the show's star who, presumably, had already established a rapport with the audience. *Soap Opera* (D5510) used Garry Moore and two of his sidekicks in a funny spoof of Wagnerian opera to deliver a message about the convenience and potency of S.O.S. pads – Moore so enjoyed himself that he thanked McCann-Erickson on air for the script. But such a success was not preserved for another showing, and there was never a guarantee that a later performance would equal its initial freshness. Besides, a live commercial might be flubbed: June Graham, a spokesperson for Westinghouse, was nearly defeated in <u>Can</u> You Be Sure …? (D5461) when the door of the refrigerator she

Figure 1.1: _Can You Be Sure ...?_ One of the staples of the fifties was the product display where an earnest spokesperson showed the consumer just how marvellous the brand really was. So prosaic an approach embodied the idea that the commercial was a surrogate for the 'salesman.' Here June Graham extols the virtues of a Westinghouse refrigerator. This ad, by the way, had no title when aired live in 1954 – TV ads were more a form of commercial news than commercial art then. Lincoln Diamant used 'Can You Be Sure ... ?' in his book, and the ad itself was entered in the Clio's U.S. Classic Hall of Fame under the title 'The Stuck Door.' (Courtesy of Westinghouse Electric Corporation)

was praising stubbornly refused to open until forced by an unseen assistant. That kind of failure could only provoke laughter at the expense of the advertiser.

The switch to film ensured ad-makers more control over the look and feel of the commercial, allowing them to leave the TV studio to shoot anywhere money could take them. That switch was necessary to enhance the artistic properties of commercials, since only film and, later, videotape could free the imagination of ad-makers to represent whatever seemed appropriate to their purpose. An immediate result was an escape from the constraints of radiovision: the directors could now indulge in all kinds of visual play to catch the viewer's eye. That explained why animation was so popular with all kinds of advertisers, not just manufacturers of kids' products: the twenty-four Clios using animation, in whole or in part, included ads for Winston, Black Label beer, Bank of America, Skippy peanut butter, Heinz Worcestershire Sauce, Pepsodent toothpaste, Raid, the Yellow Pages, and so on. Animated spots could indulge in all kinds of shenanigans that just weren't possible using the cameras and the editing of the day. Other advertisers tried such techniques as stop-motion, where the object was moved slightly after each frame-at-a-time exposure; step-printing photography, where objects leave behind a visual echo as they move;

multiple screens and extreme close-ups; or speeded-up motion. Foote, Cone & Belding's *Good Manners* (D5712) actually miniaturized a butler to extol the virtues of Kleenex napkins. From the beginning the making of commercials drove ad-makers to experiment with the most novel methods of producing visual images.

Likewise, they soon fashioned a host of different vehicles, often borrowed from the offerings of TV and other popular media, in which to house their messages. One small group of ads showed the influence of vaudeo, the best of these, *Somewhat Subliminal* (D5866), using Pat Boone and Dinah Shore to sing the praises of the '59 Chevy in a spoof of the scare over subliminal advertising. By contrast Bardahl financed an animated minidrama (D5350), based on Jack Webb's hit cop show *Dragnet*, to sell the merits of its automobile oil. Detroit's Grant Advertising created for Chrysler a news documentary set to ballad music, called *I Built Me a Dodge* (D5536), which now seems both pretentious and funny. Westinghouse (D5662) and RCA (D5459) presented demonstrations of their superiority over rivals, and Bulova Watches offered what may be the first ever torture test (later associated with Timex) when in *Over the Falls* (D5560) its Clipper went through the punishing waters of Niagara Falls to emerge 'still ticking away!' Then there were the testimonials: whether generic, such as *Smoker* (D5505) for Philip Morris, which (in a foretaste of the 'Marlboro Country' campaign) featured a 'real man,' tattoo and all, working on his car; or celebrity, like *Sporting Shaves* (D5521) for Gillette Safety Razors with baseball stars Roy Campanella, Don Zimmer, and Pee Wee Reese to show boys how grand shaving was.

The prominence of demonstrations and testimonials highlighted one of the distinctive features of the era, namely the reliance upon a strategy of reason-why, which treated the viewer as a rational consumer who liked argument and proof. Well over half the Clios used reason-why more than emotion or irony, and this strategy was especially common in ads for health and beauty aids, household products, tobacco, and appliances. A classic of the type was the minute-long spot *The Great A & B Race* (D5215) to demonstrate how Bufferin was better than ordinary aspirin. The commercial mixes live action and animation, overlaid images, superimposed text, an apparent comparison, and a lot of words. It opens with a picture of sticks beating on a drum, upon which is superimposed the face of a man in obvious distress. Meanwhile, the announcer asks, 'Headache throbbing like a drum? Don't let it last and last! Get quick relief with Bufferin. It's fast … fast … fast!' That promise is proved a moment later when two diagrams of tummies appear on the screen, one labelled ASPIRIN and the other BUFFERIN. The pills drop down, creating *A*s and *B*s, which struggle to get out through a trapdoor into the bloodstream. The *B*s naturally do it first

Figure 1.2: *The Great A & B Race*. Health ads were famous for their little stories of distress and relief. This image is a classic 'before' shot: people could see how the ills of a headache had upset the mood and mind of this poor man. (Courtesy of Bristol-Myers Squibb Co. Inc.)

and fastest, transforming themselves into *Os*, presumably bringing speedy relief to the sufferer. All the while the announcer tells how Bufferin's special formula makes this miracle possible, and without upsetting 'your stomach as aspirin often does.' At the end we see, now in live action, a few clips of a man taking a pill, before closing on a shot of the bottle of Bufferin.

Consider two elements of *The Great A & B Race*. Both were common to the hard sell, and not unknown among soft-sell ads in the reason-why camp. The announcer spoke in a style I can only label as earnest enthusiasm, loudly and incessantly hyping the product's virtues. In *The Great A & B Race* the announcer was unseen, a voice of authority, as he was (and rarely was the disembodied voice a she) in such other examples as *Killer Raid* (D5611), Chesterfield's *Smoking Cowboys* (D5708), or Johnson & Johnson's *Boil an Egg* (D5617) for Band-Aid. But in other spots the announcer could be a macho smoker (the Marlboro ad), a mannered butler (Kleenex), a hardbitten news-caster (Bulova Watches), a supercompetent and ever-polite Betty Furness or

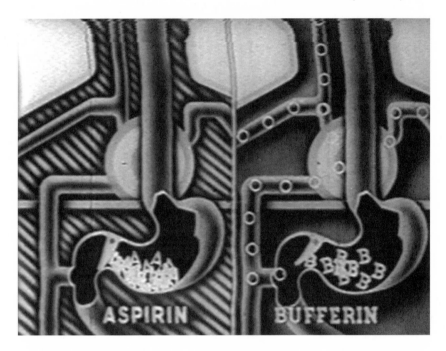

Figure 1.3: *The Great A & B Race.* Comparative advertising on television was rare in the 1950s. But the vigorous battle for market share in the patent medicine industry made ad-makers innovative. So Young & Rubicam give viewers a neat image of just how fast Bufferin was in delivering relief to the tummies of two headache sufferers. (Courtesy of Bristol-Myers Squibb Co. Inc.)

June Graham (Westinghouse), some happy pixies (Ajax), a friendly clown (Ked's Shoes), even a slightly mysterious female spy (New Mum's Cream Deodorant). Either way, the reason-why ad featured an aggressive, insistent salesman whose manner and occasional presence worked to compel the viewer's attention.

The salesman strove to involve the viewer through the use of direct address. Direct address could mean eye contact: Bulova Watches' newscaster or Westinghouse's Furness stared straight into the camera, and so into the face of the mass audience. That was supposed to convey honesty and enhance credibility. Then there was the repetition of the word 'you' and its variations, a most useful tactic in English because 'you' is both universal and intimate. *The Great A & B Race* referred to 'you' twice, and added 'your stomach' as well. Alka-Seltzer's talking tablet called 'Speedy' (D5316) in a commercial of the same name used

Figure 1.4: *Life of a Baby*. It was a commonplace belief among ad-makers that the image of a baby was sure to capture the attention of female viewers. Gardner Advertising went a step further here to show the obvious affection of a mother for her baby. That kind of juxtaposition of image and brand worked well: Pet milk became a surrogate for a mother's love. (Courtesy of Pet Incorporated)

'you' eight times, and included such claims as 'you know' and 'you bet.' Finally, direct address might require the use of questions, like 'How are you fixed for blades?' repeated three times by Gillette's parrot in *How 'R Ya Fixed* (D5219), or short imperatives, like 'Get Speedy Alka-Seltzer for fast relief ... ' or 'So don't buy several bug-killers. Get Raid ...' The whole purpose was to make the consumer think of his or her needs and to prod that person to make the purchase. At its worst, though, direct address amounted to a method of hammering the message into the mind of the hapless viewer.

The emotion of the mood ad was a striking contrast to the logic of the hammerhead school. Only a quarter of the Clios used emotion first and foremost, notably four of the six automobile ads and eight of the eleven beverage ads, where the appeal was to the heart as well the mind. In the parlance of the craft and the social sciences, the mood ad treated the consumer as irrational or illogical, though that criticism discounts the importance of metaphor. Interpreting the mood commercial required another kind of reasoning, an appreciation of association, analogy, and symbol. The classic of this type was the minute-long *Life of a Baby* (D5533) for Pet Evaporated Milk. Instead of a rapid sequence of different shots, *Life of a Baby* has only five separate visual images; instead of a torrent of words, there is Brahms's Lullaby and only near the end a short twenty-four word message by a voice-over. *Life of a Baby* opens with a medium shot of a sleeping baby, the very picture of innocence. That picture dissolves into a second medium shot of the awakened baby in the mother's arms, which dissolves into a similar shot of mother and child from a slightly different angle: he plays with her face and she laughs and loves him. Then a dissolve back to the picture of the sleeping baby: roughly midway through this scene, the announcer says, 'Your baby. Yours to love, protect, care for.' As he goes on to tell the viewer to get 'the best of milk,' the scene shifts through a V-wipe (an expanding V shape erases the old to reveal the new) to focus upon a picture of the product and a nursing bottle. The announcer concludes, 'Ask your doctor about Pet Evaporated Milk.'

One element of this strategy was a pleasant tone – thus the Brahms's Lullaby. Ogilvy & Mather achieved the same end by using classical music in *Was It Paris?* (D5545) for Schweppes Quinine Water. The tone persists throughout the conversation between an upscale Commander Edward Whitehead and a glamorous mystery woman about a past meeting, and the virtues of 'Schweppervescence.' Even soft sells using reason-why adopted this congenial pose: a mellow Arthur Godfrey (*Chicken Zoop*) or a relaxed Rex Marshall for Maxwell House Instant Coffee (D5639) strove to seduce the viewer.

But mood ads were normally richer in metaphor than their logical rivals. Consider *Life of a Baby*: the visual cliché of the sleeping baby conjured up images of vulnerability and the pictures of baby playing with mom an idealization of motherhood. The much heavier *Bear Beer* (D5242) for 'Hamms, the beer refreshing' used a bear, live and animated outdoors scenes, 'Indian' music, the label 'The Land of Sky Blue Waters,' all to evoke some mythological northland, the home of purity. The very lengthy *Alcan Champs* (D5664) tried to create an epic poem out of its documentary about the way a fleet of Chevrolet trucks had successfully conquered the Alcan highway: the screen was full of scenes of tough driving, the soundtrack boasted trumpet flourishes and a chorus, and the announcer Joel Aldred spoke in rhyme *à la* Robert Service. The purpose was to animate the trucks, to make them heroes in the age-old story of man's conquest of Nature.

Both hard and soft sells could use humour to support their spiel. In fact roughly half of these Clios had at least a touch of humour. One especially popular approach was to highlight a funny stand-in for the brand, particularly an imaginary animal whose madcap actions could entertain: Alka-Seltzer's 'Speedy,' Kroger Eggs' chicken, Gillette's parrot, Kools' penguin, or Hamms's bear. Humour served to disarm the viewer. Only nine commercials went a step further to employ a strategy of irony, though. The ironic ad positioned the viewer as a knowing consumer, an experienced veteran who was familiar with the ways of hype. Witness the animated *They Oughta' Advertise* (D5853), a sixty-second ad made by Batten, Barton, Durstine & Osburn (BBDO) to move Standard Oil of California into the national market and to mark the change of its brand name to Chevron. Like most of the animated advertising of the day, the visuals are simple, stark, semiabstract. Crucial to the humour is the contrast between the video and audio dimensions of the commercial. While an earnest and enthusiastic voice-over explains how excited the American motorist had been when the news of Chevron Supreme hit the market, our hero 'Hy Finn' remains blasé, walking through the routine of his day – that is, until he fills his gas can at a Chevron pump. Then, while the announcer extols 'the invisible bond' between motorist and Chevron, Finn rips the pump off its base and carries it to the back seat of his car. Does that mean he has been won over by the advertising? No. While driving down the highway, Finn still ignores the Chevron signs in the background and proclaims, 'They oughta advertise it.'

One feature of the ironic ad, often apparent in humorous spots as well, was a taste for exaggeration, incongruity, and in particular the absurd. The American viewer knew that Hy Finn didn't really make off with the Chevron pump. That same understanding operated for *Soup Twins* (D5737), where two workers split the peas for Andersen Soups, as well as Bank of America's twenty-second marvel, *Instant Money* (D5554), where the obliging manager pours a cup of instant money to quiet the jangled nerves of a customer.

These ironic ads often took the shape of a satire, at times a satire of advertising itself. *They Oughta' Advertise* spoofed both the earnest enthusiasm of the announcer and the indifference of the consumer. Heinz's $%&()* (D5428) mocked the pompous spokesman who couldn't pronounce the words 'Worcestershire Sauce' properly. One in a series of animated ads for Piel Bros. beer featuring the voices of radio comedians Bob Elliott and Ray Goulding, *Bert & Harry* (D5544) poked fun at the celebrity testimonial: the loud Bert mistranslated the comment of a French-speaking hockey star to hype the virtues of Piel's. Diamant reported that the series was enormously popular with viewers, but failed to sell much brew, making it an 'object lesson' of the dangers inherent in creating too entertaining an ad. Even so, the self-satire was a clever way of stroking the collective ego of consumers by exploiting the suspicion of hype to get across some message about the brand.

Figure 1.5: *They Oughta' Advertise.* Then and later, ad-makers have loved to show how enthusiastic are users of the brand advertised. This kind of excess, apparently, is proof of the brand's virtues. Such a display of excitement is mocked in this image where the happy driver has actually taken the Chevron gas pump back to his car. (Courtesy of the Chevron Corporation)

Diamant argued that the Classic Clios reveal 'the seedtime of a permanent TV style.' That judgment was substantially correct. Hard sell and soft sell, straight talk and funny talk, reason-why and emotion and irony, a taste for special effects, all would persist in later years. But never again would animation enjoy such great favour among ad-makers. The acting and the voice-over in live-action spots were so often overdone that they looked staged rather than natural – the ad-makers may have mastered hyperbole, but not subtlety or wit. Most important, the Classic Clios worked to extol the virtues of the product, less so to highlight the user, and few paid much attention to lifestyle. Many of them were caught up in the craze for things and the pose of loud belief that characterized the public rhetoric of the 1950s: gee-whiz, they said, look at this amazing cleanser, that brand of gasoline, the new model cars for 1958, and so on. Such a quaint enthusiasm for the brand, label it an idolatry of goods, was even more pronounced in other, more ordinary ads I have found embedded in the programs of the time. The move to the abbreviated commercial and the dominance of colour would bring in their wake an increasing emphasis upon both the user and the lifestyle. The revival of public cynicism in later decades would compel ad-makers to explore other ways, notably humour and the bizarre, to win over the consumer. There are two more reasons why the Classic Clios seem to be the equivalent of naif or primitive art in the history of television advertising.

Exploring the Affluent Society

When John Kenneth Galbraith published *The Affluent Society* at the end of the 1950s, he added a new phrase to the language. Galbraith wasn't being complimentary to his country. He saw America as a land of abundance where private goods were valued over public goods, where the leaders emphasized individual satisfactions rather than social justice. The Classic Clios are a valuable guide to understanding this affluent society. That doesn't mean these sixty-eight commercials mirrored the realities of the 1950s. Rather, they reflected many of the assumptions, aspirations, and by implication anxieties of the social mainstream. Put briefly, these ads presumed a classless and homogenized America in which satisfied folk lived a life closely defined by family, age, gender, and above all consumption. Living here was like being trapped in a script for the hit sitcom 'Leave It to Beaver.' There is a charming simplicity and wholesomeness about this America, especially in the light of the world later commercials of distinction would portray.

   Let's take a close look at life in one Clio. General Motors' *Boy Meets Impala* (D5868) was an elaborately produced two-minute mood commercial, boasting a very soft sell for the new Impala. Much of the meaning of the ad was conveyed through body language since the announcer only uttered twenty-one words. *Boy Meets Impala* tells the story of how a son gets his father's Impala to take his date to the high-school prom. Everything is supposed to be standard American: whites only; middle-aged, comfortable parents; a teenage boy and a younger sister; a blonde girlfriend; a private home; a suburban setting. Going to the prom is one of the rituals of high-school life, an occasion for looking good, which explains why the teenager is dressed up and carrying a corsage. He can go in his own hot-rod, an ugly looking black jalopy with scrawled white lettering on the outside. But that vehicle hardly suits the occasion. Fortunately, further down the driveway, there is an Impala convertible: a long, low, gleaming, white machine that seems to shout glamour; he yearns to drive the car. Father shakes his head, but mother and daughter give him imploring looks. Father smiles and hands over the keys. Son rejoices, blows a kiss at mom, thanks dad, even kisses sister (a bit reluctantly), and jumps into the Impala. The action

Figure 1.6: *Boy Meets Impala.* In retrospect, the American car enjoyed its greatest fame as a symbol of modernity and glamour back in the 1950s. Here are two shots of an Impala that everyone was supposed to admire. (Courtesy of Lintas:Campbell-Ewald and Chevrolet Division, General Motors)

then shifts to the inside of the Impala where our young hero is driving with his beautiful date beaming happily beside him. He's proud and she's impressed. After finally parking outside the high school, his date gives one last admiring look at the Impala. 'What a gal. What a night. What a car,' says the announcer.

This snapshot of Americana opens up a wealth of avenues to explore. It probably won't come as any shock that the ad-maker's America was almost uniformly white and Anglo. Only in one Clio, *I Built Me a Dodge,* was there a brief shot of a black face. There were few traces of ethnicity, although Speedway 79's *Dry Bones* (D5442) made use of the 'Negro spiritual' of the same name to enliven its animated display of how a car operated. The famous *Chinese Baby* for Jell-O (D5766) did offer a funny stereotype of an exotic infant saved from starvation by the Western invention of the spoon, complete with an announcer speaking with a fake Chinese accent. Nor is it surprising that the occasional Clio which suggested place presumed all Americans lived, or wished to live, in the suburbs in a single-family dwelling, preferably a ranch-style house. The family portrayed in *Boy Meets Impala* was supposed to be representative of all Americans, or rather all affluent Americans with money to spend. By and large, the Clios did not make class appeals (something very common in ads of the 1920s, by contrast) but called upon consumers to emulate the habits of so-called average Americans. Conformity was a virtue in a society where class consciousness had apparently lost its force and just about everyone could enjoy the democracy of goods.

Where the Clio's version of reality might not fit expectations was in its fascination with the group. Outside of the testimonials, and a few other ads (notably Marlboro's *Smoker*), the commercials showed little interest in hyping the individual. The actors were nearly always represented as part of a team, a couple, and above all a family. Togetherness was more than just a shibboleth: Americans were depicted as social beings, their identities defined by the stage on which they acted and the people with whom they mixed. David Riesman's 'other-directed' personality had triumphed in this America where people were moved by social cues (and hopefully advertising) rather than by some individual will. 'Today ... all little pigs go to market,' suggested Riesman in a reinterpretation of the old nursery rhyme; 'none stay home; all have roast beef, if any do; and all say "we-we."'

Consider the way in which the family operated. There were well-defined rules at work here, conventions about what was right, plus a kind of hierarchy that allowed different persons some power or privilege. One source of personal and social definition was age. Kids were allowed a certain licence to play and disobey. A topless girl frolics in the sand at the beach, while her ever-smiling mom hangs out the clothes to dry in Procter & Gamble's weird fantasy of washing, *Cleanest Clean* (D5814). In General Motors' *Brand New Door* (D5867), a girl sticks out her tongue at a boy who responds by pulling down his eyelids. The boy in *I Want My Maypo* (D5636) becomes a brat, resisting the efforts of his father to feed him the new cereal. But the adults reign supreme in the end. The dad of *Boy Meets Impala* grants his son the special privilege of driving the Impala, which brings a prompt expression of gratitude: the son pumps dad's hand and the daughter hugs dad. The adults, or at least one of them, are competent, ready with advice and an answer to every problem. In *John & Marsha* (D5634), it's Marsha's aged mother who gives the worried housewife the secret to baking a light cake, namely Snowdrift shortening. There is no sign here of any serious generation gap.

The more important source of definition, however, was clearly gender, not age. There is a lingering Victorian flavour to the idealized home. Like so much of popular culture, these Classic Clios embodied a highly sexist view of men and women with roots that stretched back to the nineteenth century. Even in the ad world, where women were so valued as the chief buyers of the household, men were more often represented than women: males appeared in fifty-seven of the Clios, but women only in thirty-three. In theory, woman's domain was the home, man's domain the workplace. Certainly women were not shown going out to work or being active in the office, even though the percentage of women in the labour force rose in the fifteen years after 1945. Rather, they were portrayed in the kitchen, the bathroom, the living-room, the backyard, and so on. Yet even at home they might play second fiddle: recall that it is dad, not mom, who grants son the Impala. On the other hand, mom and daughter

Figure 1.7: *Meet Mr. Clean.*® Fifties television offered the homemaker a host of assorted male helpers to ease her tasks: Tony the Tiger, the Pillsbury Dough Boy, the Jolly Green Giant, and other such cartoon characters. Procter & Gamble Co. introduced a friendly and very masculine genie in 1958 to represent its new All Purpose Cleaner. This expert could make everything in the house shine like new. Indeed Mr. Clean® swiftly became one of the most formidable weapons in the North American war on dirt. (© The Procter & Gamble Company. Printed by permission.)

exercise 'feminine' (meaning emotional) power to melt dad's resistance. Similarly, the family's purchase of a new Chevy in *Brand New Door* isn't certified till the mother becomes enthralled by its style and utility. The father is clearly the official head of the household, the mother often the power behind the throne.

There was a further twist here. Almost invariably the experts who advised women on the virtues of new household products were men. Thus in Procter & Gamble's *Meet Mr. Clean*® (D5813) the female singer asks the questions and the male singer supplies the answers. It is Kleenex's well-mannered butler who explains to the befuddled and gullible mother the virtues of the new napkins. The three marvellous pixies for Ajax Cleanser who scrub the bathroom so clean are, of course, men. Indeed with rare exceptions, and Betty Furness and June Graham were the most obvious, women didn't fulfil the crucial role of mediator between consumer and commodity, even domestic commodities, except in the realm of beauty products.

What conditioned women's lives were the pursuit of beauty and the cult of domesticity. Understand that the ad-makers didn't advocate these, they just assumed that every woman (and every man) would accept them. Women were nearly always on display, even in ads that had little to do with their personal appearance. A female announcer in *Does She ... or Doesn't She?* explained how the sad state of a new mother's hair so distressed her. 'Then she tried Miss

Clairol. Now she looks as wonderful as she feels,' enthused the announcer, acting as a confidante to all female viewers. 'Miss Clairol really covers gray, keeps hair young, radiant, sparkling with life.' That's why it was safe for the mother to be outside playing with her baby for all to see. You would expect that the woman in Chemstrand's parable about nylons, *A Lady Isn't Dressed* (D5858), would look attractive and fashionable. But why was the mother made up, complete with painted nails, in Tide's *Cleanest Clean?* Why did the wife in *Brand New Door* have perfect hair, sport a dress scarf, and wear fancy white gloves, even though hubby was casually attired and the family merely on a routine shopping trip? Simply because women were expected to look their best. Indeed femininity meant beauty, grace, style, sometimes glamour. So the mysterious woman in *Was It Paris?* added to the overall impression of an upscale lifestyle. In a different vein, *Sexy Cigar* (D5103) 'gendered' the Murial Cigar, presenting it as a Mae West figure, in a sixty-second, animated vaudeo aimed at men. Missing from the Clios, though, was any blatant example of sexual display in which a woman's body, or parts thereof, was portrayed in a particularly suggestive fashion.

But she was presented as something of a domestic drudge. Women were forever being shown shopping, cleaning, cooking, and looking after others. Sometimes the ad-makers actually celebrated such domesticity, as in Pet's *Life of a Baby*, where mother happily nurtures, or in Tide's unbelievable *Cleanest Clean*, where mother gleefully washes. But there were exceptions. General Foods tried to tap into a vein of female resentment with *Busy Day* (D5531): a distraught mother in this animated nightmare was shown on a kitchen tread-mill, trying to clean house, calm baby, answer the phone or the door. Similarly, Carling's cartoon *Hey, Mabel* (D5443) for its Black Label beer contrasted the way hubby came home to rest in a hammock while his wife furiously weeded the garden, mowed the lawn, painted the window, fixed the glass, even ground the axe – and eventually brought him a beer! The ad-makers presented such scenes as a statement of a problem that could be solved with their product.

The code of masculinity dictated a very different set of images for men. Rarely were men portrayed at work, at least in the normal office or factory, perhaps because the workplace was not deemed an important site of con-sumption in those days. They were associated with outdoors (*Smoking Cowboys* and *There's Bud*, D5747), sports (*Sporting Shaves*), cars (*Smoker* or *Dragnet?*) and driving (*They Oughta' Advertise* or *Alcan Champs*), relaxing (*Hey, Mabel*), or entertaining at home (*Pour, Pour the Rosé*, D5849) – a more varied, exotic, and leisured existence than their helpmates. They could be debonair (Rex Marshall in *Flavor Buds*), classy (Commander Whitehead in *Was It Paris?*), macho (*Smoker*), casual (*Brand New Door*), clever (*I Want My*

Figure 1.8: *Killer Raid.* Raid was another of those new and powerful masculine figures who arrived on the scene in the 1950s to assist homemakers. But Raid was identified right from the beginning as a potent source of death. Here he posed in a display of power, ready to defend the home against all manner of bugs. (Courtesy of S.C. Johnson & Son Inc.)

Maypo), generous (*Boy Meets Impala*), and so on. But with rare exceptions they were instrumental. They played out a special role as experts, mediators (notably in testimonials), and announcers, representing the embodiment of authority. It is worth emphasizing that when the manufacturer or ad-maker wished to make the brand appear potent, as in the case of Mr. Clean or Raid, its gender was emphatically masculine. Although some commentators in the fifties might have worried about feminine power, the Clios offered reassurance that it was still 'a man's world.'

It was also a world of goods. The signs of affluence, of course, were best represented in the handful of Clios that actually had a lifestyle orientation. The *Smoker* found his greatest pleasure working on his personal toy, a sports car. 'I like to take it apart and put it back together,' he asserted. 'I get to working on it, and I forget where I am ... what time it is. I even forget to eat.' The background for Maxwell House's *Flavor Buds* was a well-appointed playroom, complete with an easy chair, the necessary television, a wall unit, books, paintings and other wall ornaments (including some crossed swords!), and a desk upon which rested an ornate lamp. The quality of these goods illustrated the standing of their owners: by a literal reading, *Brand New Door* suggested that the typical American family should buy a new Chevy because the door of their old car was broken. How else could they take pride in owning a car? Possessing and enjoying the best, the brightest, the newest was a decent working definition of the good life.

A recurring image in these commercials was the satisfied consumer. A happy girl rushes home to mom waving her perfect dental report (Crest's *Look, Ma!* D5825); husband John starts smooching with wife Marsha after tasting her cake, made so superbly with Snowdrift shortening (*John & Marsha*); the injured dummy Danny O'Day revives after drinking a glass of milk laced with Nestlé's Quik (*Battlin' Danny*, D5635); a woman gains instant relief from a night of excess by taking Alka-Seltzer in a glass of water (*Speedy*). In food ads the lucky person is sometimes overcome with emotion: a once-frenzied husband calms down when the wise wife soothes his addiction with a new box of Ritz Crackers (D5427); a father who has tried in vain to encourage his brat to eat the new Maypo cereal has a feeding frenzy once he discovers how delicious it is; two animated heads get mighty excited over the prospect of freshly popped popcorn (D5530).

These are signs of consumers paying homage to the magic properties of the brand. Advertisers were hell-bent on building brand loyalty for all the new products out on the market in the 1950s. Some of the commercials, especially for machines and the like, called upon the consumer to share in the pride of the manufacturer. So *I Built Me a Dodge* took the viewer on a two-minute tour of an assembly plant, where happy and efficient workers put together a Dodge in record time. 'It's a proud name. Proud in tradition, proud in service,' intoned the narrator, a Broadway baritone. 'Swift and mighty in action.' With that, the camera switched to a shot of a sedan driving down the highway. The even longer General Motors' documentary, *Plane in Fog* (D5751), showed how a Delco battery saved the day at an air force base in the Arctic, when a power failure threatened to close down ground control for an aircraft attempting to land. And GM's spot, *Alcan Champs*, demonstrated how the company's fleet of mighty Chevrolet trucks conquered the wilderness 'against all Nature's might.' All this could be put down to the fetish of technology, which enjoyed so much public favour. These were machines with a social and patriotic purpose, proof of the industrial prowess of the United States.

The advertisers of more prosaic or trivial goods tried to share in the glory of

Figure 1.9: *Look, Ma!* In 1958 Procter & Gamble Co. launched Crest,® a fluoride toothpaste. This six-year-old was the first of many happy kids who would run from a car, across a lawn, and into a suburban home, brandishing a dental report card, to greet mom with the amazing cry 'No cavities!' It was yet another visible manifestation of the battle for cleanliness, this time directed at the body rather than the home. (© The Procter & Gamble Company. Printed by permission.)

science. Westinghouse's *Dirty Sand Test* proved, beyond a shadow of doubt, of course, how the new 'revolving agitator washer' was far superior to the old-fashioned 'centrepost agitators' of leading rivals in that difficult task of getting sand out of towels. RCA had all competitors beaten with its 'non-breakable Impac case,' according to the enthusiastic announcer in *Ladder Drop*: 'So rugged, it's the only radio case with a five-year guarantee against chipping, cracking, or breaking in normal use.' Dropping an RCA portable and a rival proved how tough the brand was, though the announcer admitted a tube might jar loose. The commercials for health and beauty products boasted a variety of special ingredients with weird names. New Mum's Cream Deodorant had 'M-3' to stop odour for a full twenty-four hours. Pepsodent's 'IMP' and 'Irium' did battle with Crest's 'Fluoristan' to keep teeth shiny and healthy. Even beverage ads claimed their brands had some special quality: Piel's 'Cool-Brewed' technique, Ballantine's 'Brewer's Gold,' Maxwell House's 'miracle Flavor Buds,' or 'Schweppervescence.'

What the commercials touted was a new era of convenience and ease that would take the stress out of ordinary living. Many Clios, like many print ads, swiftly presented a problem and just as swiftly solved it. In *Chalk Talk* (D5555) the New York Telephone Company showed how its Yellow Pages helped people: Mary finds a taxi for Jock who's slept in, and she later discovers the neighbourhood stores that carry the brand name goods she fancies; Jock finds the name of the employment agency that can send a typist to his office; and back home the maid uses the same source to locate someone to repair the faulty alarm clock. The friendly genie in *Meet Mr. Clean* would swiftly 'clean your whole house,' no matter how great the amount of dirt. *Take Tea* (D5640) told consumers how they could so easily find a refreshing and restful drink, which wouldn't result in the indigestion, nervousness, or sleeplessness of the unmentioned coffee. Two Jell-O spots, *Busy Day* and *Chinese Baby*, show how mother can satisfy children with a quickly made dessert. Gallo Wine's *Pour, Pour the Rosé* demonstrates how simple it is to ensure the success of a formal party or a casual barbecue, merely by offering this beverage, itself a sign of sociability. There seemed to be no ordinary difficulty that couldn't be solved with a purchase in the market-place.

Another set of Clios presented their products as badge goods that would convey status and signify belonging. Johnson & Johnson's *Funny Bandages* (D5718) tells kids how they can get special coloured Band-Aids to cover up their hurts – 'Ooooh!,' 'Ahhhh!,' 'Wow!,' and 'Woooo!' goes the chorus. Gillette explains how shaving with a safety razor is a sign of maturity. Buying a beautiful new Chevrolet station-wagon in GM's *Brand New Door* or owning a shiny Impala in *Boy Meets Impala* means possessing an objet d'art that signifies you've arrived. A woman's look can never be perfect, according to Chemstrand's *A Lady Isn't Dressed*, unless she always wears nylons that suit the rest of her costume. Both *Smoking Cowboys* and *Smoker* tell men how they can show their masculinity simply by smoking a Chesterfield or a Marlboro. Such ads explained how people could build a public self and assuage private insecurities by consuming the right brands. But none of the Clios indulged in the kind of scare copy that was common back in the print ads of the troubled thirties.

There was an implicit contradiction here. The rhetoric of some Clios indicates advertisers were trying to sell 'universal' goods to a mass market. R.J. Reynolds doesn't even try to deliver a message in its *Winston Tastes Good* (D5607), only to remind consumers via some complicated animation and a happy jingle that here is a cigarette for all tastes. Mr. Clean is for every household, Gallo Rosé for every occasion, Alka-Seltzer will cure the indigestion of high and low, Raid is good for house and garden. Admittedly, these brands lacked the longevity, the changeless quality, never mind the market leadership associated with true 'universals' like Ford's Model T (1908–27) or Coca-Cola (up to 1955). But the same goal was present, in TV advertising anyway. Another group of marketers, especially of badge goods, were aiming their messages at a segmented market, however. General Motors persisted on TV, as it had for decades in print, to market a different Chevy for different people, the station-wagon for the family-minded and the Impala convertible for the high flyers. Johnson & Johnson employed a simple form of demographics, targeting its new bandages at children. Philip Morris was experimenting with psychographics in its print and TV Marlboro ads: this smoke was meant for true men.

Whatever the market strategy, though, one crucial result of television advertising was to spread brand consciousness much more widely and more deeply through the American population. According to Richard Tedlow, a marketing historian, the demand for 'nationally branded grocery products' significantly increased during the 1950s as a consequence of their exposure on television. Slogans, sayings, and jingles like 'the cleanest clean under the sun' (Tide), 'the foaming cleanser' (Ajax), 'You'll wonder where the yellow went' (Pepsodent), 'Winston tastes good like a cigarette should,' 'Does she ... or doesn't she?' (Clairol), or 'How are you fixed for blades?' (Gillette) were on the lips of all sorts of people, including children. A new generation of Americans was being conditioned to accept the gospel of branded goods by their favourite medium, TV.

On Materialism

'While the author was preparing this chapter,' wrote Vance Packard, commenting on the importance of television commercials, 'he heard his own eight-year-old daughter happily singing the cigarette jingle: "Don't miss the fun of smoking!"' Packard was the author of *The Hidden Persuaders*, a 1957 exposé of the way motivational research (MR) was turning advertising into an omnipotent tool of manipulation. He quoted from a range of MR practitioners, notably the enthusiast Dr Ernest Dichter, to demonstrate that this new brand of psychology enabled researchers to design products or create ad campaigns which consumers would find impossible to resist. They had discovered ways to use colours, shapes, words, our fears and our dreams to tap into people's unconscious. These psychologists, or rather the agencies they advised, could then skip past our conscious defences to place triggers in our minds that would compel a purchase. A lot of this was hype, the argument relying too much on information from the fans of MR. Indeed what MR really amounted to was a preliminary exploration of the symbolic meaning of goods.

No matter – the book enjoyed extraordinary popularity, reaching the top of the best-seller list for six weeks and selling over 100,000 copies during its first year. Packard's worries seemed validated by the sudden scare over subliminal advertising when James Vicary, one of those fans of MR, announced he'd successfully implanted a trigger in the minds of some hapless movie-goers to buy Coca-Cola and popcorn, by flashing a message on screen so fast it didn't register on their consciousness. There is good reason to think Vicary's experiment was a hoax, and certainly his results weren't replicated. But the upset was sufficient to lead the National Association of Broadcasters and Britain's Institute of Practitioners in Advertising to ban subliminal advertising in 1958. Packard's success and the Vicary scare owed much to a renewed sense of alarm over the power of hidden forces to use the mass media to program the public mind. Fears of conspiracies and brainwashing rested, in part at least, upon a perceived loss of independence in the postwar era of big government and big corporations. Such fears would persist, inspiring later authors like Wilson Bryan Key to denounce advertising and the media for manipulating our desires to suit their purposes.

Galbraith's *The Affluent Society* tapped into the same kind of sentiment, which may help to explain how successful it was with the more literate public. But Galbraith's book was a much more sophisticated and erudite treatment of the whole structure of the postwar economy of abundance, in which he identified advertising as one of the key tools corporate managers used to tailor consumer demand to meet the needs of mass production. His chapter 'The Dependence Effect' was a forceful restatement of a widespread view that advertising worked 'to create desires – to bring into being wants that previously did not exist.' One problem with Galbraith's account was that he made a distinction between 'necessary' and 'unnecessary' goods, and therefore differentiated between 'wants' that were legitimate or illegitimate. These distinctions not only neglected to explain who would decide just what was 'necessary' or 'unnecessary' but denied the cultural dimension of goods, the way they carry meanings about a person or lifestyle that were important to individuals. The other problem was that his argument assumed a passive audience, rather than a group of people able to use advertising messages to suit their purposes. But there is no doubt his strictures were well received, not only in the United States but western Europe as well. And they too would persist in the public discussion of advertising, periodically updated by scholars like Stuart Ewen.

Both *The Hidden Persuaders* and *The Affluent Society* were part of a more general critique of materialism that captured the fancy of all sorts of people in North America after 1945. The critique now seems ironic, given that America was experiencing a boom of extraordinary proportions which appeared to realize the promises of industrial capitalism: expenditures on kitchen and household appliances, noted Roland Marchand in an article on postwar popular culture, rose from $1.9 billion (1946) to $5.0 billion (1960) in constant dollars. Yet wherever a person looked, she or he could find hand-wringing over conspicuous consumption, opulence, self-indulgence, vulgarity, debauchery. It wasn't always clear just what people meant by materialism, except that they suffered from a vague sense of unease over the fascination with things rather than with art, religion, public affairs, or family. Witness this lament from Ernest Van Den Haag (1957):

While immensely augmenting our comforts, our conveniences and our leisure, and disproportionately raising the real income of the poor, industry has also impoverished life. Mass production and consumption, mobility, the homogenization of taste and finally of society were among the costs of higher productivity. They de-individualized life and drained each of our ends of meaning as we achieved it. Pursuit thus became boundless. The increased leisure time would hang heavy on our hands, were it not for the mass media which help us kill it.

The obvious target for everyone's obloquy was Madison Avenue. According to the Department of Commerce, advertising expenditures jumped from $3.3 billion (or $23.70 per capita) in 1946 to $11.9 billion (or $66.04 per capita) in 1960. Many would have agreed with Packard's assertion that the question of where 'the pressures of consumerism' were taking America was destined 'to become one of the great moral issues of our times.' Fully 80 per cent of Americans, according to one 1950 poll cited by the historian Stephen Fox, believed advertising led people to buy goods they shouldn't. A series of novels had cultivated the image of the crass and immoral adman who worked to debauch the public mind on behalf of clients: *The Hucksters* (1946) alone sold some 750,000 copies. In 1951 Marshall McLuhan published *The Mechanical Bride*, which identified Madison Avenue as the instrument of a business conspiracy against all that was good and true in life. His thesis fitted into the highbrow assault on mass culture as a debased form that threatened the moral and mental health of North Americans, a view amply expressed in *Mass Culture*, edited by Bernard Rosenberg and David Manning White. Advertising itself not only worked to foster materialism, its rule perverted the agencies of mass communication by turning them into vehicles of mass entertainment that would produce the largest audiences and so the most revenue.

In such a climate of opinion, the reputation of the television commercial was bound to be low among the nation's intelligentsia. TV was already under attack for being too commercial, too trivial, too violent, too powerful. That eccentric master of advertising David Ogilvy expressed his deep ambivalence in his *Confessions of an Advertising Man* (1963). Though he made 'most of his living' from TV ads, 'as a private person' he would have preferred to pay for the privilege of noncommercial television. 'It is television advertising which has made Madison Avenue the arch-symbol of tasteless materialism,' he lamented. Increasingly the commercial was identified by social and moral critics as the most visible and significant carrier of the virus of materialism. The very display of abundance that TV could do so well seemed in itself sinful.

There is reason to doubt, however, that the American public was as exercised over commercials as the critics were. Gary Steiner carried out a survey of the views of nearly 2,500 people about television in the spring of 1960. He didn't probe their attitude towards materialism, which may well suggest that it was a nonissue to most viewers, whose satisfaction with TV was shadowed more by a concern over its display of violence. But he did devote a chapter to commercials. Yes, many of these viewers disliked the timing of commercial breaks – they interrupted, they came on too often, they were too long – and the content of many commercials – they were boring, misleading, or stupid. But only a quarter was willing to pay, like David Ogilvy, for ad-free television. Instead three-quarters agreed with the statement that commercials were 'a fair price to pay for the entertainment you get.' Over half claimed they found some spots supplied them with useful information. Fewer, around 40 per cent, added that the best ads were 'more entertaining than the program': one viewer found Piel's beer commercials 'clever' and 'amusing' – 'I look forward to seeing them.' Most popular were beer and wine ads because they amused; least popular were medicine and drug ads because they were in bad taste and/or exaggerated. So another pattern had emerged in this first decade of television advertising: a viewing public that was both annoyed and tolerant, with definite likes and dislikes, which would have preferred less hard sell and shorter breaks and more tasteful messages. What they got was a bit different.

2

Studies in American Excellence

When you reach for the stars you may not quite get one, but you won't come up with a handful of mud either.

— Leo Burnett, cited in Eric Clark,
The Want Makers

Lifestyle advertising came into full bloom on TV during the 1960s. Three of the best examples of this genre had their origins in that decade: the campaigns for Marlboro cigarettes, Coca-Cola, and Pepsi-Cola. All promoted badge goods, meaning these brands said something about their users. In a 1984 interview on the 'Pepsi Generation' campaign, the veteran ad-maker Tom Dillon, past president of BBDO (1964–77), explained how people make judgments about who they are, and who others are, based on the cigarette smoked or the soft drink enjoyed. Twenty years earlier, his agency had argued that very point to Pepsi-Cola in 'The Necktie Memo,' which presumed the purpose of a soft drink was not just to quench thirst but also to express the personality of the consumer. So Pepsi advertising had worked to link the consumer to a particular way of life, Dillon noted. In his interview Allen Rosenshine, then head of BBDO, added that the images and attitudes embodied in lifestyle advertising weren't supposed to be taken literally. His examples: a lot of women smoked the macho brand, Marlboro, which used a cowboy as its symbol; most Pepsi customers lived in the cities, though most Pepsi commercials were shot 'in the country, on beaches, or in the mountains.' According to Dillon, the ad-makers were out to construct a 'daydream' where the consumer might play. The hope was to capture what retired Philip Morris executive Jack Landry called a 'share of mind,' to get the attitudes and images associated with the brand established in the imagination of consumers.

Living in 'Marlboro Country' (1963–71)

The ad-maker Leo Burnett, who told his people to 'reach for the stars,' certainly proved his point with the 'Marlboro Country' campaign of the 1960s. Witness the 1965 colour commercial entitled *The Tale of the Marlboro Brand*. Against a soundtrack of ballad music, an unseen announcer in a singsong voice, complete with a twang, tells how Marlboro cigarettes came out of Richmond, Virginia, to sweep 'clear across the land.' The screen fills with panoramic shots of mountains, trees, lakes, a snow scene, even the towers of Manhattan. Everywhere there is the trademark cowboy, sometimes riding the range, sometimes posing on his horse, and usually smoking. The distance shots are balanced by close-ups of rugged cowboy faces and the Marlboro brand. One of the shots is directly into the sun, giving the image a halo effect. Another sequence superimposes the enlarged face of a cowboy on a landscape. The voice-over keeps emphasizing the product's USP, real flavour: hence the slogan, written on the screen, 'Come to where the flavour is, come to Marlboro Country.' The commercial ends with another trade mark, music from the hit movie *The Magnificent Seven*. (For the record, let me state here that I smoke Marlboro when in the United States, so you should realize I am a happy consumer of both the meanings created by Leo Burnett and the brand name by Philip Morris.)

The Marlboro brand actually came out of the fertile imagination of managers at Philip Morris. Back in the mid-1950s, Philip Morris was ranked a lowly fifth among the Big Six companies dominating the cigarette market in the United States: compare Philip Morris's 8.5 share with those of the two leaders in 1955, R.J. Reynolds's 25.8 and American Brands' 32.9, according to figures cited by analyst James Overton. But the health scare brought on by reports that smoking caused lung cancer, and popularized after 1952 by articles in *Reader's Digest*, shook up the whole business. Total cigarette consumption even fell in 1953 and 1954, wrote historian Robert Sobel, from 435 billion units to 401 billion. Tobacco companies correctly decided that they could meet the threat and capitalize on smokers' fears by offering filter-tip brands, which presumably reduced the health risk by removing whatever was toxic in cigarette smoke. Thus began the filter wars.

Reynolds came out in 1953 with a new brand called Winston, stunning observers by its rapid success. The ad campaign made famous the slogan 'Winston Tastes Good, Like a Cigarette Should.' By contrast, Philip Morris decided to reissue Marlboro, an old brand from the 1920s languishing with less than 1 per cent of the domestic market, once positioned as an upscale cigarette especially for women. The firm commissioned the Elmo Roper agency to conduct some ten thousand interviews in 1953 on just what people wanted in a smoke. That led Philip Morris to design a new red and white logo and a special flip-top box, to create a new blend with a lot of flavour, to add its own version of a filter, and to hire the Leo Burnett advertising agency. It was Burnett's task to make over the brand image at an initial cost of some $750,000.

The Burnett agency, based in Chicago, was winning a reputation and clients during the early 1950s. Burnett specialized in appealing characters: one of the agency's first successes was the Jolly Green Giant for the Minnesota Canning Company, and later it would create the Pillsbury Dough Boy, Kellogg's Tony the Tiger, and the Maytag Repair Man. According to Jack Landry, once a brand manager for Marlboro (1957–65), Philip Morris wanted Burnett to overcome doubts about filters among male smokers, who perceived them as a 'sort of dilettantish product,' hardly fitting for a 'real guy.' The answer was to make Marlboro a macho cigarette. According to John Benson, an account executive, Burnett himself came up with the initial idea of the cowboy and that was used successfully in a print campaign in New York. But when the campaign went national on TV early in 1955, the cowboy character was supplemented with a variety of other rugged, mature types, usually sporting a tattoo, which suggested (in Landry's words) an air of 'mystery and intrigue,' 'an interesting past.' The self-absorbed hero of that 1955 Classic Clio *Smoker* was just one of these heavily masculine figures.

The campaign worked, or so the jump in sales from 6.4 billion (1955) to 19.5 billion (1957) suggests. The upward march, however, was slowed by the effects of two more *Reader's Digest* articles in 1957 that tested the effectiveness of filter cigarettes, ranking the full-flavoured Marlboro stronger than some plain-tipped brands and touting the rival Kent as the lowest in tar and nicotine. Philip Morris and Leo Burnett tried to undo the damage with a new 'Settleback' campaign, featuring relaxed settings where a variety of mature men, sports and television celebrities, and even the ultrafeminine singer Julie London were on display. The intent was reassurance, to talk to 'the anxieties that scared smokers have,' claimed Landry. Maybe that helped sales, though hardly market share: in 1962 Marlboro sold 25.7 billion cigarettes, far behind the leader Pall Mall at 72.1 billion.

This problem led Landry, Burnett, and their respective teams to remix elements of earlier efforts in a new 'Marlboro Country' campaign. The phrase 'Marlboro Country,' superimposed on a map of the United States, had been used effectively some years earlier to dispel rumours that Marlboro cigarettes were banned from military installations because the brand caused cancer. Reports from Starch Research had demonstrated that people always liked 'seeing cowboys' in Marlboro ads. Tests in selected markets using newspapers confirmed this fact in 1962. Although doubters in the agency and the company feared the campaign was too macho and too limited (just how much could you do with cowboys and landscapes?), the new campaign appeared on TV in late 1963. Television, then and later, was the chief medium in this advertising effort: roughly 80 per cent of the increasing budget for the Marlboro brand was spent on making and displaying commercials. Leo Burnett produced colour and black-and-white versions of particular titles, in sixty-, thirty-, and fifteen-second formats. He filled these with a cluster of slogans and sayings to underline the full flavour of the brand: 'A man's world of flavor,' 'You get a lot to like,' 'The flavor that won the west,' 'Flavor you can get hold of.' Cowboys and western landscapes, sometimes paintings of the Old West, prevailed throughout Marlboro Country. A crucial element was the theme music from 'Mag 7' – indeed Landry thought this was the key to bringing everything together.

The campaign took a while to jell, however. Bits of the 'Settleback' ads cropped up in a few commercials, including Julie London on one occasion . At first some ads had a surreal quality, evoking a land of legend and myth. According to Norman Muse, one of the 'creatives' at Leo Burnett, the campaign was initially 'very stylized' with shots of city streets and Hollywood style cowboys. In one of the early efforts, for instance, an urban cowboy in a darkened city scene lights up and is transported instantly to Marlboro Country. Another commercial tied the 'Man from Marlboro Country' directly to the mythic history of the Old West: the ad used paintings and stills to explain how he'd ridden out of Richmond in some past time to leave 'his brand throughout the country.'

This taste for fantasy declined after a year or so when the agency determined to emphasize realism. Out on another shoot (for Camay soap!), the art director Neil McBane discovered the Four Sixes Ranch in Texas, which seemed a perfect setting for Marlboro Country. So Marlboro ads featured more and more lush pictures of life out west, which of course showed very well on colour television. Shots of the city, especially the canyons of New York, virtually disappeared. Around this time the 'creatives' also decided to use only real, not 'plastic,' cowboys, in short, no actors (though one of these would find work later as a Camel man). Darrell Winfield was discovered on a Wyoming ranch in 1968, and his part-time work for the Marlboro brand would take him to Texas, Idaho, Montana, Oklahoma, and Colorado in search of new landscapes for the campaign. The Marlboro cowboy was shown at work driving the cattle or riding the range and at rest drinking coffee or having a smoke. Much attention was paid to getting the details right: the cowboys wore 'chaps' when roping steers, for example. Winfield and the boys were told to act natural, in particular to smoke only when that seemed appropriate. The great boast became authenticity, a true representation of 'the poetry and nitty-grittiness' of the real West, in the words of Norman Muse.

Yet Marlboro Country was as much a dreamland and a state of mind as it was a description of the real West. Here was a place of panoramic vistas, of tall trees and grand mountains, of pure streams, of wide-open prairies, untouched by the clutter and mess of urban society. The imagery suggested simplicity, ruggedness, health, even rejuvenation. So a cowboy muses, 'This is my country. It's big, open, makes a man feel ten feet tall.' A voice-over claims, 'This land makes a special breed of man. He likes its big, wide-open spirit.' In each case Marlboro has that same quality – 'it has spirit.' A mid-sixties spot followed a cowboy riding through a furious thunderstorm to safety at his camp; once comfortable, he thinks 'the simple things mean a lot out here: a dry blanket, hot cup of coffee, a good smoke – Marlboro.' Another commercial of this vintage is soft, almost gentle, depicting a cowboy who rides slowly through a virgin forest enjoying the view and a smoke. One of the last TV ads, this about fly-fishing, has the announcer telling viewers, 'Now and then, no matter who he is or what he does, a man's got to get away by himself – and afterwards, afterwards everything seems a whole lot easier.' There was an ambiguity about Marlboro Country: both wilderness and frontier, full of beauty, sometimes harsh and sometimes peaceful, a place of testing as well as a refuge, but very much a man's realm. And it was always available to the smoker – 'Wherever you go, that's Marlboro Country,' proclaimed an announcer.

A similar mix of romance, myth, and reality conditioned the image of the cowboy. The cowboy was a hero, an American original: he was 'the last free American' (account executive John Benson), a man who 'commands his own destiny' (art director Kenneth Krom), 'a wonderful symbol' (copywriter Norman Muse) of escape, of clean air, but above all of masculinity. Close-ups emphasized his tough, weathered face, more experienced than handsome; medium shots showed him riding tall in the saddle – at work he was swift and effective, at rest calm and thoughtful, always he was central. Right from the beginning, the campaign employed visions of domain: the cowboy rides his horse up a bluff, pausing to look out over the prairies; he flies a plane or helicopter, giving him a panoramic view of the ranch; the outline of his body or face is superimposed upon the landscape – such visual clichés signal mastery and possession, that he is the lord of all he surveys. Sometimes this rugged individualist appeared among his companions: so *Heading for the High Country* celebrated the bonding of three cowboys, who chatted and smoked, about to go off to hunt in winter time. Much the same theme of male comradeship informed ads in which a team of cowboys prepare for a day's work, or drive the cattle, or herd the horses. Only rarely did a woman enter this man's preserve, and on one occasion she is specifically called 'my kind of gal' because she accepts a Marlboro from a cowboy on horseback. Time and again, the commercials emphasized one fundamental message: the cowboy, whether alone or with his fellows, enjoys a satisfying life, work that is meaningful and pleasures that are simple, and on his terms. To the viewer was left the task of comparing such an ideal lifestyle with the frustrations of working and living in the cities of the 1960s. That contrast was crucial to the impact of the campaign: the Leo Burnett agency expected people to bring their own negative experiences to the task of decoding these commercials.

'Marlboro Country' was by no means an instant hit. Sales remained sluggish in 1963 and 1964. Around 1965, recalled Jack Landry, two research agencies warned Philip Morris the campaign would actually put the brand 'out of business.' Not so. Thereafter, the campaign swiftly built momentum, sales doubled to 51.4 billion units in five years, and Marlboro rose from seventh to third position among the top brands. This advance was all the more impressive because competition was now so heated: whereas there were only eighteen successful brands in 1950, there were ninety-three two decades later, according to industry observer Robert Miles. Little wonder that Philip Morris approved a similar, equally innovative campaign, also designed by Leo Burnett, for its new women's cigarette, Virginia Slims, which effectively exploited the much-vaunted women's liberation with the slogan 'You've come a long way, baby' (and won the campaign Clio in 1969). One of the last Marlboro commercials, *Horses*, finally won an award as the Best Tobacco Products ad in the 1971 Clio competition. It was belated recognition of an amazingly effective example of art at the service of commerce.

The success of 'Marlboro Country' owed much to the extraordinary popularity of the western myth at the movies, on TV, and in popular literature between the mid-1950s and mid-1960s. The three top Nielsen's in the 1961–2 TV season were respectively 'Wagon Train,' 'Bonanza,' and 'Gunsmoke.' But that wasn't the only reason for Marlboro's rise. The smoke had a particular appeal to those under thirty-five, so Landry speculated, because the campaign conjured up a simpler, very attractive dreamland and made Marlboro 'a friendly thing' in the disturbed sixties. 'Youth were reaching out for something, and someone they could identify with,' according to an abstract of the Landry interview. '"Marlboro Country" fit these desires, this search people were going through.' The claim strikes me as a trifle exaggerated, though there is little doubt the campaign dispelled the notion that images of youth were required to attract young people. A symbol of maturity and masculinity clearly had appeal to all ages of manhood. Even some women were seduced – they too could 'relate' to the cowboy, as John Benson put it, because the cowboy was a symbol of rugged masculinity, and of power in a male world, I would add. What is also intriguing is that the cigarette proved most popular in big cities, much less so in rural Texas and the like where people didn't much care to be called Marlboro cowboys. It was further proof that 'Marlboro Country' was displaced from reality, a land of illusion geared to the hopes and fears of city folk.

TV had been very good to Philip Morris. The company bid a fond farewell on 1 January 1971 with a final extravaganza of late night ads, at an estimated cost of $1.2 million, according to writer Susan Wagner. But the Marlboro advance wasn't slowed by the ban on television advertising. Indeed the change probably helped Marlboro because the images made famous by the TV campaign were easily translated into print, although the account group at Leo Burnett lamented the loss of the music. By contrast, the jingle-based campaign of Winston, the industry leader, couldn't be effectively repeated in magazines. Marlboro finally beat out Winston for the top spot in the U.S. market in 1976. According to the annual cigarette survey of *Business Week*, the cowboy's brand was clearly dominant by 1980: rising Marlboro sales had produced a 17.8 share, while Winston's had fallen to 13.3, though both were far ahead of the two menthol contenders, Brown & Williamson's Kools (8.9) and R.J. Reynolds's Salem (8.9).

The campaign also helped to turn Marlboro into a world brand, the sales leader in cigarettes as early as 1971, eventually outselling Coke in terms of units purchased.   The conquest of the international market would never have occurred if Philip Morris hadn't worked so effectively to build alliances with local distributors. But offshoots of the American campaign (using television wherever the laws allowed) gave Marlboro what Landry called a 'worldwide personality,' that because of tradition, movies, and television fitted what foreigners thought was so American. Note how the context changed: in the United States 'Marlboro Country' worked against a background of dissatisfaction with modern urban life, but elsewhere the Marlboro man stood out as a symbol of things American. George Weissman, onetime chairman and CEO of Philip Morris, credited Hollywood's movies and series about the old West with assisting the spread of Marlboro in Europe. The much-publicized fact that Marlboro was number one in the American market just reinforced the link. In the Dominican Republic, according to Felipe Gil, a director of publicity employed by an ally of Philip Morris, Marlboro became a status symbol of the good life, shared by rich and poor alike. The images of the campaign were sometimes tailored to suit local tastes, of course. In parts of Africa the cowboys were black. In Latin America they had to share the limelight with Formula One drivers, who at first worked better as symbols of masculinity, though during the 1980s the image of the cowboy enjoyed a renaissance. In Hong Kong he moved upscale (to avoid being seen as a labourer), rode a white horse (because horses symbolized vitality), and lost his contact with cattle (thought ignoble).

So pervasive has this campaign become that even antismoking crusaders admitted the power of the metaphor. In *Merchants of Death* (1988), for example, author Larry White claimed Philip Morris had named the smoker's heaven and hell: 'Come to Marlboro Country' was really an invitation 'to the lotus land of addiction,' where the cowboy who lights up has 'the self-absorbed look of an addict getting his fix.'

'Emotionally Marlboro owns the West' – that envious judgment came from Barry Day of McCann-Erickson (cited by Eric Clark). Yes, there were competitors: John Benson noted challenges by Chevrolet, one of the Budweiser beers, Manhandler soups, and of course 'Ford Country.' But none could claim the same degree of success. 'When you see a cowboy, people think Marlboro,' argued Norman Muse. The campaign had appropriated the national and international rights to the western myth, at least in the realm of advertising.

Less noticed was another triumph. Even if the Marboro brand could never claim to 'own' masculinity – no ad-maker has achieved that goal yet – still 'Marboro Country' came close. The campaigns on TV and later in print have embodied a vision of masculinity that remains both traditional in character and powerful in its appeal. It is hard to think of an image more 'manly' than the Marlboro cowboy: so tough, experienced, skilled, commanding, effective, and independent. Nor is it easy to find a more universal image of manhood: he may be banned from North American screens, but in the summer of 1993, he could be found riding proud in the newly 'liberated' realm of Russian television. So 'Marlboro County' must be counted among the very few ad campaigns which have a central place in the global Superculture that now bestrides the world.

Coca-Cola's America (1969–82)

Far different was the situation of Coca-Cola. While the reissued Marlboro brand was a newcomer to the cigarette market in the mid-1950s, Coca-Cola had been the leader of the soft-drink market for years and years, not only in the United States but throughout the world. Ever since the 1920s, when the ad campaign 'the pause that refreshes' debuted, Coke had been positioned as the universal cola, a single, unchanging soft drink that suited the taste of everyone – young or old, female or male, white or black, American or foreign, rich or poor. It was 'your good friend,' 'a democratic luxury' ready to satisfy whenever you needed a lift, in the words of Richard Tedlow.

Legends had gathered around its name: people wondered whether it contained cocaine (purportedly it did up to 1903, because of the method used to get an extract from coca leaves). Coke had become closely identified with America and its place in the world. 'Coca-Cola represented part and parcel of the good life the American dream guaranteed,' wrote John Sculley, a one-time Pepsi executive. A 1950 cover of *Time*, entitled 'World & Friend,' featured a drawing of a happy Coke face refreshing the globe, with the caption 'Love that American way of life.' One of the signs that greeted returning Apollo astronauts in New York's Times Square, noted Anne Hoy in a celebration of 100 years of Coke, carried the message 'Welcome Back to Earth, Home of Coca-Cola.' Sometimes its fame took on a sinister cast: witness the popularity of the term 'Coca-Colonization' among left-wing critics of America's imperial might.

But during the 1950s the dominance of Coca-Cola was threatened by rivals, notably by Pepsi-Cola, which had increased its domestic sales threefold between 1950 and 1958. It was the Pepsi surge that launched the ongoing Cola Wars, and these have helped to make the soft-drink business one of the most competitive industries in the United States, according to economists Robert Tollison, David Kaplan, and Richard Higgins. Warfare has occurred on a number of different fronts: the introduction of new products and new containers, a battle for control of soda-fountain outlets and shelf space in supermarkets, a range of special discounts and promotions, to cite the more obvious. The most public battles, however, were the competing ad campaigns over that 'share of mind' deemed crucial to success.

In the late 1950s Coca-Cola gave McCann-Erickson the task of keeping Coke number one at home and abroad. The company and the agency settled on a policy called 'one sight, one sound, one sell,' which involved taking full control over the image of Coke and adopting a single, coherent advertising campaign to update that image everywhere. The result of much research was 'Things Go Better with Coke,' a campaign that employed magazines, radio, and TV by late 1963, though it relied most heavily upon television. The whole notion was to show how life improved when you drank Coca-Cola. Company records claim that within three months, two-thirds of the public surveyed was able to recognize the all-important theme song. Shortly thereafter, the same campaign was tested in seven countries, and again with happy results – almost everywhere, 'Things Go Better' appealed. At least as early as 1966, McCann-Erickson was fashioning what were called 'pattern commercials,' sent to foreign markets for use or adaptation by local ad-makers.

In retrospect the campaign seems an experiment to see just what would work. Soon the discipline of 'one sound, one sight, one sell' was relaxed to tailor ads and even media to reach particular segments of the market. A tape of pattern commercials (1966–70) contained ads aimed at youth, housewives, the family, and heavy users. Radio advertising was largely dedicated to reaching youth with a succession of lively songs sung by popular singers or groups of the day. Some television commercials were very similar to the fun and frenzy ads of Pepsi-Cola spots: that was especially true of the vignette commercials where a sequence of different scenes were linked together by a common theme and the common song. Others used satire and humour, human interest stories, thoughtful commentaries on life, and even testimonials, for example, from football hero Jim Taylor or black singer Ray Charles (who in the early 1990s would be featured in a Diet Pepsi campaign). One especially imaginative effort in 1967, *Involvement II*, boasted only a picture of an open, wet, slightly bubbling bottle of Coke and a succession of changing sounds and words suggesting heat, refreshment, and enjoyment.

Coca-Cola's advertising strategy didn't jell until the launching of the 'It's the Real Thing' campaign in October 1969. One company document, entitled *The Pause That Refreshes*, claims the campaign's purpose was to 'reestablish the fact that Coke was the original, the best, the leader.' Another document referred to this as 'our first worldwide campaign,' though I will concentrate upon its American dimension. For the campaign and its successors ('Look Up America,' 'Coke Adds Life,' and 'Have a Coke and a Smile!') touted a distinct, coherent vision of America and Coke's place in this America, during the 1970s. It also featured two of the most famous commercials ever made, *Buy the World a Coke* or *Hilltop* (first aired in 1971) and *Mean Joe Greene* (1979).

Most of the Americana commercials told a story, either via vignettes or a narrative, about some aspect of life. A mix of stills and live action shots is used to show people of all sorts at rest or play in *Mod* (1969) or to spotlight American places where this living happens in *America* (1969); by contrast, *Honeymoon* (1971) featured country people assisting a young couple whose car has broken down, and *Country Sunshine* (1972) focused on a woman experiencing the joys of homecoming.

Every one of the commercials used a song to inform the pictures on the screen and to link the individual ad to the overall campaign. Country star Dottie West sings about being 'raised on country sunshine' in that 1972 commercial, which shared honours as one of three awarded a Campaign Clio the next year. A clean-cut group of black youngsters break out into a semigospel version of the campaign song 'Coke Adds Life' in *Street Song* (1976), to the acclaim of an audience of older folk. All commercials were characterized by exceptionally fine photography, direction, and editing, making them superb examples of the art. *Raft* (1971 or 1972), a commercial about two young people at play in summertime, manages to evoke a sense of nostalgia for simpler times with a mix of earth tones and friendly colours. *Good Things* (1974), part of the 'Look Up America' campaign, flashes a series of black-and-white (meaning past) and colour (meaning present) shots of Americana to encourage viewers to celebrate their heritage.

There was a certain preachiness to the Americana campaigns, although this was never explicit in the best commercials. No wonder: one 1982 news release boasted that 'the Company's advertising has accurately reflected attitudes of the times, often anticipating changing lifestyles and the national temperament.' Translated, that comment meant the ads had a definite mission, a desire to boost a particular conception of the nation's character. It wasn't just that the Americana campaigns sported a happy face, since this was generally true of all forms of consumer advertising. Rather these commercials championed a cluster of associated values: tradition, family life, neighbourhood, simplicity, harmony, and patriotism that, they presumed, had made America great. One purpose of *Parade* (1976), in the year of America's bicentennial, was to boost the nation's morale with a series of pictures about a small town celebrating Independence Day. Both *America* and *Good Things* called upon Americans to take pride in their country. Bill Cosby in *Have a Coke & a Smile* (1979) urged tired, frustrated, or bored people (all of whom appeared on the screen) to lift their spirits, simply by pausing to drink a Coke. Returning home in *Country Sunshine* meant recognizing one's roots, searching for what was authentic in life – like Coke itself. The appeal of the Americana campaigns lay in their contrast with the distemper of the times: the Vietnam crisis, the generation gap, racial animosities, the boredom of work, the worry about moral decay, the doubts about America's virtue, the worldwide strife. Strange as it may seem, the Americana campaigns had definite political overtones, aimed at reassuring Americans of their own virtue and celebrating their achievements. It's reminiscent of one brand of conservatism that found favour in the Reagan years of the next decade.

The themes of healing and harmony were especially pronounced in *Buy the World a Coke* and *Mean Joe Greene*, both of which are entered in the Clio's U.S. Classic Hall of Fame. To make *Buy the World*, McCann-Erickson found a group of attractive young people of both sexes and some thirty nationalities, chosen from among embassy families and international schools in Rome. Standing on an Italian hilltop, they mouthed the lyrics to a specially written song later entitled 'I'd Like to Teach the World to Sing (In Perfect Harmony)' and boldly held forth bottles of Coca-Cola. The commercial opens on the face of a pink-cheeked, blonde-haired, English lass and moves out to reveal two more singers, then pans across an array of youngsters dressed in national costumes, pausing on an American girl who sings 'It's the Real Thing.' With the outline of her image superimposed on the screen, the camera moves back to reveal the whole collection of hilltop singers. The commercial ends with the rolling of an on-screen text explaining who the singers were and noting their sponsor, the Coca-Cola bottlers around the world. The final picture features an insert of the famous Coke bottle in a panoramic shot of the hilltop.

What made the commercial so powerful was the 'anthem to amity' (*Los Angeles Herald-Tribune*, 21 January 1972), which was actually sung by a British group, the New Seekers. The tune was catchy, melodic, and harmonious. The lyrics expressed a yearning for peace, harmony, and love. The singers hoped 'to buy the world a home,' 'furnish it with love,' 'grow apple trees and honey bees,' 'teach the world to sing in perfect harmony.' And they yearned 'to buy the world a Coke and keep it company,' for what the world wanted was 'the real thing.' So simple, so uplifting a song reached back to a tradition of gentle folk-songs and Christmas carols, quite unlike the vigorous sounds and often angry, disenchanted, or protest-filled lyrics of rock.

The visuals, music, and song conjured up a vision of the magic properties of consumption to transform a troubled world into a place of togetherness. It was the sort of thing ad-makers had been saying in different ways ever since the craft matured back in the 1920s. Initially some agency people worried that viewers would conclude 'we were trying to commercialize world peace,' according to Sid McAllister of McCann-Erickson. Instead the images of clean-cut teenagers of all races singing for peace and hope reassured youth and adults alike that things would turn out all right. The yearning for harmony was indeed universal, bridging the great divides of colour and age. The Coca-Cola Archives contain a variety of press clippings and news releases that attest to the extraordinary response of the American public. People wrote to the company and Coca-Cola bottlers praising the commercial, requesting copies of the lyrics and tapes, even complaining the sixty-second ad was too short or asking for more frequent showings! It was 'beautiful,' 'really moving,' 'outstanding,' 'delightful,' 'the greatest,' 'the best I've ever seen.' An altered and extended version of the song was released for general play on radio and apparently sold more than a million records. McCann-Erickson produced some variations of *Buy the World*, one called *Candles* (1977) becoming a Christmas special for a time. In 1989 the agency assembled once more most of the initial singers and, now with their children, produced *Hilltop Reunion*, which premiered during Super Bowl XXIV in 1990.

If *Buy the World* promised a happy future, then *Mean Joe Greene* showed a person transformed. It was a superb instance of the heart-warming or sentimental commercial, that won a bevy of domestic and international awards, including a Clio and a Cannes Gold. The ad features Joe Greene, a large black man, the defensive back of the Pittsburg Steelers who had a well-earned reputation as a tough guy, and a small white boy, one Tommy Oken, who plays the role of a devoted fan. We see Greene, obviously suffering pain and frustration, limping towards the team dressing room; he's stopped by the kid who expresses his admiration and offers an irritated Greene a large Coke; Greene first refuses, then accepts and chuggalugs the Coke; the kid shrugs and turns away, upset by his hero's indifference; but a renewed Greene throws his game jersey to the kid, who of course is filled with joy. The campaign song came on towards the close of the ad, which ends with the command 'Have a Coke and a Smile,' plus the old adage 'Coke Adds Life.'

This was melodrama. The problem was quickly and deftly displayed, the solution offered, and the cure celebrated, all in sixty seconds. The ad was full of contrasts – black/white, big/little, star/fan, mean/nice, tired/renewed. It was easy to understand, to empathize with the situation and the players. What made the emotion effective rather than sappy were the performances, the irritated tone in Greene's voice or the kid's body language, both of which added a touch of realism. Tommy was especially expressive – of awe, of caring, of yearning, of thanks. The ad captured one of those magic moments in life: it had a special poignancy for anyone who'd experienced a similar kind of hero worship, especially in a sports-mad land like America. *Mean Joe Greene* also spoke of sharing, harmony, and togetherness, bridging the gap between the famous and the anonymous, between black and white, between adult and youth. Once again, Coke was effectively portrayed as 'a democratic luxury' that broke down the barriers between people.

According to a story in the *Chicago Tribune* (16 October 1981), Joe Greene told friends that the commercial 'gave him more individual recognition than he ever received as a player.' A company magazine, *Refresher USA*, noted that articles appeared on Greene's role in *Newsweek, People, Sports Illustrated,* the *New York Times,* the *Washington Post,* and so on. A number of network TV shows, notably 'Good Morning America' and 'Today,' devoted time to covering the story. Later, Video Storyboard Tests rated this commercial the best-liked since the firm had begun testing public preferences back in 1977. Versions of the commercial were shown around the world, a Spanish translation was made especially for Mexico, and the ad was reshot in Brazil and Thailand using local sports heroes. Elsewhere, I suspect viewers would have been a bit puzzled unless they fully understood the mysteries of American football.

Early in 1982, Coca-Cola rolled out its new campaign, 'Coke Is It!' A news release claimed this 'direct, positive statement appeals to the forthright stance of Americans in the 1980s,' whatever that meant. In fact the campaign seems to have caused little excitement among the public, at least after the initial flurry of interest: in 1983 and 1984 the Coca-Cola campaign was rated five and eight on a scale of ten, according to Video Storyboard's tests of viewer preferences.

The commercials had moved away from the images and themes of the Americana campaigns to emulate the high energy style of frolicking youth made more famous by Pepsi. That change marked a startling shift in corporate strategy, caused by the apparently inexorable advance of Pepsi-Cola throughout the 1970s. 'Coke Is It!' evidenced a fighting mood among Coca-Cola's managers. The new leaders of Coca-Cola broke with the past, first by successfully launching Diet Coke in 1982 and then, even more dramatically, by changing the taste of Coke itself with the introduction in 1985 of what the press and consumers dubbed 'New Coke.' Later, CEO Roberto Goizueta told the *Wall Street Journal* that the purpose was to protect 'the value of the Coca-Cola trademark.' The trouble was that Coca-Cola also removed from the market the now 'Old Coke,' favourite of millions. Within a few months an explosion of consumer outrage, fuelled by extensive coverage in the news media, compelled the company to reintroduce 'Old Coke' as Coke Classic. Shortly afterwards, Coke Classic was winning sales far greater than New Coke. The whole fiasco went down in marketing history as a marvellous example of what not to do, although there remained sceptics who believed the company had actually scripted the outrage to hype the main brand. In any case, Coke was no longer the universal cola: the presence of New Coke, Coke Classic, Cherry Coke, and Diet Coke led wits to claim 'Coke Are It.'

Coca-Cola was a victim of its own advertising. The Americana campaigns had imaginatively built on the cola's reputation to position Coke as being as American as mom and apple pie. Even if they had failed to stop the Pepsi advance, which probably had a lot to do with battles on other fronts in the Cola Wars, the campaigns of the 1970s had reaffirmed the fact Coke was 'the original, the best, the leader,' 'the real thing,' a symbol of a traditional America and its way of life. Now Coca-Cola had tried to steal something consumers treasured. That could have spelled disaster if the company hadn't surrendered. Ironically, the first campaign for Coke Classic, called 'Red, White & You,' harked back to the glory years of the Americana campaigns. One of these commercials, *Celebration* (1986), mixed scenes of people caught up in a mood of happy abandon with a song proclaiming the good times were 'coming our way.' In 1986 Coca-Cola advertising, presumably both 'Red, White & You' as well as New Coke's 'Catch the Wave,' earned a ranking of one in the Video Storyboard Tests.

Pepsi's 'New Generation' (1984–6)

Early on in *The Other Guy Blinked: How Pepsi Won the Cola Wars* (1986), Roger Enrico, then president of Pepsi-Cola U.S.A., crowed about how his 'New

Generation' campaign deserved recognition for encouraging the New Coke debacle and so finally giving Pepsi victory in the Cola Wars. His brag was wrong on both counts. If any one ad campaign had influenced Coca-Cola, then credit had to go to the 'Pepsi Challenge,' the most galling sign of the Pepsi advance. Besides, by most measures, Coca-Cola remained the industry leader, and its sales of Coke Classic (1.5 billion cases in 1988) swiftly regained a slight edge over Pepsi (nearly 1.4 billion). Yet Enrico deserved his share of plaudits for shepherding the 'New Generation' campaign through corporate channels to its appearance on American TV screens, for this bold strike proved to be a brilliant renewal of Pepsi's twenty-year-old 'Pepsi Generation' campaign.

There is an undated speech about this famous two-word phrase in the Pepsi-Cola Advertising Collection at the Center of Advertising History in Washington. That speech briefly sketched how journalists, essayists, academics, congressmen, even a decorated Vietnam war hero made use of the 'Pepsi Generation.' The phrase had acquired a variety of overlapping meanings: the baby-boom generation, an ever-renewing collection of teenagers, or (and more appropriately) a label for the young and the young at heart. It could be used as a term of opprobrium, to denote people who couldn't grow up and face the rigours of life, as well as a description of social identity, to denote a special group defined by age, values, and habits. In either case it presumed a generation devoted to a fundamentally hedonistic lifestyle.

The phrase was born back in the 1960s when Pepsi-Cola's new agency, BBDO, was attempting to reposition a brand once sold as a bargain drink, later as an upscale beverage. First came the 'Think Young' campaign, which around 1965 mutated into 'Come Alive' where the term 'Pepsi Generation' was introduced amid scenes of lively youth enjoying the good times. Ironically, the copywriter who is credited with inventing the phrase, John Bergin, would take charge of the Coca-Cola account at McCann-Erickson in 1980. Although the tag was briefly shelved – some executives feared Pepsi would be identified too closely with youth – the 'Pepsi Generation' was resurrected for the expensive and sophisticated 'Live/Give' campaign (1969–72) and continued through a series of other campaigns into the early 1980s. BBDO had managed to appropriate the California lifestyle, that dreamland of leisure and play where the eternally young frolicked till the sun went down. 'The commercials subtly positioned Pepsi as the modern American soft drink,' claimed John Sculley, 'and by contrast, Coke as the old-fashioned cola.' The downside was that they couldn't work their magic in other countries, recalled Alan Pottasch, the company's long-time advertising manager, where sales weren't enough to justify naming a whole generation after Pepsi.

In the mid-1970s, though, Pepsi-Cola also embarked upon a reason-why campaign known as the 'Pepsi Challenge.' Blind tests indicated that under certain conditions people preferred the taste of Pepsi to Coke by a significant margin, as much as sixty to forty recalled Dick Alven, a Pepsi-Cola executive. (If people knew which brands they were drinking, though, Coke was the winner!) This finding was expressed in a series of local commercials intended to boost dismal sales in the Dallas area: ordinary folk were shown taking the test and choosing Pepsi. 'Take the Pepsi Challenge' proved so effective that the idea spread to other places, influenced national advertising, and even moved into Canada ('Look Who's Drinking Pepsi Now' campaign, 1981). In its various forms, the 'Pepsi Challenge' was an aggressive form of comparative advertising that used a product difference – a smoother taste – to attack a named rival. There remains some dispute over the consequences of the campaign: it helped to fuel the Pepsi advance in some markets, though Sculley believed that was really at the expense of other, weaker brands, not Coke. It may also have improved the overall image of Pepsi, which by 1977 was outselling its rival in supermarkets across America. It certainly infuriated Coca-Cola: during the early 1980s the company began to threaten dire action (special promotions, deep discounts, and the like) against Pepsi bottlers who utilized the 'Pepsi Challenge' in its original form. Richard Tedlow concluded that neither Pepsi nor Coke wished to turn the Cola Wars into a no-holds-barred conflict that might well devastate profit margins.

In any case Pepsi-Cola shelved both the 'Pepsi Challenge' and the older lifestyle advertising because they just weren't working very well. Apparently people found the image ads of the two rivals were becoming much the same: Pepsi sometimes used scenes of Americana, Coke offered its own version of fun and frolic. Sales of both stagnated in 1982 and 1983. Were consumers getting bored with the Cola Wars? In 1983 BBDO creative director Phil Dusenberry and chairman Allen Rosenshine came up with the idea of identifying the brand as 'The Choice of a New Generation,' putting Pepsi 'on the leading edge of what was happening' in Enrico's words. The aim was to make a series of spectacular commercials, better yet, mini movies: original, unusual, full of special effects, and trendy images – all to cause a sensation. That required bags of money, roughly $20,000 a second for the first batch of ads, plus $5.5 million to buy the talents of the newest superstar, Michael Jackson. The 'New Generation' campaign itself was a story of exuberance and excess that suited the spirit of Reagan's America.

The plan worked. Few campaigns in the history of television advertising have enjoyed so successful a launch. Hiring Michael Jackson proved the key to grabbing the attention of the media and the public. Even before the airing of *Jackson Street* and *Jackson* Pepsi-Cola got a massive amount of free publicity simply because Jackson was such a big news story. These commercials were premiered on MTV, and segments replayed even on news shows, all free of charge. The day after their debut, an advertising research outfit discovered the two spots had a higher recall than any other commercials in history, Enrico boasted. Overall, the 'New Generation' ads won a host of awards, including an amazing eight Cannes Lions in three years: one runner-up, two bronze, two silver, two gold, and one Grand Prix (in 1985).

In some ways the 'New Generation' campaign was a continuance of past television advertising. It certainly traded upon the currency of all those images of a swinging Pepsi generation. Pepsi-Cola was still positioned as the modern, indeed the ultramodern drink. Pepsi people were certifiably 'cool,' in tune with the times. There was still a preference for young faces, though not so pronounced as in, say, 'Live/Give' – perhaps a sign of the aging of the baby boomers? Pottasch, quoted in *The Best of Ad Campaigns!* (Blount and Walker), emphasized that the company sought performers who were full of energy, who acted young. There were often echoes of the Cola Wars: an alien spacecraft selects Pepsi over Coke in a replay of taste tests called *Spaceship*, the Grand Prix winner, *Archeology*, posits a self-indulgent view of the future where even the memory of Coke had gone, and *Robots* sees Pepsi and Coke vending machines mutate into battle robots preparing for a mortal combat forestalled by the arrival of a carload of teenagers.

But the design of the 'New Generation' differed markedly from earlier campaigns. It was more image than lifestyle advertising: now the chief focus was on the product or the user, which were positioned as 'winners' (to use a term much favoured in the eighties). Thus the glee of the Pepsi vending machine in *Robots* when a teenage boy selects a Pepsi instead of a Coke – a little head pops up and snickers. The old staple of the vignette commercial where snapshots of happy times were linked together disappeared; instead, each commercial employed the design of the playlet, a ploy that aptly suited the tastes of a generation brought up on TV's stories. Even the fairly straight *Jackson* commercial was organized around the excitement building behind the scenes and among the audience over the beginning of a rock concert, an excitement realized when Jackson makes his grand entrance. There was no single campaign song or jingle, although new lyrics were written to Jackson's 'Billie Jean' in praise of 'the whole new generation' and 'the Pepsi way' for his spots. The sell was kept well-hidden: there was little use of the voice-over, except to repeat the campaign slogan at the end of a commercial. The very clever *Archeology*, for example, makes its point when even a know-it-all professor cannot tell his class of teenagers just what a newly unearthed Coke bottle was. There was much greater use of humour to hook the audience: so *Sound Truck* shows how a young entrepreneur excites the thirst of a beach full of people by playing the sound of drinking a Pepsi over loud speakers – before offering to sell all comers a bottle of their favourite refreshment. And each of the commercials was a distinct entity, rather than the product of a common format or the vehicle of one or another story-line. *Reflections* focuses on reflections – from a motorcycle's gas tank, a rear-view mirror, a Pepsi can; by contrast, *Floats* has two astronauts engaged in a comic struggle to capture the last bottle of Pepsi on board their starship.

What gave a special quality to the 'New Generation' series, however, was its display of proven images of significance, styles, and representations that pleased the public. This involved much borrowing from the realms of popular music, movies, and the like. Superstar Michael Jackson was the embodiment of cultural power, even among viewers who found his style distasteful. And in 1985 Pepsi-Cola employed another singer-as-celebrity, Lionel Ritchie, to tout its virtues. *Jackson Street* was shot like a music video where a group of black and white, male and female youngsters begin an exuberant dance in the street, led by a Jackson 'wannabe' (complete with glove) who backs into the Real One (the kid's eyes grow big), which leads to an orgy of dancing and posing. *Shark* uses music from the movie *Jaws* to enliven scenes of a fin (actually a kid with a surfboard) moving through a crowded beach of umbrellas. The bright spaceship and the rural setting in *Spaceship* are reminiscent of *Close Encounters of the Third Kind,* just as *Basement Visitor* takes from *E.T.* the notion of a gentle alien befriended by children. The menacing machines in *Robots* are modelled upon the Japanese 'transformers' so popular in the mid-1980s. *Shuttle* evokes memories of an actual launch of the Challenger: ground control 'talks' a pilot through the enjoyment of a Pepsi during a delay in the take-off procedure. The 'New Generation' exploited that common experience so many Americans had with the products of mass culture, a fact which gives some credibility to the claim by Alan Pottasch that these commercials depicted the Americana of the eighties.

Dusenberry and his staff had created stylish spectacles that put Pepsi on the 'leading edge' of everyone's imagination. So popular was the 'New Generation' that it continued throughout the decade. Pepsi continued to hire celebrities, Michael Jackson again in 1986 (this time at an estimated $15 million), 'Miami Vice' star Don Johnson and Eagles singer Glenn Frey, and movie sensation Michael J. Fox (for Diet Pepsi). And it continued to tease Coke and tout the Cola Wars. In 1990 Pepsi won a Silver Lion at Cannes for the wickedly clever *Shady Acres:* we see a lot of happy oldsters gyrating to the rhythms of rock and a small group of solemn college boys playing a quiet game of bingo – it seems the delivery truck had made a mistake, dropping off the Coke at the frat house and the Pepsi at the retirement home. Pepsi invigorated, Coke ossified. The public kept applauding: between 1984 and 1990, Pepsi beat Coke six out of seven times in the yearly consumer ratings of advertising conducted by Video Storyboard Tests, reported the *Economist* (14 September 1991).

But good things really do have to end sometimes. Pepsi-Cola chose the 1992 Super Bowl, when around 100 million North Americans were watching, to replace the 'New Generation' campaign, at an estimated cost for airtime of $6.4 million in the United States and $1.5 million in Canada. The first spot piqued viewer interest: it depicted the actions of a farmer, purportedly on 12 January, who was compelled by some unknown impulse to drive off a country road and plough into a 'New Generation' billboard. The second spot explained how the event provoked a grand party *à la* Woodstock where people of all generations started celebrating with Pepsi – one cute girl said, 'Maybe it means the taste of Pepsi is so big, it should be the choice of everybody.' The third used a mixed group of celebrities to search for a new slogan, though it was the girl who declares, 'Gotta Have It.' The last spot treated the 'Gotta Have It' movement as a news event, where a series of vignettes attested to the popularity of the drink, the accuracy of the slogan, and the wild abandon of Pepsi addicts. A marvellous touch: one female speaker, playing out the role of the psychologist and critic, intones, 'The phrase "Gotta Have It" strikes a cord deep in the human psyche.' All this before the first quarter of the game had ended.

A later report in the *Toronto Star* (29 January 1992) made clear the change was a marketing decision. The 'New Generation' campaign may have remained popular, but sales figures didn't prove it remained effective. Pepsi's share of the U.S. soft-drink market had actually fallen from 18.8 to 18.4, while Coke Classic had held steady with a 20 per cent share in 1991. So Pepsi had symbolically closed the generation gap, declaring instead that Pepsi was a drink for everyone.

About Campaigns

There are moments when Enrico's *The Other Guy Blinked* reads like the work of an artistic impresario, so often does he talk about hiring performers, campaign themes, the merit or weakness of commercials, and so on. Even he admitted his account sometimes left the impression that Pepsi-Cola manufactured commercials first and foremost.

But his preoccupation wasn't at all unusual. The same concern comes through in John Sculley's *Odyssey* and the interviews with Jack Landry of Philip Morris or Donald Kendall of Pepsi-Cola. So much was invested in the success of a campaign. The authors of *Competition and Concentration* reported that ad expenditures on American network and spot TV in 1988 alone were $55.8 million for Coke Classic and $47.3 million for Diet Coke versus $60.8 million for Pepsi and $46.1 million for Diet Pepsi.

Besides the money, there was the personal reputation of the reigning executive at stake, which leads to what Hall Adams, Jr., leader of Leo Burnett U.S.A. in 1986, called the struggle to preserve 'the integrity of an idea.' Campaigns that don't appear to generate sales soon get dumped. That's to be expected – advertising is an obvious scapegoat. But there was a hidden danger that always faced the successful campaign: Adams worried about new people coming in on the account, whether at the agency or the company, who 'want to screw around,' to 'add something new,' just to put a personal stamp on the campaign. He cited the instance of the Pillsbury Dough Boy campaigns, in which he feared newcomers had been too clever and so hurt the idea. Adams, like the 'creative' Norman Muse and the executive Jack Landry, ranged himself among the 'keepers of the flame' who worked hard to ensure no one tampered with the Marlboro Man or Marlboro Country.

Philip Morris proved ready to take dramatic action to prevent any outsider from devaluing its campaign. The English antismoking advocate, Peter Taylor, recounted one such incident in his book *Smoke Ring* (1984). In 1976 he was intimately involved in the production of a Thames Television documentary with the revealing title 'Death in the West – the Marlboro Story.' The documentary employed material from Marlboro commercials mixed with interviews of real American cowboys dying from cancer or emphysema. Apparently it caused a sufficient sensation in Britain to elicit interest from CBS's 'Sixty Minutes' in a rebroadcast for the American public. But Philip Morris secured a High Court injunction preventing Thames Television from selling or showing the documentary again, largely on the grounds that the cigarette company had been misled into allowing the use of its commercials. An out-of-court agreement handed over all but one copy of 'Death in the West' to Philip Morris, and that last copy was to stay locked up in the bowels of Thames Television. When Taylor went out to the American West much later on to see again the families he'd interviewed, he learned that some had been visited by representatives of Philip Morris to check whether they were really cowboys and victims. In the end a pirated version of 'Death in the West' got out to anti-smoking groups and media in the United States and Australia. But, whatever the denouement of this story, it illustrates how far one company would go to protect 'the integrity of an idea.'

The career of Pepsi-Cola advertising sheds a different light on the problems of maintaining a coherent brand image. For nearly two decades Pepsi-Cola executives intermittently debated the merits of lifestyle versus reason-why advertising. 'Taste That Beats the Others Cold' (1968–9) represented an attempt to use images of youth to underline the taste superiority of Pepsi for everyone. The 'Smilin' Majority' was another upbeat campaign that didn't make it in part because it seemed to echo Richard Nixon's slogan of the day, 'the silent majority,' recalled Tom Dillon, and that could have mixed Pepsi in the morass of politics. The later 'Pepsi Challenge' was a much more direct effort to tout the claimed taste advantage of the brand to an audience of all Americans, to represent Pepsi as a universal product that should replace Coke. By contrast the successive waves of 'Pepsi Generation' campaigns targeted a segment of the population defined according to demographics (youth) and psychographics (think young). The genius of the 'New Generation' was that it melded elements of both into a novel kind of campaign that was sensational, entertaining, and open-ended, enabling Pepsi to speak of its taste superiority, its modernity, the claim it was the in-drink, the choice of people living in the fast lane. While the character of 'Marlboro Country' had been settled and frozen at an early date, the image of Pepsi has undergone a series of changes to keep it fresh and lively.

The Coke story highlights a third aspect of the same struggle. The previously mentioned *The Pause That Refreshes* made much of the fact that advertising had to suit the prevailing expectations of consumers:

Consumers see every ad or commercial for Coke as an extension of the product itself. Time and again in research studies people will comment, 'that's not Coca-Cola' when the ambience of the commercial or ad is not 'quality' or 'tasteful' or misses the way people see the product and how it fits the pulse of their daily lives.

So it follows that a commercial for Coca-Cola should have the properties of the product itself. It should be a pleasurable experience, refreshing to watch and pleasant to listen to. It should reflect quality by being quality. And it should make you say, 'I wish I'd been there. I wish I had been drinking Coke with those people.'

The special difficulty facing McCann-Erickson was to realize this imperative within the confines of 'one sight, one sound, one sell' (a discipline finally relaxed in February 1993 when Coke went after targeted audiences with the 'Always Coca-Cola' campaign). A tape of 'pattern' and foreign commercials for the 'Coke Is It!' campaign of 1982, preserved at the Coca-Cola Archives, demonstrates how the agency strove to maintain the 'integrity of an idea' as well as to satisfy local expectations. Because most of the commercials were vignettes, the task of tailoring the foreign version was much easier than would have been the case with a continuous drama. The pattern *Fireworks* featured a collection of fun-loving Americans preparing for an evening celebration that would be topped off with a fireworks display. Its Korean variation retained the distance shots, but substituted close-ups of Asian faces. The minute-long *Sidewalk Snack Bar* told the story of a day in the life of two male waiters serving patrons and watching women: it ran as a thirty-second spot with the necessary cuts and a change of language for Belgium, but was totally refilmed for Argentina, presumably to capture the particular spirit of café life in that country. The abbreviated Greek version of *Soccermania* retained the same shots as the pattern commercial but changed the music track. The very lively *Song*, about some shapely female performers who burst out into song and dance, ran in the United States and Ireland; it was shortened and translated for the French market; and it was totally reshot with a new troupe for Brazil. Because there was no exact translation of 'Coke Is It!' in Spanish, the slogan became '¡*más y más!*' ('More and more!') in Chile and '*Coca-Cola es así!*' (roughly 'That's the way it is!') in Mexico. Even so, the foreign versions of the 'Coke Is It!' campaign remained remarkably true to the originals because the prevailing themes of sociability and pleasure could be easily expressed in a variety of different languages and societies. Here was an instance of global marketing.

This brings me back to the question of advertising as art. The campaigns I've discussed worked their magic because they managed to mythologize aspects of American life: the cowboy and the West, the 'great American traditions,' a California lifestyle, the cult of youth, the pursuit of leisure. They made concrete fantasies that could feed the imagination of people at home and abroad. Let me conclude with one example supplied by the psychologist Dr Carol Moog in her '*Are They Selling Her Lips?' Advertising and Identity* (1990). Dr Moog tells the tale of a young, hard-driving lawyer she calls Amy who'd suffered from depression because of the break up of a long-lasting relationship. During the course of the therapy, Amy declared, 'This is great. Here I am – the Pepsi generation – and I feel like jumping out the window.' What did the Pepsi generation mean to Amy? It meant yelling over Michael Jackson, 'going crazy,' 'having fun,' breaking loose from the normal routine of work and obligation to indulge herself in the headlong pursuit of leisure. This was the very lifestyle Amy had avoided to achieve success in college and in the profession. But that fact made the myth of the Pepsi generation all the more seductive because it promised an escape from present troubles into a realm of permanent joy. The point is that Pepsi-Cola's advertising, directly or indirectly, had established a set of images about the good life that evoked a response even from someone who'd chosen a far different course. Amy's story was just another illustration of how art can affect what we perceive is 'reality.'

3

Art in the Service of Commerce

Only in imagination does every truth find an effective and undeniable existence. Imagination, not invention, is the supreme master of art as of life.
                                         – Ascribed to Joseph Conrad (1857–1924)

That quotation graced a congratulatory ad placed by CHCH Production Facili-
ties (an offshoot of a private Hamilton TV station) in the catalogue of the 1988
winners of Canada's Bessies. I say 'ascribed' to Joseph Conrad, since someone
(an anonymous copywriter?) had actually dropped one word, the adjective
'men's' before 'imagination,' presumably to make the language gender-neu-
tral. The original had appeared in Conrad's *Some Reminiscences* (1912), later
reissued as *A Personal Record*, from whence it made its way into at least one
thesaurus of quotations.

There are a number of ways to interpret so cryptic a claim. Conrad was
actually explaining why he wanted to describe two family moments from his
earlier days, referring in the next sentence to the virtues of 'an imaginative and
exact rendering of authentic memories.' But once processed by a thesaurus, the
aphorism was open to a variety of meanings, dependent in part upon its new
context. I read the quotation as an assertion of the supremacy of art. Truth is
what artists perceive to be such. Implicitly, the quotation questions the
importance of other forms of communication, such as news, which claim
objectivity. The aphorism celebrates the ascendancy of the image, downplaying
the significance of fact. Carried further, the contrast between imagination and
invention suggests others: art and commerce, mind and body, soul and brain,
metaphor and reason-why.

How fitting that Conrad's assertion should be employed by an agent of the
advertising industry to support a claim of cultural value in the contemporary
world. Conrad's meanings are altered by this usage. We have here an excellent

example of appropriation: the way in which ad people can take any idea out of context and turn it to their own purposes. The quotation in the context of the advertisement amounts to an assertion that the Bessies are a work of the imagination. The very act of attaching Conrad's name, and so reputation, to the Bessies is as important as what the quotation says or doesn't say – for the Bessies are thereby linked to quality, to art, gaining stature through association with the cryptic thought of a cultural luminary. Fact and argument have only a secondary place in this process, a process which implicitly contradicts the modernist assumption that art and commerce are distinct if not antagonistic realms.

The use of the quotation also implies that television commercials are, along with other works of the imagination, the source of what we should consider Truth. This notion disputes the prevailing distrust of ads and hype. Hype is a form of communication that, among much else, uses the power of metaphor over logic, of image over fact. The quotation amounts to an assertion that the messages of commercials – about life, about behaviour, about us – reach to a deeper reality. So making sense of Conrad's perplexing comment leads us into an exploration of commercials as art.

The 'Creative Revolution'

The cover story of *Newsweek* (18 August 1969) surveyed what people had come to call a 'creative revolution' that was causing such excitement on Madison Avenue. That upheaval had begun at least a decade before, though only in the last five or six years had it become so noticeable. It represented the response of the ad industry to the moods of the sixties, to the so-called youth movement and the opening up of American society, to the attack on convention and the zeal to experiment. 'Whatever it may be called,' wrote *Newsweek*, 'the fact remains that creativity has emerged from writers' cubby holes and artists' bullpens to become a dominant factor on the nationwide advertising scene.' The result was a new style of advertising, much more artistic than before. 'One thing seems certain: Madison Avenue is more often intriguing the U.S. consumer these days than boring him.'

Legend has it that the man behind the 'creative revolution' was Bill Bernbach of Doyle Dane Bernbach. The historian Stephen Fox has identified such other giants as Chicago's Leo Burnett (of Marlboro fame) and the British born David Ogilvy (who designed the Hathaway Man) as co-pioneers of the new advertising. But neither can match the stature of Bernbach in advertising's memory, for Bernbach gave 'creatives,' meaning the copywriter and the art director, a place in the sun.

This master's views on his craft have been outlined in *Bill Bernbach's Book*, a compilation by his friend and admirer, Bob Levinson. 'Advertising is fundamentally persuasion and persuasion happens to be not a science, but an art,' Bernbach declared back in 1947, when he was at Grey Advertising. Later he extolled the virtues of the poets in humanity's past, 'the real giants who jumped from facts into the realm of imagination and ideas.' Indeed 'the very thing that is most suspect by business, that intangible thing called artistry, turns out to be the most practical tool available to it.' Why? Because 'it is only artistry that can vie with all the shocking news events and violence in the world for the attention of the consumer.' Bernbach was no proponent of art for art's sake; he championed advertising as useful art, a way of engaging the heart and mind of the consumer in the age of the information explosion.

At DDB, a new agency launched in 1949, Bernbach had been able to implement his philosophy. He worked to produce original, charming, and usually witty or humorous ads, winning fame in the 1950s for campaigns for Ohrbach's department store and Henry S. Levy's bakery in New York, Polaroid's instant camera, and El Al Airlines. He strove to attract 'creatives' who trusted their intuition more than research, who were willing to experiment, to break with the prevailing ethos of the hard sell, which was closely associated with Rosser Reeves at the big-time Ted Bates agency. Above all, Bernbach refined the concept of the creative team. Before, the normal practice was to develop the copy before the art; after, the copywriter and art director were accorded equal status, and both were given the task of designing the ad – the result was not just a more integrated advertisement but an ad with greater visual impact. So that most famous of DDB campaigns in the 1960s, the Volkswagen 'Beetle' ads, came about through the combined efforts of Julien Koenig (copywriter), Helmut Krone (art director), and Bill Bernbach (adviser). Indeed the ad or campaign became the property of the creative team, something with which neither the account executives nor the research people were allowed to tamper. Bernbach had liberated the 'creatives.' No wonder Marvin Honig, one of these souls, recalled much later that it was an honour to be hired by DDB.

The DDB approach won kudos and accounts. The Volkswagen campaign was widely regarded as one of the best ever, in large part because sales of the funny little car boomed. (One caveat here: Michael Schudson has emphasized that the Volkswagon was selling well, even before DDB entered the picture, and suggests that 'the campaign caught the crest of a sales wave.') Almost as famous was the 'We Try Harder' campaign for Avis car rental, which capitalized on the fact it was number two. Despite the fact that DDB was best remembered for its magazine ads, indeed in some circles was called a print shop, the agency won fifty-one Clios (out of a possible 401 listed by Cobbett Steinberg) between 1963 and 1971. Its creative fame paid off in billings, bringing DDB into the big time: billings reached $130 million in 1965 and $249.7 million in 1970, making it the sixth-ranked agency in the United States.

The new gospel spread. Bernbach had trained a generation of young 'creatives' who moved elsewhere or started up their own shops, which then fostered a second and even third wave of agencies. Among the most famous of the 'boutiques,' as old-timers sneeringly called them, were Papert, Koenig, Lois; Jack Tinker & Partners, owned by Marion Harper's conglomerate Interpublic; Wells, Rich, Greene, noted for its television advertising and the presence of the only top-ranked woman in the business, Mary Wells; Carl Ally, a Papert, Koenig, Lois graduate, who made his name with the Volvo account; Delahanty, Kurnit & Geller, out of which came Della Femina, Travisano – all won Clios and clients. Nor was DDB's influence confined to the United States: in Toronto Jerry Goodis of the fast-rising newcomer Goodis, Goldberg, Soren looked upon DDB ('my heroes,' he wrote later) as the model for a revolution in Canadian advertising.

Meanwhile, the established agencies tried to ride the wave of creativity. In 1962 Young & Rubicam hired the youthful Stephen O. Frankfort as creative director, who then imitated the concept of the creative team, and made him president of Y&R U.S.A. a few years later – Y&R took fifty-five Clios (1963–71), more than any other agency, and boosted its billings from $212 million (1960) to $356.4 million (1970), making it number two in the U.S. rankings. The hard-nosed Ted Bates agency briefly employed Jerry Della Femina at a high salary to give its advertising some creative sparkle. Even J. Walter Thompson, then the largest agency in the world, stole Ron Rosenfeld from DDB to become the new creative director at the phenomenal sum of $100,000 a year. By the late 1960s clients of all kinds seemed obsessed with finding the best, the most exciting, the most artistic advertising. So much so, recalled Jerry Della Femina, that agencies went through a ritual of displaying their 'creatives' to prospective clients: the wackier these guys were the better, since wild hair, jeans, bold colours, no shirts or shoes, and a taste for drugs seemed proof of their brilliance.

According to *Newsweek*, this invasion of young, bizarre 'creatives' had transformed the look and style of the advertising office. That made the craft, Della Femina decided, 'the most fun you can have with your clothes on.' The surge of newcomers had more far-reaching consequences for the look and style of advertising, though, because it opened up the industry to novel talents. Once upon a time, historian Larry Dobrow claimed, 'the most important credentials anyone could bring to a job interview were an Ivy League education, a Protestant affiliation and a white skin' – he could have added, as well, a male sex. What made the 'creative revolution' was not just the arrival of a collection of people attuned to the youth rebellion, but the decline of the old WASP dominance. Often the newcomers were Jewish (mostly copywriters) or Italian (mostly art directors), born into working-class homes in New York. They were just the most numerous of a flood of 'ethnics' like George Lois (Greek background), Carl Ally (Turkish), or Tom Anderson (Norwegian), a veteran of the 'Live/Give' campaign for Pepsi, who recalled his Brooklyn years when he yearned to escape and conquer Manhattan. 'Their street-sense has helped them recreate reality in commercials,' thought BBDO executive Phil Dusenberry. 'This makes the ads believable.'

What stands out, however, was the particularly Jewish flavour of so much of the new style of advertising, whether in print or on television. Stephen Fox noted how so many DDB ads positioned the client (be that a Volkswagen or an Avis) as the little guy, 'standing up to the bigger privileged competition, using their wits and humour to avoid being squashed. The funny ads provoked smiles in the characteristically Jewish fashion of self-deprecation from strength.' Art director Roy Grace, who worked on the Alka-Seltzer campaign when it was at DDB (1969–70), stressed how Alka-Seltzer ads entertained viewers with 'a Jewish/Italian view of the world.' Similarly, Jerry Goodis, Jewish like Bernbach, claimed his ads owed much to 'Yiddish humour, which was once described by Tony Aspler, the English journalist, as having a bittersweet ring, a quality of world weariness and self-denigration.' 'The flavour is warm, deprecating, not-taking-itself-too-seriously, *shared*,' he continued, adding it was 'the flavour of *all* true underdog humour.' Success brought emulation: even gentiles, Stephen Fox pointed out, began to adopt a similar tone of 'folksy sophistication.' Advertising in North America, like other forms of expression from comedy (think of Wayne and Shuster in Canada) or literature (Roth or Malamud in the United States), was belatedly moving towards a greater cultural diversity.

One might also credit some of the change to the shock of television, which sometime early in the decade had assumed a place of dominance in popular culture. The very character of TV ads was being refashioned by a combination of factors that emphasized the importance of images in advertising. The move to the thirty-second spot, for example, compelled ad-makers to use visuals and sound more effectively to convey a message: symbols were 'in,' words were 'out.' The advent of colour meant ad-makers could enhance both the sensual and the realistic qualities of their messages: nail polish really could look red, pink, or whatever, rather than an unappealing shade of grey. The new generation of ad-makers adopted innovations in the technology and techniques of cinematography to produce more exciting, if more expensive, commercials. Tom Anderson recalled using a piece of newly developed equipment allowing 'vibration free filming from helicopters' for a shoot of one Pepsi commercial in Maine. Clients then said, 'Do what you have to do,' he remembered.

Figure 3.1: *The 1949 Auto Show*. The Volkswagen campaign was aimed at the ad-wise consumer. That person was expected to have sufficient knowledge of the pretentious style of the normal car advertising to understand the Volkswagen difference. Here the humour lies in comparing the false glamour depicted in the Hudson shot with the plain, honest statement of value presented in the Volkswagen tableau. (Reproduced with the permission of Volkswagen of America, Inc.)

The movies were a key influence on the making of the best commercials. According to Gene Case, one of the originals at Jack Tinker & Partners, one reason Y&R did so well in television was because Frankfort 'went to movies directed by Bergman and Fellini,' basing an Excedrin commercial upon Bergman's *Wild Strawberries*! Anderson admitted that he was particularly influenced by British films, especially *The Knack and How to Get It* (1965) and the Beatles' *A Hard Day's Night* (1964). Another Pepsi veteran, the director Rick Levine, thought 'an important artistic influence' on his work were the American films of the 1930s and 1940s, 'especially those of Spencer Tracy, Katharine Hepburn, and Humphrey Bogart.' He added that the spectacular television specialist Wells, Rich, Greene was 'very film oriented': indeed Mary Wells, first at Tinker and later at her own agency, was credited with making the Alka-Seltzer ads the most entertaining campaign on TV.

Even so, it wasn't the lessons of movie-making or a taste for visual tricks but rather satire which carried forward the most celebrated campaign of the 1960s: DDB's efforts on behalf of the Volkswagen 'Beetle'. That campaign has been preserved by Volkswagen itself in a case history for a college lecture kit, complete with slides of print ads, a cassette of radio ads, and a reel of television commercials. Among much else, the reel contains three award-winning commercials, *Snowplow* (1963), *Keeping Up with the Kremplers* (1967), and *The 1949 Auto Show* (1970), which embody the basic style and messages of the campaign. DDB had realized, ad-maker Marty Myers later explained (in Leiss et al.), 'that people wouldn't mind a tickle, being challenged and being made to perform what the psychologists call closure – that is, give them 'a' and 'c' and they'll put the 'b' in.' The commercials ran counter to the prevailing mood of fantasy, the obsession with the new, the glitz and glamour of much automobile advertising in the past and present.

The 1949 Auto Show presented a fake minidocumentary (in black and white to convey authenticity) of new cars on display: the viewer was treated to pictures of women draped on cars and pretentious announcers proclaiming what was in fashion, all to the acclaim of awed consumers, before he or she saw the lonely Volkswagen announcer extolling the fact his homely 'Beetle' would be constantly improved but always look the same. *Snowplow* showed how it was the unglamorous workhorse, a Volkswagen, that a driver used to get through the snow to reach his snowplough. The camera in *The Kremplers* stayed in one spot to record the action occurring outside two standard American homes in the suburbs: the commercial compared the good fortune of one family who wisely bought a Volkswagen and had money left over for a stream of appliances, while their foolish neighbours spent all their funds to acquire and maintain an expensive Detroit product. Each of these ads drove home some aspect of what the company called 'the VW mystique': that the 'Beetle' was an unglamorous, never obsolescent, dependable, durable, and inexpensive vehicle, a triumph of utility. The wit, the reverse snobbery, the comparisons could only work with ad-wise consumers who saw the mockery of the Ford and General Motors advertising.

It was during the mid-1960s, recalled Lincoln Diamant, that television commercials came of age. 'At least, people started saying with a perfectly straight face at church social and cocktail parties: "You know, the commercials are better than the programs."' Janice Tyrwhitt's article in *Maclean's* (1 January 1966), 'What Do You Mean You Don't Like Television Commercials,' was in much the same vein. She argued, perhaps a bit tongue-in-cheek, 'there are more memorable commercials and more forgettable programs than ever before.' She singled out Jack Tinker's Alka-Seltzer ads as especially entertaining and effective. She recognized, *à la* Andy Warhol, that the best commercials had become 'a highly sophisticated form of pop art, worth at least as much attention as the shows they interrupt.'

However trendy, Tyrwhitt's reference to Pop Art was apt. The sudden rise to ascendancy of Pop Art in New York during the mid-1960s radically expanded the definition of art. Pop signaled a reaction against modernist orthodoxy, especially the Abstract Expressionism of the immediate past, one reason Pop was so often despised by critics. It also represented a rapprochement with mass culture and mass consumption, as Christin Mamiya has recently demonstrated.

Figure 3.2: *Snowplow*. If the Volkswagen wasn't beautiful, it certainly was useful.
Not even a blizzard could prevent this little marvel from reaching its destination.
Here DDB presented the Volkswagen in a more realistic setting than was common in
most automobile advertising. Ten years later, the agency fashioned a similar
Canadian ad (*Winter Theme*) that showed how the car could beat winter and the
snow. (Reproduced with the permission of Volkswagen of America, Inc.)

Pop artists, a number of whom had worked in the field of advertising, drew upon
the processed images of comic strips, consumer packaging, television, advertising, and so on to produce their own work. You can read into Roy Lichtenstein's
cartoons, Tom Wesselmann's still-life series, or Andy Warhol's Brillo Boxes
and Marilyn Monroes an assortment of different meanings: an enthusiasm for
hype, the replication of TV's style, the allure of surfaces, and so on. But what
I find in much of this work is a pose of ironic celebration that both parodies and
honours the trivia of a consumer society.

That same pose of ironic celebration was present in the 'creative revolution':
'What is coming out of Madison Avenue now is often offbeat, irreverent or self-
kidding,' claimed *Newsweek*. Pop mimicked ads, ads fed on Pop, and both
expressed a particular moment in the cultural life of New York City. In the long
run the rise of Pop indicated a new tolerance towards advertising that ran

counter to the criticisms based on the fear of manipulation and the distrust of materialism.

The Young & Rubicam Collection

Founded in 1923, Young & Rubicam had become a major player on the advertising scene well before the arrival of television. Excellent management moved Y&R up the list of American agencies, ranked fourth in billings in 1960 but first in 1980, and during much of the 1980s it shared with the Japanese giant, Dentsu, the honour of being the world's largest single agency. Unlike rivals J. Walter Thompson and Ogilvy & Mather, Y&R retained its independence through the acquisition craze in the late 1980s, which leap-frogged conglomerates like Saatchi & Saatchi and WPP well ahead in world rankings.

In 1988 Y&R and New York's Museum of Broadcasting opened an exhibit of radio and TV ads since the mid-1930s, complete with a catalogue that explained the collection and the company and identified the individual ads. I will use this collection to probe the overall techniques and styles of ad-making since the years of the 'creative revolution.' When I examined the collection in the summer of 1991, there were 109 television commercials, covering the period from the early 1960s to the mid-1980s, for a wide range of clients including Dr Pepper, Eastern Airlines, General Foods, Union Carbide, Lincoln-Mercury, Metropolitan Life, even the Peace Corps. Not all these commercials were listed in the catalogue, and those omitted I have 'named' myself, with quotation marks to indicate that their titles aren't official. Many of the individual commercials have won an award, some a couple of awards: Union Carbide's *Insulation* (Y67101) shared a campaign Clio, won entry to the Clio Hall of Fame, and received both an International Broadcasting Award and a Gold Lion. (In the case of the Y&R collection the first figure, here 67, represents the first year the commercial was broadcast.) There is another way in which these commercials differ from what has become common – over two-thirds run more than thirty seconds, most are sixty seconds long, and a few are up to 120 seconds. I suspect that when these appeared on TV screens, at least after the 1960s, they were usually abbreviated. The fact that so many of the commercials are uncut, however, merely emphasizes their stature as works of art.

Techniques

What I find especially striking about these commercials (in contrast to the Classic Clios) is just how rich they are in information. Not that this is advertising-as-news, information about the product or its use, but rather about people, their dreams, their lifestyles. The most intriguing ads are marvels of compression, chock full of nuance, allusions and illusions, stereotype and stimuli. No other form of communication seems so well suited to a distracted and jaded audience, more agreeable to taking its mental, even emotional sustenance in small bites than previous generations.

TV ads are imaginative treatments of the familiar. Often commercials borrow their shape from the popular culture to ensure as wide an acceptance as possible – they are outstanding examples of parody and appropriation, otherwise known as 'intertextuality.' Excedrin's *Tax Audit* (Y67094) portrays the anxiety of a man undergoing investigation by the taxman, Nynex's *'The What's Up Call'* (Y85027) the simple pleasures of a gossipy chat on the phone. The black and white masterpiece *Birds* (Y65078) draws upon the conventions of wilderness documentaries to show the affinity between nature and technology, all in the cause of Eastern Airlines. Many efforts refer to movies. Sometimes it's to a genre, as in the case of the sinister *Foggy Road* (Y65088), which takes on the guise of a horror flick to exploit women's fears of being alone in an emergency, or the mocking *Silent Movie* (Y73048), which harks back to the Perils of Pauline – but this time the Mountie gets neither his man nor his maiden, who's seduced by a Dr Pepper. Sometimes the reference is to a hit movie, like *Space Cowboy* (Y84016), which puts the hero in the bar from *Star Wars*, or *Help* (Y85025), which uses the music and the style of the Beatles' film of the same name. There's a mock wrestling match between husband and wife, asleep on an uncomfortable mattress (*Wrestling*, Y67095) – a comic allusion to bedroom troubles and the sports contest; a slow pull back from a field of dots to reveal a woman of style and elegance, reminiscent of Pop Art (*Dots*, Y69109); a NASA-style news brief, partly in grainy black and white, of life in some lunar colony (*Lunar Mountain*, Y77067); the birth of Unisys (*Creation*, Y86039), rendered in a fashion that recalls both sci-fi and religious imagery. Each of these ads referred to some other text(s), usually manufactured or popularized by magazines, newspapers, movies, or TV. I am struck by the analogy of the warehouse: everything current is stored, ready for use in one spiel or another.

That said, the commercials somehow had to hook viewers. One way was to employ a celebrity, and Y&R was especially keen on comedians: Jack Benny in *Jack Benny* (Y63077); Bert Lahr in *Devil* (Y67086), Tim Conway first for Lay's potato chips (*Diver*, Y76063) and then for Manufacturers Hanover Trust (*Auto Loan*, Y77059), or Bill Cosby in the Mafia spoof, *Godfather* (Y85022). Another way was via sexual innuendo and display. An ad for Vitalis (*Heads Are Turning*, Y78069) reverses things by turning a well-groomed male into a sex object ogled by women. More common were women, or rather bits of them: shapely legs, bare arms, red hair, a bosom in a tight dress, pouty lips, or a sultry face. The male voyeur might be especially titillated by scenes of beautiful, stylish, young women wearing high boots in the desert, to a soundtrack dominated by Nancy Sinatra's 'These Boots Were Made for Walkin',' all for a Goodyear Tire ad of the late 1960s. A third ploy was to spring some striking visual on the unwary. *Clapping Hamburgers* (Y66084) features a crowd of animated burgers at a political rally cheering the news of two new ketchups; Irish Spring's *'Man in Desert'* (Y84008) flashes some fearful images, a vulture and a lizard; Southland Corporation's *Billy Olson* (Y84017) honours an Olympic hopeful with a slow-motion vault into the air.

Often commercials encourage viewers to participate in the little story being played out on the screen. That's obvious in the satirical or humorous ads where we're supposed to get the joke and so win a little jolt of pleasure. But there are many other techniques. She, that is the 'typical' female viewer, might be asked to identify with the heroine's persona, such as the female reporter who decides to become an independent writer in Mercury's *Proud Mary* (Y84014). He might be asked to fill a void, to become the absent male in *Foggy Road* who must protect his wife by buying the right tires – 'When there's no man around Goodyear should be.' And then there's the ad-as-puzzle where the opening sequence is sufficiently enigmatic that it requires us to figure out just what is going on. That common ploy was carried to an extreme in *Montreal* (Y70042): a boy cavorts in unknown streets amid sights both traditional and modern, none of which is explained till the Eastern plane flies out of the sun and viewers learn they've watched a retelling of the joys of being in an exotic place. Here, and in such other examples as *Dots*, *Silent Movie*, or *Space Cowboy* (to name only those previously cited), the pleasure comes from working out the mystery of what the ad wants to say.

Commercials often come in the shape of playlets. That shouldn't occasion much surprise: it has become almost a truism to state that television is the grand storytelling medium that excels as a vehicle of drama. Slightly less than two-thirds of the Y&R *oeuvre* offered viewers minidramas, sometimes to shock, but usually to entertain. Thus the public service announcement entitled *Karen* (Y72073) was a poignant story of the perversion of love: a teenaged daughter deceived her anguished father to extract money from him for the purchase of drugs, all of this filmed in black and white, with a grainy finish to the pictures, which evokes the style of the documentary. In a much lighter vein, *Front Porch* (Y73047) showed a young man trying to entice and seduce his girlfriend with a Dr Pepper, while the father is keeping watch from the window – 'You've got to try it to love it,' is the message. These and many other examples dovetail nicely with the prevailing wisdom about television programming.

But not all commercials fit this pattern. The testimonial so common in the 1950s has persisted, albeit often with a humorous twist: the U.S. Postal Service used a series of celebrities to announce the coming of the Zip codes (Y77066). So too has the stylized display where either the product or the user is shown in a fashion that highlights the virtues of the brand: Canada Dry managed to convey the ideas of play, pleasure, and freshness with pictures of beautiful people, male and female, swimming in effervescent water (Y84015). More novel was the vignette, which first won favour during the 'creative revolution' and, you will recall, proved especially common in the 'Pepsi Generation' and Coke's 'Americana' campaigns. Rather than 'presenting a generally coherent narrative,' as Michael Arlen put it, the vignette commercial 'consists of a sequence of only slightly interlocking scenes and situations.' Y&R employed a series of vignettes for its client Eastern Airlines. One such, 'Acapulco' (Y67087), proved to be an incredibly rapid succession of pictures of people having fun on the beach, in the ocean, at nightspots, etc., joined together by occasional shots of the famous Acapulco diver showing his bravado to the world at large. About ten years later, *Vacation Island* (Y78049) repeated the experience through a superfast travelogue, more than 150 images in sixty seconds: a collage of shots of nature, people, buildings, play, and food from the Caribbean, all to convey the ideas of pleasure, abundance, and novelty. The significance of this design is that it depended so heavily upon pictures to make its point, so many different pictures that they tumble over the viewer. The viewer is invited to construct his or her own narrative out of what could be absorbed. The vignette, and to a lesser extent the display, emphasized the visual dimension of television, its ability to communicate by overwhelming viewers with striking images, sometimes a stylized single image and sometimes a torrent of images.

Once you had their attention, how do you get them to swallow the message? Y&R's ad-makers were adept at building their commercials around contrasts to highlight the preferred reading, such as dark/light, slow/fast, cold/warm, old/young where the juxtaposition of opposites serves to simplify and to explain. Spic and Span's *Custodian* (Y68102) relies upon the image of an old pro instructing a young novice in the ways of cleaning. A winter-weary male in Eastern's *Jogger* (Y73050) compares the sorry state of affairs around him with visions of a bright sun, beach life, and beautiful women. The Dr Pepper spoof *Silent Movie* was shot in black and white (peril) until the heroine succumbed (happiness): she discovers 'once you try it, you'll love the difference.' A later spot, *Godzilla* (Y84013), was wholly in black and white except for the can of Dr Pepper. 7–Eleven's *One Potato* (Y85021) compares the frustrating wait at a supermarket checkout (underlined by slowed motion and a greyish tinge) with the cheeriness and speed of service at one of its stores.

Presenting opposites also allowed the ad-maker to work the theme of transformation. Sad gives way to happy, and silence to music, in *Deaf Child* (Y67092) when a young girl overcomes her disability with the help of Union Carbide. On the other hand, *Crying Babies* (Y84012) shows how Anbesol soothed, and so silences, a host of infants suffering teething troubles. Two 1984 spots for Mercury Cougar, *Proud Mary* and *Born to Be Wild* (Y84014), note how a woman and a man escaped the corporate routine to seek pleasure in their freedom machines. In the story of the *'Red Dress'* (Y85023) the harried housewife turns into a ravishing beauty, once she uses Colgate-Palmolive's Fresh Start to clean her evening wear. Likewise our *'Man in Desert'* swiftly converts from a state of distress into a state of glamour, once he defeats dirt with Irish Spring. *'Upscale Eating'* (Y86032) employs a series of contrasts – old/novel, blah/exciting, plain/upscale – to prove 'Dinner Will Never Be the Same': faced with peas again, we were relieved to see the array of treats offered by Birds Eye Deluxe Vegetables. None of these ads was ambiguous: in each case the preferred reading was obvious, the focus on contrasts presented the consumer with a stark choice between before and after.

But that wasn't the only attribute of the Y&R *oeuvre*. The ad-makers owed an enormous debt to metaphors and similar suggestive devices. I use the term 'metaphor' loosely to mean a sign (a word or phrase, a saying or a pun, a picture, a tune, a sound, a person, etc.) that common parlance deems will refer to something beyond its apparent or literal meaning. Many a scholar has noted how advertising has a distinct liking for metaphor. (Witness the discussion of the link between Catherine Deneuve and Chanel No. 5 in Judith Williamson's classic, *Decoding Advertisements*.) Using an image or symbol allows the ad-maker to suggest what she or he cannot say. At best it encourages viewers to glean the meaning that the ad-maker intends, in short, to make viewers complicit in their own seduction.

There was a myriad of ways in which the Y&R ad-makers employed metaphor. How simple, how corny was the metaphor used by *Clapping Hamburgers*: putting the image of the leaning tower of Pisa in a spiel about a new pizza-flavoured ketchup. Birds Eye demonstrated its new Italian-style vegetables were really authentic by placing the announcer in *Venice* (Y76065) in a gondola! This was done tongue-in-cheek, the ad mocking itself, but the purpose was to link the Italian setting with the product. Goodyear Tire's *Torture Test* (Y72056) carried an array of metaphors to suggest toughness: block letters, a harsh voice, heavy music, and a polysteel tire riding unharmed over a bed of nails. Johnson & Johnson's feel-good spot, *New Babies* (Y78071), had mothers holding and fondling babies, a sign of tenderness, that easily translated to its infant products. AT&T equated phoning home with giving love in *'Goodbye/Hello'* (Y87030), a metaphor that remains a cliché of telephone ads.

Still this persuasion through metaphor could be a good deal more subtle. In the justly famous *China Shop* (Y80002), which won both a Clio and an International Broadcasting Award, a bull (meaning both power and clumsiness) wanders safely through a china shop (meaning fragility and peril), guided presumably by the wise counsel of Merrill Lynch, to prove these advisers were 'sensitive to your investment needs.' Southland Corporation's spots celebrating two contenders in the 1984 Olympics, *Tyrell Biggs* (Y84011) and *Billy Olson*, equated the athletes with America, for 'The Dream Begins with Freedom,' the freedom to be your best, to struggle and achieve. What the exhibits catalogue referred to as 'new wave' advertising for Ford's Lincoln-Mercury division exploited the beloved rock tunes of yesteryear to capture the fancy of baby boomers and position the cars as *their* cars.

I found particularly clever *Come Back to Gentility* (Y81003), which provoked a fierce critique by TV critic Mark Crispin Miller because he decided that the commercial was full of racist allusions. This ad piled one metaphor on top of another. The Jamaican Tourist Board was trying to persuade Americans it was safe to visit Jamaica again, though it could hardly declare outright that the downfall of the then socialist Michael Manley meant an end to the troubles hurting tourism. Instead *Come Back to Gentility* accentuated the positive. It talked about gentility, beauty, hospitality, bounty, tranquillity, romance, the way things used to be – Coming Home. We were treated to vignettes of motherly figures (hospitality), a beautiful woman offering flowers (welcome — and availability?), a wise elder telling us to come back (serenity and security), and to signs of plenty (a fruit stand) and pleasure (a dance). The ad's purpose was to evoke ersatz memories (for how many had experienced the real thing?) of a colonial past where the affluent played and the natives served. The same effort to exploit a nostalgia for the good times informed other 'come back to' spots: *'Writer'* (Y86035) where a man escapes to the simplicity of his island home, and *'Jamaican Fun'* (Y86035) where two young women rediscover the fun of vacationing in a land of sun. The ads, in particular *Come Back to Gentility*, might be interpreted on a number of levels, some a bit sinister (as Miller made abundantly clear).

'Might' is a key word here. None of this creativity guaranteed that the viewer would absorb the preferred meaning. Even the most closed ad was in fact open to a different, perhaps contrary reading(s). Let me dwell on one specific example: the very different responses of William Henry and myself to Eastern's *Birds*. Henry is a much accomplished critic of the media and culture employed by *Time*. He wrote a superb account of the exhibit's collection in the catalogue.

Figure 3.3: *Birds*. One of the more innovative features of *Birds* was the way in which the camera contrasted close-ups and distance shots. Here we have an extreme close-up of the watchful eye of a bird, a picture of an owl whose feathers (and peace of mind) have been ruffled by the passage of the plane, and a distance shot of the Eastern jet overhead, streaking away from the natural paradise. (Courtesy of Young & Rubicam)

He was especially enthusiastic about *Birds*, which he decided 'may be the single most daring and impressive ad ever made for a major corporation.'

It is the antithesis of the hard sell. It works almost entirely by implication. The spot begins with glimpses of a riverine terrain, swirled in mist, dotted with lush and mighty trees. There are birds in flight, storks in pools. Birds in the distance, a bird in closeup. Then a plane. Just when the viewer might expect the ad's focus to shift and the sales pitch to start, the ad crosscuts to an owl and a deer. The ad copy intones with Emersonian romance, 'To fly ... to hover serene, beyond reality ...' The message is that flight, even air travel, is a part of nature rather than at war with nature, that airplanes are not part of an ecologically destructive 'progress' but a form of beauty at one with the universe. And, of course, although airplanes move from city to city and epitomize technology, they do enable passengers to go commune with nature. Virtually none of this is actually said; instead, it is felt. That makes the message vastly more effective. If the rational part of the brain were engaged by formal argument, the weaknesses inherent in the sales spiel would quickly become apparent. Because the appeal instead is to emotion, and the implicit pitch is something viewers would like to believe, spectators go with the flow. They accept the juxtapositions, the nonlinear substitute for argumentation, and come away with a far more positive impression of Eastern than if they heard a minute of aggressive salesmanship about the convenience and affordability of air travel.

Henry clearly got the preferred meaning. His appreciation of the technical wizardry and creative excellence of this celebration of flight is understandable. His reasoning about the appeal of the ad is also persuasive. But I had a very different reaction when I first viewed *Birds*. What upset me was the awesome sound of the jet plane as it rushed overhead (sadly just after the ad had featured the cry of a loon). I took this as a sign that the plane was a monstrous intrusion in an otherwise unspoiled wilderness. Indeed that sound alone converted the ad into a critique of technology. For me the sound was a metaphor of modernity, the dark side of modernity. Why? Was this because I am swayed more by Green ideas than Henry? Perhaps so, perhaps not. More important here was my personal experience. I relish the silence of the lakes in Canada's north. I despise the powerboats and the like that pollute this natural paradise with their terrible noise. *Birds* evoked this hatred and anger. No matter how clever the pictures, how poetic the voice-over, how imaginative the metaphors, my response was dictated by my background, and that the ad-maker could never counter.

Schools of Art

Since the early 1960s there have emerged formulas, which condition the way most messages are framed. These run the gamut from 'stick it in your face' reality to outright fantasy. No one scheme can encompass the full variety of commercials: some are definitely hybrids, employing a mix of formulas, and a few are unique so they cannot be labelled. But such exceptions aside, most commercials fit into a distinct school of art, sharing a particular purpose, moods, and styles. I have based my description of these schools upon already accepted terms employed in art history and literary criticism.

The naturalist and the essentialist schools are both brands of realism. Commercial reality is not the same as experienced reality, a point I'll return to in a moment. What I wish to emphasize here is that such ads endeavour to persuade the viewer they are indeed telling the truth about a situation, a problem, or a product. This approach of 'telling it like it is' grew out of the live demonstrations, minidocumentaries, reason-why spiels, and the like that were common in the 1950s.

Almost half of the Y&R collection falls into the naturalist school, which is indicative of the American style of ad-making. (Recall, for example, how the 'Marlboro Country' campaign moved away from fantasy towards an obsession with authenticity.) The naturalist ad pretends to represent what the eye might see, strives for photographic accuracy, in a word, for verisimilitude. It may take on a number of different shapes. Straight talk: *Lady Shopper* (Y67098) follows the struggle of wits between a pleasant but determined woman and a glib salesman in a clothing store – she refused to buy anything that lacked the Sanforized trade mark. Heavy drama: the very powerful *Slumlord* (Y68105), made for the New York Urban Coalition's 'Give a Damn' campaign, uses the technique of cinema-verité. We are the camera, taken through a run-down tenement by an uncaring landlord. At the end the camera swings around to reveal a young black man, whom circumstance forces to take the apartment. Action-adventure: Mercury Cougar's rock-oriented spots (1984) are fast-paced stories of energetic thirtysomething people living life to the fullest. A bit of humour: the three spots for Dr Pepper's 'Throw Your Diet a Curve' campaign feature a female executive (Y86028), a male body-builder (Y86031), and a black female singer (Y86038), all sexy, all successful, who compose in their minds a personal ad to seek their kind of companion.

But the commercial reality is censored, condensed, and touched up. Even *Slumlord* used dark lighting, with a slightly greenish tinge, to suggest the bleakness of the tenement. The slices of life served up weren't complete. All distracting elements, such as furniture or background noise, are removed, as are most unique markings that might identify a character as a real individual. People usually represent particular types: the wise veteran (*Custodian*), upscale trendies (*Gatsby*, Y73052), the independent woman (*Proud Mary*). Even the athletes in 'The Dream Begins with Freedom' are turned into metaphors of America, not the least because we are able to eavesdrop on their musings. Michael Schudson has called this a process of flattening that makes everything standard, expected. The naturalist ad embodies what the ad-maker believes we think is real.

The essentialist school narrows the focus even more. Such ads provide only a simplified portrayal of reality where background data is left meagre to concentrate attention on the product or its stand-in. Consider Union Carbide's award-winning *Insulation*. The purpose was to tout the technological sophistication of Union Carbide. *Insulation* used a single striking image: a baby chick (meaning vulnerability) was placed inside a super-insulated box (strength), which was then gently inserted into a pot of boiling water (danger). While the viewer watches to see whether the chick gets cooked, the voice-over explains the virtues of the insulation. Eventually (for the ad runs two minutes) the box is raised and the chick removed unharmed. Here was the hard sell with a vengeance: no music, no sight of a person, only a bare setting, nothing to distract our focus on the fate of the chick. Excedrin's *Shoe Store* (Y67089) achieved a similar effect by presenting a tired salesman and a pigheaded shopper in silhouette, except this time there was some humour – the viewer is treated to a little story of comic frustration, labelled 'headache 39.' Y&R's *Leontyne Price* (Y84009), for the United Negro College Fund, features the opera star in performance, using low light and interesting camera angles to enhance her look and the drama of the occasion, before she talks directly to the viewer about the fund's needs. Often commercials contain one essentialist shot, near or at the end, where a frozen image of the product is left on the screen for a few seconds to drive home the brand name and appearance. But however common it is on TV, where it seems the chosen method of local advertisers (because it can be made so cheaply?), the essentialist ad clearly didn't impress the people who assembled the Y&R exhibit: there are very few samples in this *œuvre*.

The romantic school has found much favour in North America. If the bias of the essentialist school is towards the hard sell and reason-why, then the romantic school is very definitely soft. The romantic commercial offers a highly idealized or sentimentalized version of reality where the signs accentuate some particular emotion or sensation, such as satisfaction, happiness, joy, celebration, and occasionally poignancy or sadness. The music track in such commercials is necessary to identify and maintain the mood. Similarly, ad-makers will use soft lighting, pastel colours, and dissolves for much the same reason. Both *Birds* and *Come Back to Gentility* belong to the romantic school. In the mid-70s Metropolitan Life sponsored two romantic ads for its 'Where the Future is Now' campaign: *Partnership* (Y74055), winner of a Gold Lion at Cannes, and *School Bus* (Y5061), winner of a Silver Lion. Both were vignette commercials, which is common (though not inevitable) in the romantic repertoire. *Partnership* told of two boys, Tommy and Bobby, who grow up together to run a major company; *School Bus* follows a boy up to manhood and independence, when he finally frees himself of adults. In each case the metaphor of shaking hands is repeated, signifying friendship, harmony, love. Pop music, dissolves, and slow-motion are used to emphasize the warmth of these commercials.

But the best samples were three ads, all narratives, made for Hallmark Cards in the early 1980s, *Music Professor* (Y82004), '*Sister and Brother*' (Y82006), and *Christmas Wish* (Y82005), a campaign that would win an International Broadcasting Award for the best campaign in twenty-five years. In the first two spots the card became a symbol of friendship, even love; giving one represented giving a part of yourself. A kindly Lisa presents a birthday card, meaning both respect and affection, to her gruff music teacher. In 'Sister and Brother' a woman reminisces about her youth and her brother (these scenes are in black and white), recalling fondly the togetherness of yesteryear. Giving a card here meant not just love, but recapturing the old times. The real weeper, however, was a corporate ad, Christmas Wish, which reminded all to 'give the greatest gift of all, give a little of yourself,' especially at Christmas. The story probes the relationship of a cute Katie and her harried father: he is so caught up in the hectic pace of getting ready for Christmas that he has no time for his daughter. Here again are the contrasts, a kid's simple desire for a sign of love and her father's preoccupation with the trivial. Of course the ending is happy: Katie's distress is transformed into joy when father realizes his error and lavishes attention on his daughter. Even if you knew the ending was too pat, still the spot has enormous impact, at least for a man with daughters. It was an extraordinary rendering of that ideal bond between father and daughter.

The absurdist school (well represented here: roughly a quarter of the ads) is quite the opposite. Where the romantic ad honours, the absurdist ad mocks: typically it represents something weird or outlandish, if barely possible – though very often what is shown is impossible. This type aims to evoke mirth. Why? Because humour can both entertain the casual viewer and disarm that person's defences. The absurdist ad lets us know it's kidding, leaves room for us to decipher its meaning, puts us on the inside, the people who know what's up.

That kidding is obvious in Clapping Hamburgers, Wrestling, Silent Movie, 'Man in Desert,' Space Cowboy, Godfather, and Godzilla. It was, at least until the mid-1980s, a favourite approach of the Dr Pepper campaigns, where well-remembered characters or settings from pop culture were cleverly spoofed. But let me highlight a slightly different treatment, this of a lovable icon from the seventies' hit 'Sesame Street.' The Advertising Council sponsored this public service announcement, entitled Cookie Monster (Y74057), to sell the virtues of good eating habits to children. An off-stage reporter interviews Cookie Monster in an outdoor restaurant, allowing him to explain how he eats all kinds of nutritious foods. At the end such preachiness is replaced with farce: a load of cookies is dumped on his head, his reward for being so good. The humour depended on knowing what an obsessive creature Cookie Monster was.

That example has taken us away from the self-conscious realism of the naturalist ad. The last two schools, the mannerist and the surrealist, move us into the realm of fantasy. Both types of ads strive to evoke a sense of awe or reverence in the viewer, to make the product or its user appear sublime, exalted, omnipotent, or even mythic. (Not that other types don't sometimes attempt to do the same, just that this purpose defines the two schools of fantasy.) These ads, no more than a tenth of the *oeuvre*, employ the imagery of religion and mythology, the rhetoric of the numinous, following a tradition of appropriation identified by Roland Marchand in his study of American advertising in the 1920s. Here television advertising eliminates the boundary between the sacred and the profane, elevating the gospel of consumption to a higher plane of transcendence.

Each type of commercial does so differently, however. The mannerist ad grows out of a fascination with style or elegance. It bears the marks of artificiality, of careful staging because it is so conscious of its artistic quality: the maker takes special pains to produce pleasing shapes that will strike the viewer as beautiful or potent. For example, the Pop Art clone *Dots* was highly visual, eventually focusing attention upon the woman as the embodiment of elegance (since showing the product Modess might have offended). Equally visual but more bizarre was the placement of that large bull amidst the racks of delicate ornaments and the like in *China Shop*. In the first ad the woman became the source of awe, in the second Merrill Lynch because it could manage so delicate a situation. But the most 'artistic' treatment in the exhibit was *9 Months* (Y67093). The intent was to surround Bulova Watches with an aura of distinction, and the voice-over makes reference to the firm's devotion to craftsmanship, often used to assign prestige to an item at a time when mass production is associated with mediocrity. The spot employs the analogy of giving birth, equating not only the term of a normal pregnancy but the process itself to the time and work involved in making a Bulova watch. The visual is an overhead shot of a table on which are successively displayed, month by month and always very stylishly, the pieces that go into the final product. What had been something of a puzzle at first – it was difficult to figure out just why the viewer was treated to so unusual a display – was resolved at the end when the camera shows simply a ticking watch, itself an *objet d'art*.

The surrealist school (which I admit is my favourite) allows the widest and wildest range of images, notably visuals since the ad-maker often indulges in all manner of special effects. Sometimes the surrealist ad offers up a simplified fantasy, sometimes an ambiguous or open-ended scenario, sometimes a series of lush, overlapping symbols, but always that ad has a dream-like quality, inviting the viewer to suspend disbelief and imagine what life might be like in the programmed fantasy. What makes 'Acapulco' surreal is the mix of slow motion, silhouette, and overexposure, especially the latter, which conveys the impression of 'the dazzling glare and heat of the tropical sun,' in Henry's words. By contrast, Unisys's *Creation* portrays a man humbled before the majesty of technology: alone, in the office, he turns to witness a blinding explosion of light, backed up by trumpet music, which announces the birth of Unisys Office Systems!

The most stunning of the surrealist ads was *Capri Magic* (Y80001), made for Ford's Lincoln-Mercury division. Its producer called this 100-second commercial, initially intended for release in cinema houses, 'a cross between a Fellini movie and a Monty Python sideshow.' It was an extravaganza of brightly coloured images and bizarre juxtapositions. A man wandering through the desert encounters a series of mirages: the car, nuns, football players, beautiful women, all of which disappear – as does our traveller. The rock music track had one-word lyrics, superimposed on the screen: 'magic seductive sexy exciting wild elusive.' The male viewer, and it is clearly aimed at men, could make his own set of fantasies out of this openended story-line. What remains behind, though, is a sense of excitement and mystery, a feeling of awe if only because the spot is a superb expression of the art of film-making.

Britain's Creative 'Breakthrough'

Ironically one ad-maker judged *Capri Magic* an imitation of a European style, not a native American product. In an *Adweek* survey of American creativity (17 September 1982), Richard Henderson of Cole, Henderson, Drake detected efforts to emulate the surreal look of European films, where viewers were left to complete the story – 'Mercury was the first, with the TV spot in the desert ...'

That sneer at what other commentators called 'new wave' advertising reflected a malaise afflicting the creative community in the United States during the early 1980s. 'I'd say right now we're rife with mediocrity,' complained Martin F. Puris of Ammirati & Puris in the same survey. 'The last risk-taking here was in the mid-1970s,' lamented Jerry Della Femina to the *New York Times* (8 December 1983), 'and that was when we started giving away the creative crown to other countries.' The British ad magazine *Campaign* (20 January 1984) even published 'Is US Creativity Dead?', a story in which reporter Ann Cooper asserted that Chiat/Day and Ally & Gargano were 'virtually' the only agencies 'which could lay claim to being either creative or hot.'

Ad-makers could come up with a host of explanations for the decline of creativity. Perhaps it was the arrival during the 1970s of a host of MBAs, who lacked any artistic sense. Perhaps it was the fact that the 'creatives' themselves were now older, more conservative, and no new people were taking over. Or maybe it was the reliance on the committee system to craft a commercial ('There are a lot of people to say no,' Jeff Epstein told *Adweek*) or the tyranny of research ('Everything that can be measured, weighed, counted, evaluated, corroborated, confirmed, or quantified, is: to the point of sterilization,' declared Ann Cooper). Nor could one discount the changed mood of clients who were made cautious by competition and recession; they weren't willing to risk big money on creativity. There did seem to be a consensus, though, on the fact that the much-touted 'creative revolution' had fostered a backlash. Account executives and brand managers had decided creativity didn't necessarily pay off, and the pendulum had swung back again towards hard sell, reason-why, and safe advertising.

The standard of creative excellence had shifted across the ocean. 'It has become fashionable to concede that Britain now rules the waves of advertising creativity,' intoned the *New York Times*. A one-time leader of the 1960s, Steve Frankfort (now of Kenyon & Eckhardt) told the *Times* the Brits were just more innovative, reaching into books and movies for ideas, not so bound to research. One advantage was that a number of top-notch film directors had taken on the task of making commercials. Even Americans were beginning to hire these folks. One such, Ridley Scott, who had made *Alien* (1979) and would direct Apple's *1984*, had won much fame for his work on an ultraromantic campaign for Hovis bread, set in the north of England in the 1930s. A better sign of preeminence, however, was the success of British ad-makers in international competitions. In the Cannes festival of 1984, for example, they won over one-third of the awards, far more than the Americans and the French.

Some Americans weren't about to admit that any of this proved the United States had been toppled from its pedestal. Award-winning commercials weren't always good ads from the marketing standpoint. An anonymous creative head told Ann Cooper there was a lot of 'cuckoo creativity' in the U.K.; another ad-maker, Charles Moss of Wells, Rich, Greene, told the *Times* there was 'a lot of junk' on English TV. Perhaps the ultimate put-down came from Larry Dobrow in his celebration of the 'creative revolution,' *When Advertising Tried Harder* (1984). He agreed the present state of the American commercial was sad, and that British work was much more imaginative. But British efforts were just 'clever 1980s adaptations and applications of Bill Bernbach's well-established principles and techniques,' he wrote. 'The best of current British work finds its roots in our creative revolution and bears a remarkable resemblance to a whole generation of American antecedents.'

This was little more than sour grapes. No doubt all 'creatives' owed something to the example of Bill Bernbach, though his principles were no more correct and certainly far less definite than those of his rival, David Ogilvy. Anyway, the British had produced their own distinctive style of advertising, with a look and feel qualitatively different to that of the American product in the 1960s or the 1980s. That look and feel had two leading characteristics. First, it grew out of a commitment to building a brand image through long-running campaigns that boasted a continuing shape, tone, and sometimes characters, quite different from so many American campaigns (excepting those featured in the preceding chapter) where the aim was to make powerful spots. Second, the individual commercials displayed a passion for the humorous, for satire and parody and spoof, for caricature or farce, for wit and ridicule. This humour could be gentle or hard-edged, subtle or broad, very ordinary or very bizarre, against people or against convention; in short it could encompass an enormous range of types. No wonder the prevalent strategy of British advertising was irony: indeed, the British revitalized that pose of ironic celebration which had first surfaced during the 'creative revolution.'

The evolution of the British style took time. Initially, back in the mid-1950s, agencies like Y&R and JWT had simply imported the American style into Britain. Just a glance at some of the historical showcase reels at the ITV Library demonstrates that there was a lot of earnest enthusiasm on the British airwaves up to the early 1970s. But the British Egg Marketing Board was making use of comedian Tony Hancock in 1966 and Schweppes Bitter Lemon had Benny Hill in 1968. Campaigns such as 'The Randalls' (1962–7) for Fairy Snow ('Forces Grey Out – Forces White In') mixed a modicum of comedy with a serious display of the virtues of the soap powder. As early as 1958 Oxo introduced its 'Katie' series of commercials, which amount to a serial drama about the trials and tribulations of a typical family that used the product to prepare delicious meals. The series lasted until 1974, and was revived with a new 'Katie' in 1983. In 1976 Birds Eye sponsored the 'Ben & Mary' campaign for its Beefburgers: this serial featured two youngsters growing up, Ben obsessed with his Beefburgers and Mary interested in Ben. That sequence ended in 1982 with *Goodbye Ben and Mary* (1982), an especially poignant commercial, in which Ben and Mary, now adults, finally parted ways. These and other such campaigns appealed to viewers as soap opera, and they were remembered, as was the brand image.

In retrospect Heineken's 'Refreshes' campaign, launched in 1974, seems particularly crucial to the 'breakthrough,' winning a lot of international recognition, even a Campaign Clio in 1982. The campaign was famous because of its determination to make the viewer laugh. It revolved around the slogan 'Refreshes the parts other beers cannot reach,' and so it played with the motifs of renewal and transformation. Drinking Heineken awakened the monster (*Frankenstein*, 1974), made Scrooge mean again (*Scrooge*, 1975), saved the Star Trek crew (*Astroship*, 1975), renewed the power of the lamp (*Aladdin*, 1977), made a gardener so potent that his plant became huge (*Green Fingers*, 1978),

Figure 3.4: *Casino* & *Changes*. During the late 1980s Volkswagen in Britain ran a much celebrated series of wryly humorous ads that portrayed people victimized by bad luck. The man, who was a loser at the casino, had also made a bad choice in marriage; the woman, who was a loser at love, proceeded to shed the gifts acquired during her relationship. But he drove away in his Volkswagen; and she kept her Volkswagen. Some things were too precious to lose. (Courtesy of Volkswagen [United Kingdom] Limited.)

invigorated Houston so a launch could proceed (*Columbia*, 1981), empowered a poet (*Windemere*, 1982), and taught a refined woman how to speak with a cockney accent (*Water Majorca*, 1985). One character, an Australian aborigine, in *Boomerang* (1980) was brought back by popular demand in *A Real Charmer* (1983). Only limited by advertising regulations, the ads lampooned all kinds of texts, including the campaign itself. Rarely was there a creative concept that allowed ad-makers so much freedom yet ensured the campaign would retain its coherence.

By the mid-1980s the British 'breakthrough' was in full swing. I have chosen to use the 119 British winners of Cannes Lions (out of 384 winners), 1984 through 1986, to survey all this creativity. I concentrate exclusively upon the humour: three out of four Cannes winners used humour, and roughly 60 per cent fit into the absurdist school. I recognize that this approach exaggerates the amount of humour in British advertising as it appeared in real life: a one-day survey of all spots in the London ITV region in 1985, according to Eric Clark, learned only slightly 'more than a third were designed to make viewers laugh or smile.' My approach also neglects the other kinds of commercials, such as the highly sensual spots for cosmetics, which were a part of the whole scene. But the fact is the passion for humour had become the British trade mark, the source of British ad-makers' fame as the creators of the world's most outstanding commercials.

It would be possible to adopt a very sophisticated mode of analysis, to consider the ways in which these ads fit such traditional formats as the comedy of character, manners, or ideas. Instead I will show how the British tickled people's funny bones. One source of material was ordinary life, the habits or poses of people, exaggerated for effect. Hamlet's *Pink Shiny Dome* (C85010), also part of a long-running campaign, displays the embarrassment of an older man in a restaurant when his younger companion accidently brushes off his toupee – only by smoking the cigar can he escape from an unwelcome reality. BarclayCard's *Restaurant* (C84042), by contrast, portrayed one of life's little triumphs: after being subjected to a harangue about British failure and Yankee success, the British businessman wins out when the restaurant refuses the American's credit cards but accepts BarclayCard. Similarly an upscale pipe smoker enjoys a moment of revenge in *Submarine* when he launches his model submarine against a tiny, noisy powerboat some punks have brought to disturb the peace of a quiet park (C86102). But Ronald in *Naughty Boy* (C86092) faces a cruel fate when his failure to use Delco auto parts stalls his car in the countryside, leaving him at the mercy of his passenger, a plain but eager Joy.

A second technique was to employ the unexpected or incongruous, which often gave the commercial the shape of a puzzle. That applied to *Hotel Lift* (C84084): a beautiful woman with truly stunning hair enters an elevator; a fat, older, upscale man touches her hair; she takes out her penknife; as she leaves the elevator, we see she has cut off his pants! A series of three Bronze Lions (C85071/2/3) for Creda Appliances, the 'Science for Womankind' campaign, used reverse sexism: in each, the men are confined to the home, they're the sex object, drudge, or neglected spouse, while the women work outside the home and determine the couple's destiny. What was the point? If men had to suffer this treatment, then they would build better appliances, leading into Creda's spiel. *Cocoa* (C84055) weds Sony's well-known mastery of technology with British humour. A skinny robot with the voice of John Cleese explains the virtues of the Sony CD player, near the end pointing out that if you need to

Figure 3.5: *Girls*. Do these images embody the fantasies of the heterosexual male? Not only were the female attendants on British Caledonia flights beautiful, they were also marvellously attentive to every need of the business traveller. (Courtesy of British Airways PLC)

replicate the sounds of the old stereo then munch a cookie and slurp a cup of cocoa. British Telecom won four Bronze Lions (1985) for 'It's for you-hoo' ads in which Robin Hood, Quasimodo, Custer, and Tarzan have their lives altered (briefly) by a phone call. The funniest involved an embattled Custer, who is first told that reinforcements are coming, then that they won't arrive till tomorrow, bringing joy to the Indians.

Of course, the last example might just as easily be counted as spoof or parody, the third brand of humour. As Frankfort had noted, the British ad-makers were very adept in using literature and drama to establish a connection with the audience. In *Prisoner of Zenda* (C84082) a tired young monarch sends a look-alike onto the balcony so that he can enjoy a Grandee Cigar. Then we hear a shot, the applause stops, the monarch pauses, the ministers blanch, but not for long – the monarch returns to his smoke. 'No one's too grand for a Grandee,' says an urbane, if mocking, voice-over. In *Waiting*, Yoplait Yoghurt (C84037) offered up a version of *The French Lieutenant's Woman*, showing a women waiting on the cold wharf for her man and his yoghurt to arrive, before a kind soul tells her it's available in town. Holsten Pils won three Silver Lions (C84116/7/8) for *Wayne*, *Bogart*, and *Cagney*, using bits of their movies to demonstrate how desirable its brew was. The spots were done largely in black and white, except for the requisite shot of Holsten Pils at the end. The agency for Tonka Toys decided to spoof that old stand-by of advertising, the product test, to prove how durable its little truck was, in the aptly named *400′ Cliff* (C86053). The Tonka and a real heavy-duty truck are dropped off the cliff at the same time; slow-motion is used to highlight the spectacular demolition of the monster, complete with all the sounds of destruction; the Tonka, of course, simply bounces around, largely unhurt.

Finally, there's farce where the charge of 'cuckoo creativity' may have some merit. By North American standards, even in the mid-1980s, the two commercials *Girls* (C84102) and *Cabin* (C84103) for the airline British Caledonia were a bit offensive. The ads were clearly aimed at the business traveller, assumed to be male and middle-aged. They are an affirmation and a parody of grossly sexist and mildly racist views, embodied here in the way the white males extol the virtues of flight attendants. In *Girls* a male passenger sings the merits of assorted 'stews' to the Beach Boys' tune 'California Girls.' A sample of each brand of 'girl' is shown serving him – the solicitous Asian, the sexy Latin, the loquacious American, and the motherly German – followed by his appearance at Gatwick airport, where he goes to British Caledonia, which has the best 'girls' of all. The final sequence, back in the plane, has all the male passengers singing the praises of the beauty and style of the British 'girls.' A female off-stage, in a soft and slightly sexy voice, mentions this is the airline that never forgets 'you' have a choice. In *Cabin* a series of men extol the virtues of the product: British Caledonia 'girls.' The 'girls' giggle – the men are so ridiculous, though their praise is welcome. Every male on the whole plane sings, loud enough so that a housewife on the ground hanging out her laundry hears and pauses, puzzled. This time a male voice-over delivers the punch-line. Both spots could be read as a mockery of male attitudes – the men do act like fools. The ads can also be read as a celebration of the male gaze, turning each kind of 'girl' into an object.

Other examples of this genre are even more peculiar. Woodpecker Beer in *More Taste* (C84005) throws a series of nonsense images at the viewer, all to a rock tune, 'I Hear You Knocking,' before the voice-over and superimposed text claims that Woodpecker has much more taste than its advertising. Radio Rentals' spot, *The Screwdriver* (C86070), finds the cabin of a submarine pierced by a giant screwdriver. The crew, who happen to be in a televised movie, discover the owner of a malfunctioning TV has called in a repairman. They smash the screen from the inside to escape, flooding the house with sea water. Meanwhile, of course, Radio Rentals has been able to deliver its message that renting a TV is far better than owning one. Or consider another Hamlet ad, this entitled *AC/DC* (C86080): Frankenstein awakes, looks down to his private parts, discovers a surprise, lights up a Hamlet for relief, and crosses his legs, complete with nylons and high heels. Here the reliance upon irony has been carried very far indeed.

Why did the makers of the British 'breakthrough' become so infatuated with designing ads that amused, jeered, satirized, and relished the offbeat? Observ-

Figure 3.6: *Cabin*. While the men sing the virtues of the 'girls' of British Caledonia, these 'girls' laugh and coo in delight at such an emphatic sign of admiration. (Courtesy of British Airways PLC)

ers have speculated that the answer lies in the British character itself. According to Martin Davidson, who was once involved in advertising, the style of whimsy and irony represents a response to the widespread antipathy of the consuming public to 'trade, selling and huckersterism.' He cites the comment of Gilbert Adair in *Myths & Memories* who argued that his people 'distrust, even despise, advertising.' The task of the ad-maker was to hide the sell: 'in a fair proportion of British TV commercials the product on offer becomes almost a McGuffin, as Hitchcock would say, a narrative factor of no great significance in itself except insofar as it generates a brief fragment of fiction.' That way the commercial takes on a pleasing disguise that avoids awakening the contempt of potential buyers.

But some part of the answer, I suspect, lies also in understanding the popular culture of England, or perhaps just of London. For centuries now, British patriots have taken a certain pride in their country's tradition of wit and humour, even claiming a preeminence in the world of comedy. Whatever the merit of that claim, there's no doubt that the British have produced more than their fair share of humorists and that they have allowed these people much licence to mock. The British appear to value eccentricity more than most, to honour the iconoclast when he or she comes as a satirist. Ivan Fallon, one of the biographers of the Saatchi brothers, has pointed to the revival of satire in Britain during the 1960s, what with the revue *Beyond the Fringe*, the famous TV show 'That Was the Week That Was,' and the appearance of 'Monty Python's Flying Circus.' Their 'new style of irreverent humour would influence the ads made in Britain over the next decade and later their style of wit and humour made an impact on the straighter ads of the New York agencies.' The revival of satire conditioned television advertising at the moment when ad-makers were developing their own tradition and established conventions that have persisted to the present day.

If in New York the demands of commerce forced constraints on art, indeed fostered a return to the hard sell of the 1950s, in London those same demands apparently encouraged ad-makers to push the boundaries of the permissible. Witness this comment by Bob Levinson of DDB International about his British colleagues in the *New York Times* (8 December 1983): 'They do a brilliant job in a country that tolerates and encourages eccentricities. It's a wonderful country to practice advertising in.' You can detect the note of envy in his statement.

The Canadian Accent

On 21 April 1992, about a thousand people gathered at the glitzy Sheraton Centre in downtown Toronto to celebrate the year's eighty-seven winners (out of 426 single and ninety-five campaign entries) in the Canadian Television Commercials Festival, otherwise known as the Bessies. That's been an annual affair (except in 1972) for nearly three decades now. The first festival was held in 1963, at the initiative of Wallace A. Ross, the founder of America's Clios, who worked with the Radio & Television Executives Club. Soon, the renamed Broadcast Executives Society (from whence comes the term 'Bessies') and the Television Bureau of Canada took over management of the competition.

The judging in 1992 was done by nine ad-makers, seven men and two women, four of whom were creative directors and another four from the production industry, nearly all from Toronto. Males have always predominated, though back in 1981 six of a thirteen-person panel were women — quite a change from 1976 and 1977 when all the judges were men. That imbalance has a certain logic, since the top creative people were and remain largely men. I used the credits listed beside the Bessies '90 to identify the sex of key agency personnel (which was not possible in every case): the creative directors (fifty-nine out of sixty-three) and the art directors (forty-six out of fifty-one) were overwhelmingly male, the writers largely male (forty-five out of fifty-seven), and only the producers mostly female (thirty-four out of fifty-one). Likewise, Toronto people have always dominated the judging committees: on the five occasions between 1976 and 1982 when the working addresses of the judges were published, fifty-nine listed Toronto, five more listed nearby places, and only one came from outside the province – Montreal. This, too, may seem fitting: Toronto is the headquarters for business, advertising agencies, and network television in Canada. Located here are the major production houses, notably

The Partners, which has been credited with producing over one-fifth of all the commercials that won Bessies between 1979 and 1992.

Only English-language commercials in which 'the creative concept' and 'the production supervision' are deemed Canadian are eligible to win Bessies. Gold, Silver, and Bronze awards, as well as certificates of merit, may be bestowed on commercials in a host of categories: automotive and automotive accessories, alcoholic and nonalcoholic beverages, food and fast food, government and media, public services or charity, corporate, travel, etc. The highest honours go to three single commercials and, since 1985, up to three campaigns. According to the 1990 judging chair, John McIntyre, of Camp Associates, the awards are given to 'work that stands out, that's original, fresh, cuts through, is technically flawless and advances the art' (*StarWeek*, 21–8 April 1990). That's not just hyperbole: the overall quality of the Bessies since the mid-1980s has been exceptional. For the record, I think the 1989 Bessies are the best exemplars of innovation, imagination, and sophistication so far.

Only the 1963–71 Gold Bessies and a selection of entrants survive from the early days of the competition. The main collection numbers, by my count, some 1,299 different commercials given certificates or Bessies between 1973–4 and 1976–92 (most of the 1975 winners are unaccountably missing). Note that awards are usually given to advertisements first telecast in the year before, although it has been possible in times past to award certificates to commercials not yet shown or aired early in the award year itself. Slightly more than half of this collection is composed of ads up to and including the 1984 award year. The realist formulas predominate (41 per cent are naturalist or essentialist), there is a large number of both absurdist (26 per cent) and romantic (17 per cent) ads, and least common are the mannerist (9 per cent) or surrealist (6 per cent) spots. Most Bessies look American: that is they employ the same styles, share the same approaches, adopt the same fads that won favour in the United States.

No wonder. It was the Americans who taught Canadians, like the British, how to make television commercials; unlike the British, the Canadians never broke the imperial link. How symbolic that the luncheon speaker at the 1992 Bessies was the American Marty Cooke, a creative director with Chiat/Day/Mojo, who had just completed a tour of duty at the Toronto office and was now off in New York. A lot of the biggest TV advertisers are American multinationals, like Procter & Gamble, General Motors, Coca-Cola, or Pepsi, though often the Canadian and provincial governments through their agencies and departments have topped the list of overall advertisers. Most of the major players in Canadian advertising are now foreign-owned. Back in 1968, only two of the top ten agencies were American. In the next two decades, and especially during the merger madness of the late 1980s, however, the industry was taken over by outsiders, in part because many multinationals have preferred working with branches of their main agencies. The *Globe and Mail's* annual run-down of corporate Canada in the *Report on Business Magazine* (July 1992) listed Young & Rubicam number one in 1991 with billings slightly above U.S $375 million. When the U.S. firm BBDO Worldwide announced in January 1992 that it was buying up two old Canadian agencies (that were already partly owned by Americans), McKim and Baker Lovick, only one top-ten agency remained fully owned and managed by Canadians: Cossette Communication-Marketing. The fact that some of the once American agencies were now owned by Britishers did not change the reality that New York was the metropolis for the Canadian advertising industry.

So, increasingly, Canada's best 'creatives' have been employed by foreign agencies. True, such stars as Jerry Goodis in the 1970s and Graham Watt and Jim Burt in the 1980s were independents. Some of the most artful and distinctive campaigns of the recent past have been created by people at agencies largely or wholly Canadian-owned: Michael McLaughlin and Stephen Creet of MacLaren ('Makes the Ordinary Extraordinary' – Hellmann's Mayonnaise) or Bob Hawton of McKim (Bell Canada's 'Natural Campaign'), for example. But, overall, counting the total number of awards since 1973, branch-plant firms have been the biggest winners in the Bessie competitions: J. Walter Thompson (118 ads), McCann-Erickson (ninety-nine), and Ogilvy & Mather (ninety-four). Once prominent Canadian-owned firms like Cockfield, Brown (forty-one ads, 1973–82) or Foster Advertising (thirty-eight ads, 1973–88) haven't survived. MacLaren Advertising, which was the leading Canadian-owned contender, was far behind the Americans at sixty-two Bessies, and it became MacLaren: Lintas in 1989.

Little wonder the recent Bessies have a distinctly international flavour. In the past decade or so many have traded on the extraordinary popularity of the global Superculture. You can find stars past, present, and sometimes future playing out their personae: a sexy Kathleen Turner for Arrow Shirts; Bea Arthur as the loud-mouthed Maude for Shoppers Drug Mart; the British comedian John Cleese for Pepsi Free; the Smothers Brothers in their characteristic comedy routine for spoon-size Shredded Wheat; the down-to-earth Australian Paul Hogan touting his country's brand, Foster's beer; or that tough lady Grace Jones for Canada Dry. There have been look-alikes (Mick Jagger), sound-alikes (Jack Nicholson), or even name-alikes (Burt Reynolds). Some Bessies borrowed the look and feel of hit movies or movie types: a Midas Muffler spot *Moose II* (B8314) offered a variation on the spaghetti western, complete with its own Clint Eastwood look-alike; Speedy Muffler King replied with *Dangerous Journey* (B8510), based on action-adventure movies like

Romancing the Stone and the tall tales of Indiana Jones; Coca-Cola's *Workout* (B8414) for Tab, a diet product aimed at women, was modelled on *Flashdance*; the style of *Close Encounters of the Third Kind* was used first by Honda (B8312) and then by Imperial Oil (B8608). Other spots relied on the world of popular music: the sound and look of an early rock star, Jerry Lee Lewis, helped to sell Certs breath mints; a Beatles song and a parody of the Beatles' Abbey Road record cover, hyped Molson's Canadian, a brand of beer, in the rock video style; even the musical *Cats* lent its aura to an ad for Ralston Purina's Cat Chow. Similarly, agencies tried to capitalize on popular crazes: McKim's *Video Games* (B8307) for Hostess Potato Chips; J. Walter Thompson employed Britain's Spitting Image to satirize the British royals (*Chuck & I*, B8750) and that other dynamic duo, Reagan and Gorbachev (*U.S. & Them*, B8752); two campaigns, Harrod & Mirlin's 'California Cooler' (1988) and later J. Walter Thompson's 'California House' (1992) used the mystique of California to sell alcohol.

There's one particular spot that suggests how international an ad can be: *Trouble in River City* (B8610), part of the 'No Trouble' campaign made by MacLaren Advertising for Imperial Oil which won the Campaign Bessie in 1986. The commercial was, in the jargon of the trade, a big production number with all kinds of singers and dancers performing on a stage (a style popularized back in the late 1970s by Young & Rubicam). The client was a Canadian branch plant of Exxon, the agency was Canadian, the production house was British (Jennie & Co. of London England), and the model was American, a hit musical of years ago with a Jimmy Durante sound-alike as the narrator.

All of this is reminiscent of the approach used by BBDO in the 'New Generation' commercials to hype Pepsi. Canadian ad-makers have proved more and more adept at appropriating names, styles, or icons from the other domains of popular culture, especially from entertainment: the Bessie winners endeavoured to link their clients' products with images of significance or favoured sounds or popular fashion. Witness the case of *The Kid* (B9130), an excellent spot made by McCann-Erickson and The Partners for Coca-Cola Classic that has been widely used outside Canada. A young man proves his skill with a guitar in a try-out for a rock band. The action occurs in some nameless tavern. What matters is that the Coke energizes his performance and concludes his success: Coca-Cola Classic is 'The Real Thing' everywhere. The reference here is to the youth culture, a state of mind, not an actual place. So you can look through the Bessies to see just how 'global' Canadian advertising and, by implication, the culture itself has become.

Such a fact does not mean that all distinguishing marks of their origin have been eliminated from the Bessies. Yes, the early Bessies were more parochial: that is, there were lots of direct and indirect references to Canada, its people, and their experiences. The 1970 Gold Bessie went to a Javex ad simply entitled *Hockey*, a reference to a sport that was then a national passion. A 1973 ad for the Bank of Montreal (B7315) had Leslie Nielsen extolling Canada, its spirit of enterprise, and the way the bank helped the country remain a winner. Molson's asked beer drinkers to *Raise a Glass* (B7304) of Canadian in honour of their marvellous country.

Indeed a few ads traded upon the anti-Americanism of the times. So *Pool Hall* (B7310), part of a popular campaign for the antidandruff shampoo Resdan, contrasted a plump, flashy, loud 'Chicago Fats' against a lean, handsome, masculine, and ever polite 'Canada Kid.' He showed the American how to keep his hair clean and how to play pool. More subtle was the approach of *Friendly Invasion* (B7348) for Canadian Pacific Hotels: the commercial offered up images of an American invasion of tourists, complete with what looked like an American general standing up in his command car, only to solve the mock problem by welcoming the horde to a newly opened CP hotel. That way the fear of an American take-over of Canada was turned on its head.

These signs of bombast and anxiety receded in the more ironic eighties. What persisted was the gentle touch, a particular kind of inflection that marked many of the Bessies (though by no means a majority). A single example here will do a better job of illustrating my meaning than a rushed list of ingredients. There's one beautiful spot, entitled *Rose* (B8472), which won both a Bessie and a Cannes award in 1984. It opens with a shot of a single, perfectly formed but blackened red rose, a symbol of beauty tarnished by dirt. Playing in the background is a gentle melody, the clear, soft sounds of a classical pianist, which serves as a sign of quality. A very white cotton swab appears from one side and begins to clean a petal. The camera shifts to an extreme close-up of the flower, and as the swab gently removes the dirt from the petals, a woman's voice-over explains. 'There's only one cotton swab with a touch this delicate, There's only one this gentle, this flexible, this cushiony soft and sure,' she declares in a voice both sweet and firm. 'There's only one cotton swab that pampers you this beautifully too.' At which point the image shifts back to a close-up of the cleaned rose, its glory highlighted by a luminous blue circle in the background. We had witnessed a marvellous transformation – beauty had been returned to its original state of perfection. 'So why in the world would you settle for an imitation? Q-tips, the original.' A woman's hand carefully picks up the rose, and lays it down in front of a Q-tips box. Beneath this final shot appears on screen the comment 'There's only one.' Delicacy, efficacy, beauty: these were all suggested by the overlapping signs. *Rose* was very much a soft sell – it supplied the viewer with the reason-why she should purchase Q-tips and in a fashion that was tasteful.

Figure 3.7: *Obsession*. The first Gold Bessie (1965) to evidence a special Canadian style was a cleverly designed commercial for Rose Brand Pickles. The camera focused on the face and moods of an attractive young woman who was obsessed by the sensual pleasures of the rose (beauty) and the pickles (taste). Note that this light-hearted display of addiction mocked the hype of advertising: the woman wryly explained how captivated she was by the brand. Purportedly, this was the first Canadian commercial to win an award at the Cannes Advertising Festival. (Courtesy of Robin Hood Multifoods Inc.)

Rose was a mannerist ad. The Canadian accent was more often evident in commercials belonging to the romantic and the absurdist schools, however. Typically the former took the shape of a celebration, of good times, simple pleasures, family life or social harmony. So *Church* (B7307) offered a friendly look at people enjoying life, along with Salada Tea, in a small town for a Sunday afternoon get-together; *Club House* (B9268) offered a series of portraits of club members, while a voice-over extolled the fact of harmony, sharing, enjoyment, all to introduce the notion of a Sears Club, the creature of a retail giant.

Perhaps the most famous campaign of this type was that mounted by J. Walter Thompson for Labatt's Blue, then Canada's favourite brew, represented

Figure 3.8: *Reunion*. Scenes of homecoming – the reunion of husband and wife, father and son, and the whole family after the Second World War – recalling a time in legend that honoured the ideal of togetherness. *Reunion* was one ad in a continuing series called the 'Human Journey,' made for London Life by Goodis, Goldberg, Soren during the 1970s. The campaign expressed another element present in the Canadian style, namely a taste for the heartwarming, even the sentimental. (Courtesy of London Life)

in the Bessies by *Scuba* and *Snowsail* (1984), *Balloons* (1982), *Heliski* and *Windsurfing* (1983), and finally *Blue Horizon* and *Night Ski* (1984). As the titles suggest, each commercial featured a different kind of outdoor sport that engaged the energies of young adults at play, though a continuing image and at times the focus was the Labatt's balloon floating gently through the sky. (The campaign was so commonplace that people used to puzzle over just what new sport Labatt's would discover to celebrate in its next commercial.) The campaign theme song, a brand of soft pop, told viewers 'When you're smilin' keep on smilin' Blue smiles along with you.' The commercials conveyed a sense of cleanliness, freshness, and above all harmony: their images linked happy couples, good times, sports and the outdoors, and beer. Actually Labatt's

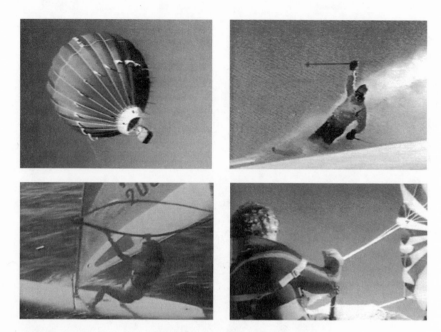

Figure 3.9: Labatt's 'Smiling' Campaign. Scenes from one of the most famous beer campaigns of the late 1970s and early 1980s, in which J. Walter Thompson linked drinking Blue to outdoor fun. Outside of the signature picture of the floating balloon, many of the images were action shots of healthy folks testing their skills against Nature. (Courtesy of Labatt Brewing Company Ltd.)

'Smiling' campaign was only one of a number of romances revolving around beer and good times that were common throughout the 1970s and the early 1980s.

By far the more pleasing examples of the Canadian accent came out of what the ad-makers did with humour. That first took the form of spoofs or satires, reminiscent of the work of English Canada's top TV comedians, Johnny Wayne and Frank Shuster in the 1950s and 1960s. Indeed Wayne and Shuster were employed by Gulf Canada to give the foreign oil company a Canadian face: *Jack-in-Basement* (B7323) put a Gulf man on twenty-four-hour stand-by in Wayne's basement, *Men's Club* (B7603) had two English chaps discussing the virtues of Gulf's Mid-Winter Service Special, and *Brother John* (B7823) told the story of two monks who discovered the virtues of Gulf's self-service stations – 'Gulf helps those who serve themselves.'

A Portfolio of Images

This portfolio reflects my own list of favourite commercials. But the actual choice of what to show was dictated by more than just my personal tastes. I could only select from a limited range of pictures available on film (since these reproduce best). I was restricted to the range of images that the companies or their agencies could offer me. And I decided to present images that in some way illustrated how advertising connects with popular culture.

Hilltop or *Buy the World a Coke* (Coca-Cola)

Mean Joe Greene (Coca-Cola)

The 'New Generation' Campaign (Pepsi-Cola)

1984 (Apple Macintosh)

Rose (Q-Tips)

The 'Butter Dance' Campaign (Dairy Bureau of Canada)

The 'Natural Campaign' (Bell Canada)

Hilltop or *Buy the World a Coke*: The collage is a photograph of a promotional picture puzzle that reproduced some of the images from this celebrated commercial. These images illustrate the themes of joy and harmony that were central to the company's message. (Courtesy of the Coca-Cola Company)

Mean Joe Greene: These images are photographs made during the filming of the commercial. They highlight the contrasts between the famous football player and his little fan – and they display the central importance of Coca-Cola as a gift of friendship and source of renewal. (Courtesy of the Coca-Cola Company)

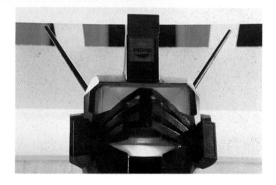

The 'New Generation' Campaign: These images are taken from *Sound Truck, Jackson Street*, and *Robots*, which were part of the first wave of commercials in the 'New Generation' campaign in the mid-1980s. That campaign specialized in images of significance: here the desire of the masses (*Sound Truck*), the superstar of music (Michael Jackson), and the mechanized warrior (the Pepsi robot). (Courtesy of Pepsi-Cola Company)

1984: One image from the single most famous commercial of the 1980s that introduced Apple's new Macintosh computer to the United States. The running female
represents the new force that was about to liberate humanity from the tyranny of
Big Brother, meaning IBM. (Courtesy of Apple Computer, Inc.)

Rose: This commercial was an especially fine example of the Canadian accent. Here are contrasting photographs of the dirty and the cleaned rose, a testament to the powers of Q-tips cotton swabs. (Q-Tips is a registered trade mark of Chesebrough-Pond's Canada. Photographs used with permission.)

The 'Butter Dance' Campaign: These photographs are taken from *Asparagus Dance, Corn Dance,* and *Bread Dance,* a campaign created by Graham Watt and Jim Burt that employed the language of romance and extolled the virtues of self-indulgence. (Courtesy of the Dairy Bureau of Canada)

The 'Natural Campaign': These images come from *Wolves, Loons,* and *One Voice,*
made for Bell Canada by what is now McKim Baker Lovick/BBDO. They embody a
love of the wild that is purportedly one part of the Canadian character. They also
attest to the beauty of nature photography. (Courtesy of Bell Canada)

Figure 3.10: The 'Pity' Campaign. J. Walter Thompson made familiar these faces of English tea 'experts' who were so impressed with the taste and quality of the Canadian blend Red Rose. Such images were supposed to express pleasure, surprise, and sometimes sadness. (Courtesy of Thomas J. Lipton Inc. Red Rose is a registered trademark of Thomas J. Lipton Co.)

Right at the end of *Men's Club*, the news the winter special was only available in Canada provoked the response 'Pity,' a direct reference to one of the most famous campaigns of the decade: the Red Rose Tea campaign. Here, J. Walter Thompson mocked English snobbery, and particularly the presumption the English were the teamasters of the world. The stories – *Tea Party* (1976), *Rectory* (1977), and *Breakfast* (1978) – took place in English settings, where a collection of tea fanatics tried out this special Canadian blend, whose purported superiority evoked cries of nonsense or heresy, until one soul would proclaim 'Pity' when he or she learned Red Rose was only available in Canada. The speech, the ways, the superiority of the English, all were spoofed in this mock revenge of the colonial against one-time lords and ladies. The hope was that if Canadian viewers were left with the impression even the English thought Red Rose was better, then they would try the brand. The fact was that the campaign embedded the Red Rose slogan in the national memory: many years later, a front-page headline in the *Toronto Star* (28 February 1993) began 'Only in Canada, you say? Pity ...'

The other, equally popular satire of the 1970s was the campaign mounted by Goodis, Goldberg, Soren for Speedy Muffler King. If anyone deserves credit as the first champion of the Canadian accent, it is Jerry Goodis. His repertoire was extraordinary: his shops produced such romances of history as *Reunion* (B7643), about the postwar homecoming, and the poetic *April Showers* (B8217), which was an extended visual metaphor on the need to save. But Goodis's forte was humour. His campaign made famous the claim 'At Speedy, You're a Somebody,' still used in the early 1990s. In *Pizza* (B7322) a rotund, expressive, and heavily-accented Italian explains how he was so well treated by Speedy before that now he really is a 'somebody,' owner of his own fleet of Pizza cars, Speedy gets all his business. Three other Bessies tell a poignant tale of a man put down by circumstances, if not by his fellows, who finds recognition only at Speedy: the weekend golfer who woke up the neighbourhood when he tried to sneak out of the house (*Golfer*, the Gold Bessie winner, 1975); Rodney Dangerfield, who explained how he never got respect (B7604); and the ordinary Joe, who believed what people told him, only to end up in impossible situations (B7916). Some years later, the Jerry Goodis Agency retooled this scenario in an inventive spot, entitled *Broken Telephone* (B8333), where a man seeking a loan is mistreated by bureaucracy, until he finds a friend in the Bank of Nova Scotia. Each of these commercials was a mock parable for the modern man, struggling to survive in an uncaring world.

You can find this brand of satire even now: witness, for example, the sad plight of the spokesman for Goodyear Canada (B9221) whose efforts to explain how the firm does great tune-ups are foiled by Goodyear's touting of a tire sale. But in the 1980s what gained favour was a slightly different species of deadpan humour where viewers were asked to laugh at the bland delivery and the strange antics of the actors. Fiberglas Canada told how a collection of cheap-skates were able to save so much money on home insulation that they could realize their dreams: a ridiculous little car (B8225), 262 pink flamingoes (B8579), a cramped summer place (B8639), or a tiny swimming pool (B8727). Factory Carpet's *Bait & Switch* (B85101) and *Samples* (B85105) showed how rival outlets tried to chisel the naifs who were foolish enough to cross their doors. IKEA's *Systems* (B8653) features a man talking Swedish who turns out to be a robot. Speedy Muffler King's *Burt & Betty* (B8745) has a deadpan middle-aged couple dispute whether or not the car needs a brake repair – it does, desperately. Recently, Doner Schur Peppler has created a set of award-winning spots (1991 and 1992) that mock the amazement, antics, or style of very

Figure 3.11: *Pizza & Golfer*. Note the contrast between the happy Italian man, who was pleased by the service he received from Speedy Muffler King, and the unfortunate golfer, whose quiet escape from home was foiled by a faulty muffler. In the third frame we see the golfer seeking Speedy's help to ensure that he won't cause a sensation the next time he wishes to leave his home on the sly. (Courtesy of Speedy Muffler King Inc.)

ordinary folk, all to demonstrate the miracle of low prices at Leon's Furniture. According to a *Toronto Star* poll (18 April 1992), about as many people hated the campaign as loved it, one respondent claiming it was 'wonderfully silly,' while another declared it was 'degrading to the elderly.' The trouble with deadpan humour is that it can easily be read as depicting people as fools.

Since Jerry Goodis retired from ad-making in the mid-1980s, the most outstanding, indeed authentic expressions of the Canadian accent have come from the alliance of Graham Watt and Jim Burt. At the 1991 Bessies they won a Campaign Third for 'Butter Dance,' plus three individual awards for these spots, three more awards for milk commercials, one award for an advocacy message on behalf of the Dairy Bureau of Canada, and the Speiss Award for lifetime achievement. Ever since 1978, first at McKim, later at Watt Burt

Advertising in Montreal, they have designed fourteen award-winning commercials for the Ontario Milk Marketing Board (in association with McKim) and three butter commercials for the Dairy Bureau (in association with Léveillé Vickers & Benson). They've tried to please viewers, to speak softly: 'Better to stand out by being quiet and better-loved,' they told Jim McElgunn of *Marketing* (10 June 1991).

It's this gentle touch that runs through their work, not a commitment to any one school or design. Watt and Burt have created romantic (B8013), mannerist (B8518), surrealist (B8933), and absurdist (B8930) spots. They've employed animation (B8412), slow-motion (B9126), the mildly erotic (B8516), sensual music (the lambada: B9145), and humour (B8934). Drinking milk has been cloaked in nostalgia (B8319), associated with health and fitness and well-being (B8120), presented as a tonic against the fast life (B8412), defined as a sign of the avant-garde (B8519), even idealized as a source of power (B9127). Their 'Butter Dance' campaign was, at one level, a celebration of excess and exuberance, of surrender to the sinful pleasures of self-indulgence. I repeat: what gives this work coherence is its mix of charm, imagination, and geniality. It doesn't shout or dazzle but instead seduces.

The temptation to explore the general significance of this accent is too great to resist altogether. Previous studies of the country's audio-visual culture have made much of the realism of filmed documentaries and TV dramas, whether that is expressed in a tradition of 'telling it like it is' (Morris Wolfe), or a fascination with ambiguity and open-ended narratives (Mary Jane Miller), or a taste for misery (Richard Collins). None of this really fits the bill here, though. Indeed I'm inclined to think the emergence of the accent was *sui generis*, a result of seeking some way to appeal to Canadian tastes within the confines of the language of advertising. Note that both Canadian-owned and foreign agencies have designed this approach. It calls to mind one side of the mythical Canadian, or at least English-Canadian character: namely that this country is a kinder, gentler place, a polite America less given to fads and frenzies than its southern neighbour. An advertising that was subtle, tasteful, calm, in a word 'gentle,' that embodied a sense of difference compared to the welter of hype coming from the south or cloned by local ad-makers was an expression of some Canadians' sensibilities.

A Postmodern Form?

What all this discussion of styles and schools has been leading up to is the claim that these commercials of distinction could be the preeminent expression of postmodern art. Readers may be excused if they should sigh, 'not again.'

Something similar has been claimed for an assortment of new/old buildings, for particular kinds of novels, for music videos, and so on. Besides, if I've grown weary of reading all those lengthy tomes on postmodernism, I can well imagine why others would greet any reference to this phenomenon with a sigh. There's a sense in which postmodernism is a fiction, created by an enormously inflated class of cultural critics (many in the ivory tower) who are bent on advancing their own self-interest by announcing the discovery of something most people can't even understand.

Bear with me, however. I presume the term 'postmodern' connotes a range of traits and beliefs that became common on the cultural scene by the mid-1980s: the confusion of what was once considered trash and quality, the celebration of the ironic tone, the prevalence of cynicism and nostalgia, a fascination with artifice, the prominence of images, the mixing of genres and forms, an enthusiasm for parody and collage, a taste for contradiction if not paradox, for the decentred or indeterminate text, a mood of playfulness rather than commitment. These have been linked to the imperialism of art (also known as 'the aestheticization of reality') and above all to the triumph of commerce. Indeed, if we are to believe the French theorist Jean Baudrillard, we now live in an era when only the simulacra are real.

Well before the term became faddish, other scholars had applied some of these attributes to advertising, and specifically television advertising. Marshall McLuhan (the first postmodern oracle?) is on record about the significance of advertising in its own right, never mind what products it moved. The ad-maker Stan Freberg, writing in the Y&R catalogue, cited with approval one of McLuhan's many dicta: 'Individual ads can be seen as the vortices of power that "put us on" as art forms do.' He thereby assigned the power of irony to advertising. Back in 1972, the British Marxist John Berger decided publicity was 'the last moribund form' of 'the visual art of post-Renaissance Europe,' borrowing all manner of images and messages from oil painting (which was, above all, 'a celebration of private property'). Some years later, Bruce Kurtz devoted *Spots* to a serious treatment of the work and thought of four American directors of commercials, all in the tradition of art history and art criticism. He detected echoes of surrealism, existentialism, and the theatre of the absurd, linkages with the avant-garde, a kind of originality, in what he termed 'the most pervasive visual imagery in our culture.' Florence Feasely corrected one of his enthusiasms in 1983 when she pointed out television commercials were really the 'Unpopular Art,' though she added that it was closer to the people and their lives than much of what was in museums. She cited a variety of luminaries like Daniel Boorstin, Neil Postman, or Martin Esslin who had discussed the parallels among fine art, literature, drama, and advertising.

The new status of advertising as the art form of the moment was widely recognized during the late 1980s. Some evidence of that was the growth of collections of TV ads in museums and archives, the nostalgic appeal of shows made up of old commercials, or the increasing attention devoted to commercials by special interest groups and the news media. In April 1989, *Harper's* opened its forum on the Second Coming with the claim 'The eighties have witnessed the flowering of the art of publicity.' It hired a few professionals to design a marketing strategy for Jesus Christ, including a storyboard for a sixty-second spot, a romantic ad, naturally. James Gorman in the *New York Times* (18 November 1990) took note of the Calvin Klein ads for Obsession. They had been made by David Lynch out of novels by Fitzgerald, Hemingway, D.H. Lawrence, and Gustave Flaubert. How would Stanley Kubrick handle Plato's *Timaeus* for Nike or Brian De Palma transform Chandler's *Farewell, My Lovely* for L'eggs Panty Hose, he went on to speculate. Indeed, 'if you want to work with the classics (and to do whatever you like to them), television advertisements may be your best bet,' he observed. That was all a bit tongue-in-cheek, of course. More serious was the work of the feminist artist Barbara Kruger, who employed the images and style of publicity to subvert the status quo. Her *Love for Sale* (1990) was a parody of parodies, wresting the signs of advertising free from their context to sell a political agenda at odds with capitalism and patriarchy.

But just how creative is advertising? For years now, ad-makers have talked up their claims of creativity. Particularly since 1959 and the birth of the Clios, there have appeared a wealth of festivals and competitions to honour the accomplishments of ad-makers. Such an awards network is essential to the development of any artistic profession: that makes it possible to recognize 'good art,' and by implication denigrate 'bad art,' which serves the function of maintaining the self-esteem of the creative staff. 'Creative people live for the awards shows,' Dean Stefanides of Scali, McCabe, Sloves told *USA Today* (19 June 1991). 'It's better than getting a raise.' Winning bolsters 'egos' and 'resumes,' stimulates 'inspiration' and 'imitation,' and may even 'please the client,' claimed the newspaper's reporter, which was the reason why agencies were so shocked when the Clios 1991 aborted because of financial troubles: the whole profession was betrayed.

Most of the awards are given out for imagination and originality. Jean Johnson, a member of the Cannes jury in 1980, recalled in *Marketing* (28 July 1980) that a clever Canadian spot called *I Remember* for Smarties barely lost out in the competition for a Silver Lion when one veteran juror claimed its particular gimmick, a shaking box, had been used by another candy manufacturer in South America. News media and adland call agencies noted for their creative excellence 'hot shops,' such as Wieden & Kennedy of Portland, Oregon, which masterminded the highly successful Nike advertising campaign in the late 1980s, and received a write-up entitled 'They Know Bo' in the *New York Times Magazine* (11 November 1990). Indeed it is possible to apply the famous *auteur* theory to the making of commercials, to search through some body of work to discover the signature of a true artist, as I have done in the case of Jerry Goodis, Graham Watt, and Jim Burt.

Nonetheless, it is dangerous to carry the *auteur* theory too far. Adland is notoriously imitative, borrowing ideas, styles, techniques, and the like from wherever – videotapes of award winners from around the world are now regularly offered for sale to ad agencies. Innovation is a lot more common than originality. Jerry Goodis, for example, admitted his debt to Doyle Dane Bernbach. Saatchi and Saatchi was a 'hot shop' back in 1979 when it handled the Conservative Party account, and shared in the glory of Margaret Thatcher's victory, although its advertising campaign borrowed heavily from the techniques and style common in American electioneering. Besides, it is often difficult to determine in any given situation just who is more authorial, the client, the creative executive, the art director, and so on, a point Michael Arlen made in his acclaimed investigation of the creation of an AT&T commercial. The ad-maker may be an artist, but he or she is at work in a collective enterprise and an incestuous industry, which is reason enough for the haters of advertising to scoff at claims of creativity. Witness this marvellous diatribe by Michael Chanan, who translated Mattelart's *Advertising International* into English:

This word 'creative', as a term of vocabulary in advertising discourse, has very little to do with what a poet, a philosopher, a psychologist or even a neuro-psychologist might mean by it. For all the differences which divide such experts, the word has in each case a real and plastic meaning which links it intimately with the faculty of imagination. 'Creativity' and 'creative staff' in the advertising world are fetishistic terms. To borrow the aesthetic terminology of the poet Coleridge, there is never any *imagination* in advertising, only the work of *fancy*, which produces nothing original, but merely recycles and recombines existing material. What Stravinsky admired in composers of jingles was not their originality but their economy of means. The only possible originality advertising could claim is in technique, and even this is doubtful; certainly never in content, which consists entirely in pseudo-speech, Orwellian non-speak.

Such a rigorous definition, of course, would consign most painters, novelists, musicians, architects, and the like to oblivion.

But paradox is certainly built into the exercise of imagination in advertising: as William Henry put it, ad-makers in America have the 'task of producing art, or at least charm, while in shackles and chains.' Feasely noted how uncomfortable some industry leaders (and at least one author of an advertising text) were with the notion of commercials-as-art. They didn't want the 'creatives' making art instead of marketing products, and all these awards merely encouraged the 'creatives' to indulge their artistic passions. From that standpoint, the 'creative revolution' had been a time when these passions overwhelmed the imperatives of commerce, a view that informed the welcoming speech the chairman of the Clio advisory board gave to the assembled 'creatives' in 1979 (a speech included in a tribute entitled the *Clio Awards*).

Often the client is in the driver's seat. Ad agencies compete vigorously to win new accounts: writing in the *New York Times Magazine* (20 October 1991), Randall Rothenberg thought the 1991 review for the Subaru of America account, valued at $70 million, was akin to a 'ceremonial dance' among six finalists involving 'supplications, professions of faith and the quest for a single defining idea that one participant likened to the search for the Holy Grail.' Agencies must listen carefully to their masters: Ingalls, Quinn & Johnson, according to the *New York Times* (24 March 1991) worked very closely with marketing teams at Converse Inc. during the fall of 1990 to design a new $22 million campaign that could make the company a serious contender in 'the sneaker wars.' The news in September 1991 that Coca-Cola had signed a deal with a Hollywood agent to mastermind a counterattack on Diet Pepsi's TV campaign shook some ad people in the United States, since it seemed to signify doubts about the creative wisdom of agencies. The point is that advertising, more than any other creative enterprise, embodies the confusion of art and commerce, which seemed one mark of the postmodern moment.

There is a lot more evidence of how television advertising suited the new paradigm. Need I emphasize the obvious: that commercials borrow from everywhere; they happily cross the boundaries between trash and quality; they love to parody, to juxtapose opposites, to rip icons out of their context, to play with metaphors; they specialize in creating images; and they are models of artifice. Consider as well the popularity of irony, which positions the viewer as a veteran consumer of hype. That strategy, apparent from the beginning, won much fame with the arrival of the British 'breakthrough.' Finally, commercials are ubiquitous: no other source manufactures so many of the simulations that bombard our consciousness, pushing us into what Baudrillard considers the state of 'hyperreality.'

So commercials seem both a product and an agent of that sensibility labelled postmodern. But there is one vitally important quality of commercials that contradicts this observation. Commercials may at times take on a pose of ambiguity, of indeterminacy, pretending that they really are open or decentred texts. That can't be taken at face value, though: almost all consumer commercials are meant to seduce or sell. Put another way, television advertising normally acts as the vehicle for an overarching ideology, the gospel of consumption. We may give commercials an alternate reading than that intended. But it would be foolish to deny that commercials strive to achieve closure. These preferred readings, the meanings TV advertising encourages, are the subject of the next chapter.

4

Reading the Bessies

Show me a nation's television commercials and I'll tell you what really turns its crank.
— Paul Knox, *Globe and Mail*, 9 July 1990

One of the old conceits of the ad-makers is that their work reflects the hopes, concerns, styles, habits, and rituals of daily life. There's merit to such claims: you can ransack the Bessies to find evidence of how hairstyles or skirt lengths have changed, the colloquial expressions of a decade ago, or what appliances were in the kitchen of the early 1970s. You can find evidence of how mores have changed as well. The 1977 Gold Bessie *You're Looking Good* for General Motors of Canada features a brief scene where a man, in public, pats the bum of the woman he is with. A few years later, during an election campaign, when Prime Minister John Turner did much the same thing, the outcry was extraordinary.

But it would be foolish to conclude that the Bessies provide either an accurate or a complete record of daily life. Ad-makers deal in stereotype: their work may embody these stereotypes, espouse them, or even mock them – never forget the playfulness of the ad-maker. The Bessies amount to interpretations of what's perceived to be reality. That reality is excerpted, condensed, flattened, pick your favourite word. What makes the Bessies different from a painting, newscast, or a movie is that the commercial almost invariably presumes a reality where the gospel of consumption reigns supreme.

Here TV advertising differs little from the ads of print or radio. 'The ideology of advertising is an ideology of efficacious answers,' noted Roland Marchand. 'No problem lacks an adequate solution. Unsolvable problems may exist in society, but they are nonexistent in the world glimpsed through advertisements.' The crucial fact is that advertising offers individual satisfactions to people *en masse*, and its success has always distressed critics since that diverts attention away from pressing social needs. The way to personal self-realization is not through the voting booth, the school, or the church, but the shopping mall.

Barring a few exceptions here and there, I intend to treat the Bessie Collection as though it were one gigantic document, a useful fiction for the purposes of analysis because I am looking for recurring images and motifs. The Bessies can be taken as a collective effort, however imperfect, to reflect and interpret the views of the social mainstream. Understand the Bessies and you understand a bit of Canada's soul? Put a bit differently, reading the Bessies is one way to investigate the ideas that appear to exercise hegemonic authority in Canada and throughout the First World. But it is also a way of probing the resistance to that hegemony, how people evade, mock, or even reject social disciplines.

One caveat: my reading of the Bessies is obviously personal. That's a difficulty with the craft of cultural history: analysts can never totally free themselves from their particular views – they fulfil the role of supercritics whose accounts must always be treated with a degree of suspicion. Besides, my reading does not exhaust the wealth of clichés, myths, motifs, and the like in the Bessie Collection. You could, for example, say much more than I will about the cult of personal cleanliness, the stereotype of seniors, or the health craze of the 1980s. In particular, I haven't treated at any length one important genre of Bessies, the public service and charitable ads. Why are they significant? Because they often express views that counter the main thrust of the consumer ads. But that very property makes them ill-suited to an effort to map the cultural landscape of the consumer society.

Identities

Back in 1979 the Silver Bessie went to a McCann-Erickson spot for Levi's Pantomime (jeans for women), entitled *Years & Years*. It's unlikely that ten years later any similar spot could have gotten on the air. A censor somewhere, whether in the agency or at the network, would have forecast the outcry any showing would provoke from women's groups.

Yet *Years & Years* has enduring significance because of what it says about both gender and age. It's a romantic little gem, shot in soft focus, with lots of quick cuts and close-ups, backed up by some gentle pop music and a male voice-over who speaks in rhyme. It might easily fit my description of the Canadian accent, except for its erotic undertones.

Featured are a handsome young man and two gorgeous young women, both blonde, who first appear walking along a sunny beach. One of the women wears a revealing bikini. This woman starts to get dressed, in Levi's of course, while

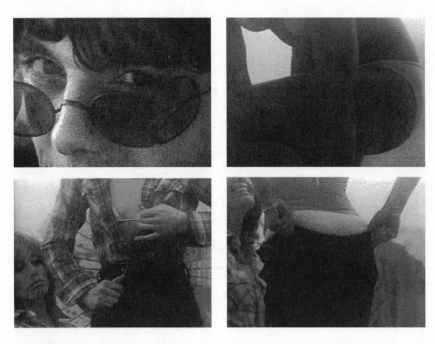

Figure 4.1: *Years & Years.* This finely crafted commercial was one of only a few Bessies that have boldly employed the art of sexual display. Here the male gaze acts as a catalyst for a series of shots exposing portions of the female body. The ad positions the viewer as a voyeur who intrudes upon a private moment in the life of two women. (Courtesy of Levi Strauss & Co. [Canada] Inc.)

the man settles back to watch.

Through the years and the years, it's been beautifully clear
That a man and a woman are different right here
A man walks in metre, a woman in rhyme.

We are treated to close-ups of the woman's crotch, bum, breasts, navel, face, back, and legs. The two women even touch parts of their bodies, a touch that serves to straighten out the clothing as well as to caress the thigh or the bum. The camera swings back and forth between the woman or her companion and the man who, on one occasion, averts his eyes – a nice touch of authenticity that.

So Levi's invented a line called Pantomime
Designed for a woman, they're snug in the waist
And shaped different behind to reflect feminine taste.
Pantomime comes in denim or cords
To beautify ladies and mystify lords
To magnetize eyes and accentuate thighs

Although one of the women is initially irritated, then aloof, at the end she blows a kiss to the watcher, who waves goodbye as the women walk off jauntily down the beach.

So remember in life through the lows and the highs
That whoever you are, you can live in Levi's.

The most obvious code at work here is gender. Not only are we told that men and women are different, that there is a definite 'feminine' taste, but we are shown how the male and the female are depicted in quite different ways. The man watches, the women display. You could read the ad as a celebration of the male gaze, where the woman becomes an object of desire. Or, given the fact the message is aimed at the female consumer, the ad becomes an expression of the female gaze where the woman is a subject, even a role model, whose look exercises power over the imagination of the man. The voice-over tells us that Pantomime has a twofold purpose, to 'beautify' and to 'magnetize,' to transform both the woman and the man. In short, Pantomime is being sold to consumers as a way to attain feminine beauty, and so feminine power as well.

Whatever the particular view expressed in any single commercial, the Bessie Collection reflects the age-old notion that 'this is a man's world.' One of the most important sources of authority in the commercial is the voice-over: throughout, the overwhelming proportion of such voices is male. Perhaps even more surprising, men are more often represented in the Bessies than women. Only in health and beauty ads do women slightly outnumber men because the discipline of beauty falls more heavily upon women; by contrast, women appear infrequently in ads for automotive accessories, since once purchased, the car apparently falls under the label of a man's thing. Overall, men and women appear together in 540 ads, men alone in 415, and women alone in 113. There's not one award year where the sexes are equally represented.

What this also illustrates is the import of gender as both a social resource and a source of personal identity. Recall the comment in *Years & Years* that men walk in 'metre,' women in 'rhyme.' At bottom the code of gender works through a form of binary logic: the feminine and the masculine can only be fully understood in relation to each other. Recognize, however, that the workings of this logic can be affected by other codes, notably of age, and that the individual expressions may at times violate convention. Furthermore, gender stereotypes have changed over the years, especially since in the mid-1980s. That aside, the code can be identified through a series of contrasts – here's a partial listing:

	Feminine	Masculine
Physique	weak	strong
Traits	emotional	rational
	delicate	rugged
	warm	cool
	sociable	competitive
	narcissistic	masterful
Display	body	authority
Domains	home	workplace
	private	public

Let's take a close look at how this worked in practice. Consider first the motif of woman as object: it was far more common to see women displaying their bodies and their sexuality than men. A wide assortment of ads – for health and beauty products, clothing, and foods – presumed the typical woman was preoccupied with turning herself into a work of art. One animated minidrama actually presents a woman as a caterpillar, who is transformed into a marvellous butterfly after she uses a particular deodorant (B7909). In another, more realistic sketch, a woman slips into a car and begins immediately to beautify herself with a cordless hair-dryer (B8478). Women lose themselves in the joys of pampering, withdrawing from the world around them (B8116) and experiencing a quiet ecstasy (B8037). Women caress – their bodies, their clothes, their children (here extensions of themselves): the smooth skin of a leg just shaved (B7616), a body newly bathed (B7816), a happy baby (B8955), sleek black boots (B9021). Men, by contrast, touch themselves only after shaving (B8953) and caress only their beautified women (B7840).

Once their charms have been enhanced, women show off marvellous legs (B8147), stunning hair (B8477), the perfect smile (B8481). Sometimes they sit, a picture of quiet beauty (B7733); sometimes they clown or cavort, caught up in the sheer pleasure of their look (B8128); sometimes they tease a watching male (B7632), act out the role of the vamp (B8063), or play to an unseen audience (B8247) – such ads position the viewer, especially the male, as a voyeur. Even where you can detect a slight feminist touch, as in one ad for Slim-Fast (B8453), the women saying goodbye to the men who've put them down nonetheless display their new slimness and so their beauty. Is it any wonder that women come to embody certain properties in all kinds of ads: glamour (a bank, B7428), sensuality (butter, B8738), radiant health (milk, B8516), or male desire (a chocolate bar, B9201)? What underpins this cult of beauty is the promise of self-esteem, even of power over other people, and especially men, a promise that is occasionally made explicit (B8566).

Consider that other motif, woman as nurturer. In the world of the Bessies, women have a natural affinity for caring about other people – that's proof of their love. So a telephone operator tells how she explained to a worried caller the right way to cook a chicken (B7935); a female chaplain visits disabled children in a hospital to brighten their day (B9158); women's voices urge upon two old gents the wisdom of a reconciliation (B9228); a female voice-over talks about friendship in an antidrug message (B9245). Typically, the women are the ones who make any occasion a social success, even a Christmas choir (B7312) or a church bake sale (B8062), though recently ad-makers have begun to depict men helping women when the family has dinner guests (B8733).

Far more common have been food, beverage, and household product ads that portray the women serving families. That's especially true of soup: after collecting the wood, father and son return to a farmhouse where mum has prepared a hearty soup (B7432); another mom adds a little milk (meaning love) to her soup to please and invigorate her children (B7735); a third makes a quick and appealing meal of soup for the family, even earning a kiss from hubby for her care and effort (B8121). That tradition of service is readily handed on to girls: a girl helps grandma bake a pie to please grandpa (B7809); a daughter serves daddy his soup when mom's out (B8630) and two daughters clean house and serve more soup to please a single, working mother (B9218); even a pretty toddler brings cereal out to dad, who is fishing off the dock (B9037). A succession of very clever ads for Sunlight detergent shows mother doing the laundry, while she chats with a teenage daughter (B8977); counsels a college-bound son, who mocks her concern (B8942); and returns a newly cleaned teddy bear to an insistent child (B8944). Scali, McCabe, Sloves won a Gold Bessie in 1988 for spoofing this cliché of the feminine experience: an anxious woman explains how she almost lost her cat (meaning her mate) to a rival, all because she failed to serve the pet Meow Mix (B8809)!

Contrast that with the commentary on masculinity. There is a 1984 winner for Old Spice After Shave lotion, entitled *Maritime Morning*, which conveniently tells us about 'the essence of a man.' The man in question is a rugged and handsome hunk who strides around his room and the outdoors, casually helps some other men pull a boat into the sea, and generally looks in command of the situation. A female voice-over explains 'he's straightforward, dependable, and honest. I feel like he could do anything. He's strong but I think it has more to do with his character – he's there when you need him.' Old Spice commercials, by the way, have always made much of the mystique of masculinity to sell their goods, especially their deodorant.

Masculinity is signified first by physique, gestures, and language. The best of men, including the cool customer in *Maritime Morning*, are tall, slim, and rugged, sometimes a bit weathered (men weather, women wrinkle) to show his experience. Perhaps this explains the taste for Clint Eastwood act-alikes (B7915) or look-alikes (B8314)? The 'real' man stands straight, legs apart (B7427), grasps rather than holds a beer (B8618) or a battery (B8636), smiles coolly (B8480), looks you right in the eye (B7633), all to indicate he's in command. His voice is firm (7315) and dry (B8816); his sentences are often short (B7345); his words sometimes sharp or hard-edged (B7917) – to convey authority, instil confidence, or capture attention.

But a man is also known by what he does. The key here is not necessarily his occupation, but rather his skills, the very fact that he can pose as an expert. So one Bessie (B8610) played off a veteran mechanic against both a wide-eyed youthful apprentice and a slightly incompetent female customer to emphasize the expertise of Imperial Oil's staff. Canadian Breweries, later called Carling O'Keefe, featured two artisans, a bottlemaker (B7303) and a drayman (B7305), as well as truck drivers (B7922) and even a master of party games (B7605), to link their brews with masculinity. Over the years, Midas Muffler has made much of its zeal to employ the most professional and macho mechanics (B8206). In a different vein, Colgate-Palmolive (B9241) portrayed two expert violinists to demonstrate the virtues of its dental floss. The point is that masculinity connotes mastery, an ability to do some valued task efficiently, whatever obstacles might stand in the way.

That leads into a third characteristic, namely the fact that masculinity is always being tested in one way or another. Men are forever engaged in competition, to best nature, circumstance, others, even themselves. The champion car racer proves his expertise and his daring with some frenzied driving, just on the edge of losing control (B7601). Young soldiers demonstrate their manhood by showing they are willing to parachute out of a plane (B9008). Sports is a favourite arena for these tests: the men strain to steer a sailboat to victory (B8117); the skier trains long and hard to triumph in competition (B8811) or bashes down a hill to prove his vigour (B9209); a man demonstrates his skill on the muddy football field before meeting with his girl (B9188). Even when males get together to play, their companionship often is marked by some contest: shuffleboard (B7736), pool (B9231), or horseplay (B7821), where the purpose is to best a friend. This trait has occasionally taken on a more sinister cast, where masculinity is linked to violence (B9001/3). But much more common is the ad-makers' preference for aggression, here deployed as a positive trait because it betokens confidence, zeal, and will.

The second major source of identity is age. Recall that *Years & Years* featured not only women and men, but youth as well, a volatile mixture crucial to the preferred reading of the ad. There is a vital distinction between the codes of gender and age: though you can't shed your sex (according to the Bessies), people are always moving along the age scale, from infancy to adulthood and eventually into their 'golden years.' Even so, the code of age also operates according to a kind of binary logic, organized around the distinction between the child and the adult:

	Child	**Adult**
Size	little	big
Sexuality	asexual	sexual
Gender	emerging	established
Skill	incompetent	competent
Social definition	undifferentiated	differentiated
Activity	play	work
Attitude	dependent	independent
	naive	wise
	irresponsible	responsible

Typically, childhood is presented as a magic time, a time of innocence, of hope, of learning (school is usually a pleasant experience), and above all of play. Mattel Canada (B85115) gives us two little girls, living in a world of black and white, who suddenly colour their world once they discover the joys of the Rainbow Bright doll. What keeps their world so happy is the parent, here cast in the role of counsellor, teacher, and servant. So two spots for Purina Dog Chow show a wise mother (B8359) and then an equally wise father (B8360), explaining gently to a daughter and a son about the health and longevity of their pet dogs. In a slightly different vein, Kraft (B8548) offers us a mother and a

father who work hard, and happily, to ensure a young girl has the necessary
food to help her continue her frenzy of play.

Children come in two guises. First, there's the Cute Kid, the boy or girl, who
charms through naivety and innocence: a boy who tries to feed his dog candies
(B7420); a mix of kids at art class munching cookies (B7943); two girls playing
ballet while dad takes pictures (B8499); a beautiful girl who explains why she
doesn't like colds (B8956). Compare that stereotype with the other variety, the
Brat, who seems particularly common in ads for food. He or she is wilful, messy,
mischievous: those tykes who turn eating into play (B7942); little Rosie
(B8760) who won't talk to mommy until she gets corn flakes; or a precocious
boy (B8916) who says what's correct but captions show us he really thinks his
parents are fools, except they did buy great cookies – 'they finally did something right.' Both varieties are allowed liberties, treated indulgently, granted
special privileges, in itself an interesting reflection on what's considered proper
child care in North America.

Adults don't have it quite so good. Indeed you might wonder why anyone
would want to grow up in the world of the Bessies: adults suffer ill health,
obesity, stress, car troubles, work at home or in the office, in short the burdens
of everyday existence. They are subject to a wide range of social stereotypes: the
housewife and mother (B8137), the working woman (B7642), the ambitious
yuppy (B8308), the slightly dotty elderly lady (B7615) or the experienced
senior citizen (B8628), the lordly business executive (B8964), the naval officer
(B9181), and so on. Ironically, some of the public service ads try to question
these stereotypes, arguing that the elderly (B8849) and even more the physically disabled (B8594) are really 'just like us' and ought to be treated as normal
adults.

Distinctions based on class and race play only a modest role in defining the
adult identity. Just one ad, Goodis's *Workingman* (B7940) for London Life,
explicitly addressed the issue of class, and this was (naturally) a celebration of
the workingman's achievement. You can find signs of a working-class beer
(B8135), even a nostalgia piece for Kellogg's Corn Fakes (B8459), which
nonetheless leave the impression of a 'typical' Canadian home. And that's the
point: where class is signified, it is placed in a context that blurs its character.
So an ad for Foster's Light beer (B8971) offers us pictures of mechanics, muscle
builders and wrestlers, an urban cowboy, ending with a collection of jean-clad
males, all identified as ordinary folks having fun. Likewise professionals or the
well-off become part of a much broader category labelled upscale, whether a
snooty food critic (B7946) or two beautiful and stylish women (B9121), though
their superiority is deemed largely the result of taste. Class, then, is divorced

from production and defined through consumption: it becomes a matter of taste, of choice, of lifestyle.

Race is subsumed in ethnicity, a less troublesome property that ad-makers can safely employ, chiefly for the purposes of mockery: the eager if hokey Japanese chef (B7623) and the sensuous French chef (B7721), the loud-mouthed Jewish wife (B8470), the ultra-macho Aussies (B8522), the loquacious Italian woman (B8705), the mysterious Asian woman (B8722), even a sensual black woman (B9109), or 'the two drips from England' (B9140). The English (but not, interestingly enough, the Americans, who presumably are 'people like us') have long been a favourite butt of humour, going back at least to the Red Rose Tea campaign of the 1970s. This treatment of national types has something of the flavour of the ethnic joke, although the bite isn't severe. In any case most adults are presented simply as Canadians, subject to the same urges as Anglo or white Canadians even when they are people of colour. In short the twin codes of race and class are masked by the ubiquity of the gospel of consumption.

What's been left out of this discussion is youth, an ambiguous or 'dirty' category (to use John Hartley's adjective), which covers people roughly between the ages of fifteen and twenty-five. Neither child nor adult, youth transgresses and at times scandalizes: it breaks down the contrasts set up by the code of age and even undercuts gender stereotypes. Youth enjoys the licence and the playfulness of childhood, the sexuality and independence of maturity, and allows men and women to be aggressive, if not offensive. Starting around 1979, perhaps because the baby-boom generation had begun to submit to the discipline of maturity, some of the Bessies came to celebrate a distinct lifestyle of play, pleasure, beauty, and excess where the young seem to be living in a time of perpetual carnival. In general this youth lifestyle is most apparent in commercials for candy bars, snack foods, soft drinks, beer, health and beauty aids, and some clothes and appliances. One of the major events of the times was the sudden switch in beer commercials in the mid-1980s, inaugurated by Molson's expensive 'Dancin'' campaign for its Canadian brand, the winner of the 1985 Campaign Bessie. The three high-energy commercials (B8523/5 and B85121) featured quick cuts, rock music, bold colours, bizarre shots, beautiful people, sexual display, frenzied actions, and loads of fun. That style reached its acme with the 'Black Label Campaign' a few years later.

The most outstanding property of this lifestyle is the liberation of the body from the rules and regulations imposed by social norms so that this body can wallow in excess. Consider the signs of youth: plenty of loud music, especially rock, whether in a soft drink (B8122) or a chocolate bar ad (B8624); lots of slang, sometimes teen speak (B8981/2/3); casual or sloppy dress (B9203); beautiful bodies, at the beach (B8701) or in a gym (B8950), usually marked by erotic suggestion; aggressive or exaggerated gestures – hectic sports (B8479), fast driving (B8622), frenzied song (B8438) and frenzied dance (B8413), sheer exuberance (B8616), intentional posing (B9123), a madcap life (B8572); images of breaking loose (B8819), mocking authority (B8932), even challenging that authority (B8927); joy in the bizarre, whether white on black (B8968) or a mix of colours and shades (B9040) or weird images (B8612) or grotesque print (B9108). Young women and young men flouted convention in a fashion that seemed to express a free spirit at play, unbounded by a fear of embarrassment or submission to rules. Such commercials indicated the ad-makers' recognition of *jouissance*, to use John Fiske's terminology, the sense of pleasure that comes when the normal breaks down and the body is freed. So great was the social esteem attached to this lifestyle that ad-makers found they could sell to all sorts of adults simply by 'talking young.'

The recent portrayal of youth is the most significant exception to the twin codes of gender and age. But ad-makers have always been willing to provoke laughter by mocking the prevalent stereotypes. Sometimes adults act as though they were wilful children (B8741), more often kids pretend they are adults – patrons at an upscale restaurant (B7812), customers at a store sale (B84109), girls playing at being women (B84122). Occasionally ad-makers will present a masculinized female, such as the English headmistress who acts as the voice of propriety and authority (B7938), or a feminized male, such as 'Felix' in a series of take-offs on the sitcom 'The Odd Couple' (B7413/4/5). In the past, some Bessies turned women into bimbos: an aggressive, clinging female at a party, more a child than an adult (B7722), or a secretary who goes ape over a new office copier, hugging the machine and declaring her love for it (B84102). Recently, a couple of Bessies have played havoc with the mystique of masculinity, showing a macho type bested by a flood of flakes (B8806), a male creep who thinks only of getting women or 'chicks' as he calls them (B8929), and a cool guy whose pose of command is unmasked by pictures of his actual performance when watching a hockey game (B9050).

These representations of the female bimbo and the unmanned male are only variations on a much more common motif in the Bessies, namely the treatment of people as fools, which I'll deal with later. What's important here is to recognize that these characters are regarded as exceptions, meant to be objects of laughter. They don't reflect any shift away from the code of gender – indeed they only work because of the prevalence of that code. The Bessies tell us that people are defined first by their sex and second by their age. These constitute the foundation of personal identity in the affluent society.

Everyday Life

J. Walter Thompson created an innocuous commercial entitled *Home from Work* for Labatt's '50,' which took first place in its category in 1974. It purported to be a sixty-second minidocumentary that tracked one man's escape from work, into the arms of his wife, and then out to the backyard to enjoy life with some friends. The man was an ordinary sort, not handsome, dressed in a jacket, slacks, and tie, the uniform of the office. By contrast his wife, and the other females shown, were all attractive. Instead of a voice-over, the agency used a special pop song to celebrate this experience, a mood piece that placed the commercial in the romantic school. The male singer explained 'it's been a long day,' but the day would have 'a new beginning' when he got 'home to my world' and 'to my beer.' After a warm kiss from the wife, he got his beer, or rather she got it for him. Now the singer exclaimed, 'Making friends over "50," yeah – the welcome taste we share.' This announced the appearance of the happy scene of couples chatting, laughing, and drinking in the backyard, or as the singer called it, 'your world.'

This ad is a good example of a standard kind of portrait. Many Bessies dealt with the routine of everyday life, sometimes in a romantic, sometimes in an ironic fashion and, occasionally, in more realistic ways as well. There are minidramas and documentaries about doing your income tax (B7302), the horrors of winter driving in Canada (B7404), getting married (B7847 and B8967) and having a baby (B7429), kids growing up (B8737), romance renewed (B9194) and romance consummated (B8911), the church bake sale (B8062), or the Christmas pageant (B8813). One of the funniest treatments of romance, or rather the failed pick-up, is Molson's 'Magic Moments' campaign (B8852/72/3), which shows an all-too-eager man who tries to woo a succession of stunning women at a neighbouring table: each time, he borrows the salt and pepper, which he liberally sprinkles over his food, but all to no avail, leaving him only with six shakers and a ruined meal – a superb send-up.

Nearly all of these 'social tableaux,' to borrow Roland Marchand's phrase, are happy or funny – the consumer ads (as distinct from public service and charity commercials) don't show unemployment, funerals, divorce, and the like, which might unduly upset. With rare exceptions (say B7922), they display the affluent lifestyles of the successful, who are able to enjoy the good things in life. It's here, then, that the markings of class are most apparent, because people who don't or can't enjoy this affluence are simply absent.

But what really makes *Home from Work* memorable is the fact that it touched, albeit briefly, all the bases of a person's existence: work, home, and play. Here, again, the messages of the Bessies indicate an underlying pattern or grid of contrasts that separates everyday life into three distinct realms:

	Work	Home	Play
Gender	masculine	feminine	both
Age	adult	all	all
Purposes	success	succour order	fun escape
Organization	hierarchy	community	equality
Ruling spirit	competition	togetherness	pleasure
Groups	team	family	family friends

Work is the least explored of these realms, chiefly because it is an important site of consumption only for a limited range of business goods and services. In beer ads, for example, work is something people leave behind, perhaps to go home as in *Home from Work*, or to celebrate an achievement (B8009), or just to escape (B8135). Those ads focusing on work emphasize, above all, that it is an arena, often an arena full of stress (B8308), frustration (B9256), frenzy (B8718), and even peril – witness the fate of 'Herbert D. Langley' in one telephone ad (B8230), who made a mistake and was never seen again. At times the Bessies employ the analogy of the contest to explain work: the duel (B7416), juggling (B7744), pool (B84103), the race (B8498), the guessing game (B8907). On other occasions, they make much of the feared power of the boss, usually in a humorous way: a man who denies an employee permission to take a longer lunch (B8544), another whose anger is marked by a roaring blue storm that devastates the victim's office (B8619), and a third called 'The Pez' who rules supreme over his yesmen (B8455). Note that all these bosses were men: women appear, and with increasing frequency in recent Bessies, where they may actually solve the problem (B8323 or B9139), but they operate in a world where men are at the top and, more important, the whole ethos is masculine. Note as well that the workplace is usually the corporate office, not the factory or the small business.

Is it any wonder that home has often been portrayed as a refuge? Home wasn't just where the heart was; more important, it was where the family lived. Back in the early 1970s, General Foods (B7311) had sponsored a paean of praise to the extended family, presenting images of a party of all generations mixing happily to feast on the company's products. In the mid-1980s, Catelli (B8627) offered a different view of the family, recognizing the changes of the past fifteen years: Catelli's families were young, mature, about-to-be, single parent, partly disabled, black, native Canadian, Asian, nuclear as well as extended, all ready for the company's 'family' of pastas and sauces. What joined these two very different portrayals was the notion that the family represented togetherness – and a crucial unit of consumption. The early Bessies might be more maudlin (see B7316 or B7411), the recent Bessies more realistic (B8942 or B9218) but both presumed home was a place where the ethos was feminine: the emphasis was upon nurturing, cooperation, warmth, peace, tradition.

What also remained consistent was the vision of the home as a place of order, and here too the primary responsibility fell upon women. 'Cleaning is caring,' declared one ad (B8466): and the visuals showed an infant crawling throughout the house, so mom must clean, deodorize, and disinfect everywhere. 'Protect your family,' cried another ad (B7828): the camera moved through a darkened house, reminiscent of monster movies, in search of the enemy – germs, mould, and mildew. Women were engaged in a never-ending war against dirt: brightening windows (B7328), washing floors (B8347), whitening their laundry (B8346), wiping up after kids (B8465), vacuuming the whole house, and hubby too (B8602), searching the house to give a reluctant dog a bath (B8818), even talking to a dirty carpet in desperate need of its yearly cleaning (B8857)! Occasionally men got dragged in as well, to keep the oil clean in the family car (B8008) or put some order into the workshop (B9006). And the couple was urged to buy a new furnace (B8482) or clean dirty ducts (B9124), or refurnish their home (B8733). The war against dirt, the old, and the messy represented a ferocious effort to control the domestic environment.

There was a class dimension to this war: though godliness had dropped by the wayside, cleanliness was still ranked among the leading bourgeois virtues. The act of cleaning was rich in meaning: of love, order, and conformity. Indeed the strength of such an obsession suggests a more symbolic reading of these ads: they become an assault upon ambiguity and the anomalous, the hidden and the unknown. Here, at least, was a place where the individual could exercise control. No matter what the state of the outside world, the good homemaker could ensure the house remained a haven of civilization where people were kept safe and secure from all threats.

Inevitably home life was satirized: one ad (B8923) focused on just what happened to a car during, presumably, a Saturday or a Sunday – it rushed in and out of the driveway, dogs and kids got forgotten, granny was brought home (as, by accident, was a cow), father tried to wash the car (but mostly got himself soaked), and so on. All this was shown in a superfast mode, and the irony heightened by playing music from the famous fifties sitcom 'Leave It to Beaver.' The ad left behind the impression home was a place of frenzy, not peace, that the couple was burdened by a host of social obligations.

Play is the reward society offers people who are fed up with the routine of everyday life or exhausted by the treadmill at the office and in the home. There's one recent, suggestive commercial for teleconferencing (B9230) which demonstrates just how important play has become. The ad features a meeting at a busy airport between two acquaintances, both businessmen, both in some sort of a corporation: the first, in a suit, has just finished apologizing to his wife over the phone because he has to make a business trip; the second, in casual dress, has just finished discussing with some business associate a recent piece of news, also via the phone. They chat, and we learn Mr Suit has to make his monthly meeting with regional managers, while Mr Casual claims he does this every week. Mr Suit couldn't do that; 'he never sees his kids now.' The key is that Mr Casual meets via phone, 'teleforum,' 'videoforum,' 'dial-up video,' all new business services. He's at the airport with his family, ready for a vacation – indeed, the boy comes over and says, 'Dad, mom says we gotta go,' and off goes Mr Casual to a happy wife and daughter, leaving Mr Suit looking thoughtful. So the promised pay-off isn't greater efficiency or more productivity or even a promotion, but more time for leisure.

The Bessies treat play as very special indeed. Drinking beer and happy times have always been locked in a close embrace. During the 1970s Molson's presented its Export Ale as the key to male bonding: a group of the 'boys' were shown enjoying themselves after softball (B7306), at a fishing camp (B7410), and playing shuffleboard (B7736). During the early 1980s, the rival Labatt's presented its Blue as the natural accompaniment to young couples off doing exotic things, from snowsailing and scuba diving to ballooning or night skiing. Similarly, driving has been linked to getting away from it all: Buick cars become freedom machines that allow people to have fun in the countryside (B7636); a rider on a trimotor recreates the excitement of the amusement park as he rushes up and down hills (B8509); drivers experience the marvels and challenges of Nature on three of the world's toughest roads, including the Cabot Trail (B9192). But the most obvious exponents of play have been the travel ads, going back to a quaint Air Canada commercial (B7347) offering jaded Canadians their own horse-drawn caravan in Europe. One marvellous ad for the now defunct Eastern Airlines (B84116) actually followed the transformation of a pair of male feet from wearing galoshes on a winter street to running free into the blue ocean. The long-running '15 Seconds of Club Med.' campaign featured a series of dreamlike sequences of men and women in ecstasy somewhere down south in the sun (B8833 and B9185).

What are we to make of such rampant hedonism? It wasn't nearly so apparent in the early 1970s, when ads presented drinking as a form of good fellowship (B7605) or travel as a learning experience (B7449). I believe that the celebration of the youth lifestyle paved the way for a reconstruction of leisure as much more central to individual well-being. Over the course of the last decade, play has become a magic realm where people are liberated from convention, encouraged to seek pleasure for its own sake, and to experience the joys of the body. We can discover such joys whether partying, drinking, driving fast, vacationing, swimming, tanning (yes, one Bessie [B9019] actually shows beautiful people baking in the sun – 'It's the way we play'). Any and all of these are represented as a sanctioned evasion of the rules and the obligations imposed by the routine of everyday life.

Tradition, Nature, and Modernity

Advertising can 'name' a country, a people, a culture. One such example was 'The World Next Door' campaign of Tourism Canada, which won a certificate of merit in 1987. The three ads were created by John McIntyre and Arnold Wicht of Camp Associates, an agency that specializes in travel commercials (for Conservative governments). The campaign was aimed at foreign markets, chiefly the United States. Studies had shown that Americans were no longer responding, at least in sufficient numbers, to portrayals of Canada as a wilderness playground, indeed that they had some trouble deciding how Canada differed from their own country. The campaign was intended to rectify this by displaying the various sides of Canada. A 1989 study, mentioned in *Marketing* (11 February 1991), reported that in fact there had been 'a sharp improvement in Americans' perceptions of Canada' since the campaign launch, though this new appreciation hadn't produced more visits.

The commercials belonged to the mannerist school, each offering a collage of staged and elegant shots of people, settings, scenes, and life, along with a musical theme and song, which called on viewers to 'come and widen your horizons.' Also common to each ad were suggestions of a warm welcome, friendly and happy folk eager to receive visitors. *Wild World* (B8761) played out the old motif of Canada as Nature: the ad offered scenes of mountains, lakes, forests, the Chateau Lake Louise and the Banff Springs Hotel, plus people engaged in such outdoor pursuits as diving, mountain climbing, fishing, trekking, horseback riding, golf, and so on. Here the campaign music and song was given a pop flavour. *Old World* (B8749), in contrast, named Canada a land of Tradition: it deployed slowed pictures of places and people that called to mind farm life on the prairies, Old Quebec, fishing villages, and the British heritage.

This time, a piano and what sounds like a harpsichord give a classical twist to the theme music. I should add that this particular commercial nicely suits that Canadian accent discussed in the previous chapter. Finally, *New World* (B8748) offers us some frenzy: scenes of bicyclists, dancers, night-life, neon lights, and the like, generally in an urban setting, accompanied by a jazz rock rendition – label Canada Modern.

This campaign employs narratives that have been used by ad-makers time and again over the past two decades. None can be counted original; none are unique to Canada. They draw together imagery from popular history, litera-ture, art and music, cinema and television, created inside and outside the country. I consider them an expression of some of the ways in which people try to understand the significance of goods, life, surroundings, and even experi-ence. Ad-makers use them as an intellectual shortcut, to label a good and to evoke a response quickly. Once more, it is possible to reduce these narratives to a series of contrasts, which receive definition from their relatives (the vertical groupings) as well as their rivals (the horizontal distinctions):

	Nature	**Tradition**	**Modernity**
Place	wilderness	country	city
Time	timeless	past/present	present/future
Scale	individual North/South	small Europe/Canada	mass First World
Knowledge	lore	craftsmanship	technology
Properties	beauty challenge	simplicity stability	complexity change
Promise	freedom	community	progress
Mood	awe and peace	nostalgia	optimism
Person	worshipper challenger	inheritor	maker victim

Of the three, the narrative of Tradition is the least common in the Bessies, probably because an appeal to nostalgia just doesn't suit most products. Exceptions to this rule are mostly confined to the categories of travel (British Airways), food (notably Kraft's Crackerbarrel Cheese and Kellogg's Corn Flakes), and beverages (milk or beer), though recently a wider range of advertisers have begun to use Tradition. The narrative evokes images of a simpler time or place where the homely virtues of family, good fellowship, warm hospitality, hard work, and fair dealing reigned supreme. That time may be solidly in the past: when beer was made by craftsmen (B7305), when the Kraft wagon served small towns (B7740), when Dr Ballard started out in early Saskatchewan helping farm families (B9210), or in the fabled Prince Edward Island of Anne of Green Gables (B9182). That time could also be a childhood memory, say when the milk tasted so grand (B8319); a special moment, like the ritual of leaving Santa Claus some food (B9144); or a special occasion, such as the return to a home town (B8059). That place might be a storied Britain (B7349) or a familiar Maritimes (B8320), an Old French Quebec (B9186) or the Aboriginal West Coast (B9187), anywhere the old ways have survived the erosion of modern times. Sometimes we are asked just to marvel at this Tradition (B7957), sometimes to recognize that what's old has lasting merit (B8055), sometimes the old ways are contrasted with a less satisfying present (B9190). In short, these normally romantic ads purvey the charming fiction that you can buy things or go somewhere to make contact with the world that was lost. They speak to that sense of unease, in some people anguish, which nearly everyone suffers at some time or other. Such nostalgia, of course, derives its strength largely in reaction to the much greater presence of Modernity.

Among the most beautiful of the Bessies are those that feature pictures of Nature. This narrative comes in various guises. First, there are the panoramic shots of mountains, lakes, and forests, less often of snowy slopes, which usually signify the Canadian wilderness. An ad for Alberta travel (B8831), for example, is full of the visual splendour of winter, of wildlife, mountains, and landscape, which at the end is magically transformed by the sun into a summer land of extraordinary beauty. Then, there are the lush pictures of sun, sand, ocean, and palm trees that signify the tropical paradise down south, the playground of affluent Canadians. The Bahamas' Ministry of Tourism (B8357) offered vignettes of happy natives, blue water, gracious living, magnificent sunsets, and warm hospitality. Third, consider the close-ups of ponds, plants, and the like, which convey the notion of a pastoral setting. A laxative commercial (B9025), of all things, lingered on beautiful pictures of water, flowers, ducks, and sunshine before moving on to highlight the outhouse where a woman finally got relief! Fourth, note the many shots of both wild creatures, especially birds in flight, as well as domestic animals, notably dogs and cats. Just about any product can make use of this design, even high-tech appliances like the Sony Handycam, which in one ad (B9102) captured the image of a bald eagle – implicitly, this ad draws the analogy between the eagle's eye and perfect vision. Lastly, there are the scenes of ice and snow in the Canadian city (compare

Figure 4.2: *Family*. During the 1970s the 'J.L. Kraft Wagon' was a familiar symbol of times past. In ad legend, this horse-drawn wagon brought good cheese to satisfy the needs of old-fashioned families (like that pictured above). Indeed the campaign mounted by J. Walter Thompson celebrated a land of small towns, happy homes, and family values. The added value these commercials attached to Crackerbarrel cheese was, of course, Tradition: the brand not only promised an old-fashioned quality; it traded upon a nostalgia for an imagined world that was lost in the rush of modern progress. (© Copyright Kraft General Foods Canada Inc. Reproduced with permission. Crackerbarrel is a registered trade mark of the Company for use in association with cheese.)

Volkswagen's B7404 and Club Med's B9259), signifying the infamous Canadian winter, which is often cast in a negative light.

Not surprisingly, then, Nature has a wide range of distinct meanings. Least common is the notion of bad Nature or Nature's revenge, say mosquitoes in the north woods or hay fever, where you must rely on the instruments of Modernity, like a bug spray (B7949) or an allergy remedy (B9180), to bring relief. The tropical or wilderness playground, itself displayed as a commodity, can be a place of escape, peace, and renewal. So Air Canada provided two dreams of 'Endless Summer' (B8654/5) where Canadians could escape not just winter but everyday life, to immerse their bodies and souls in the sensual pleasures of the south. In a different vein Bell Canada (B8817) placed three males in the north woods where they could renew their friendship. The rugged Canadian landscape can also become the site for testing oneself or a machine. The latter has become a favourite ploy of automobile advertisers: so Honda Canada (B9016) claimed its 'showroom' for the Accord was the highways of the Rockies, while Nissan (B9236) offered different views of Nature's glory to tout the prowess of its Pathfinder. Wild animals represent the pure, untainted, and original; domestic animals come to embody particular traits valued by humanity. GM (B7405) compared its Pontiac to some exotic tropical bird to suggest mystery; Union Gas (B7716) was like the squirrel, always storing up for the future; the dog, whether in the service of Kokanee beer (B8854) or Moosehead beer (B8715), has usually signified loyalty; Greb's bear (B8326) meant toughness, just like its Kodiak Wilderness boots, while Facelle Royale's kittens (B8575) represented that quality of softness found in its toilet paper. An especially imaginative rendition of this theme has been Bell Canada's 'Natural Campaign' where wolves (B9012), loons (B9053), and a variety of birds (B9225) were used to suggest the purity of sound and variety of services offered consumers. All of which is one reason why 'the natural' has become a metaphor for 'the good,' whether this means a fruit yoghurt (B7941) or a Ziploc bag (B9214).

The most emphatic meaning, however, grows out of a sense of transcendence where Nature, better yet the Canadian wilderness, becomes the embodiment of a beauty and a grandeur that all must worship and preserve. Long before the environmentalist cause caught hold of the popular imagination, this vision of Nature was advanced in a corporate campaign by MacMillan Bloedel (B7421/2/3), a logging company, the very kind of enterprise now considered one of the chief villains in the struggle to save Canada's forests. The first of the three ads was merely an explanation of the company's conservationist purpose, plus a sequence that showed how lumbermen turned work into play. But the second ad, running two minutes, covered the efforts of Tommy Tompkins, a well-known naturalist sponsored by MacMillan Bloedel, to preserve scenes of the British Columbian wilderness and bring these into the lives of city children, who were of course awestruck, especially by the sounds of wolves. And the third ad, also two minutes long, recounted how MacMillan Bloedel had set up a bird sanctuary: this commercial featured some extraordinary shots of the flight of trumpeter swans, among other birds, which gloried in both their beauty and magnificence. 'Man and Nature can live together,' the announcer declared. This meaning of Nature has been implicit in a good many Bessies over the years, and the rise of both the New Age and the Green philosophies has only given it a greater currency. Recently the mix of the two found expression in *Inconnu* (B9260), another effort by Camp Associates, where the response appropriate to the amazing scenes of natural splendour is awe.

Nonetheless, there is an inherent irony here: the celebration, even mystification of Nature is acted out against the dominant narrative of Modernity. One of the Bessies makes that abundantly clear. *Mass of Humanity* (B8564) works through a series of contrasts: many/one, rush/peace, city/wilderness. It opens with accelerated scenes of urban life, accompanied by harsh sounds and jarring music, which makes the city appear very much like a hive; it closes with pictures of a single man on a bike enjoying a panoramic view of Nature before setting off down the road. The ad, by the way, was for Midland Doherty, billed as financial advisers. And the message? – financial security inevitably leads to 'other freedoms.'

The last narrative, the most complicated of the three, presumes constant change, which ad-makers usually call progress. In the widest sense Modernity signifies little more than what's 'in fashion' or 'new,' perhaps the most overworked word in the ad-maker's lexicon. Products as diverse as an 'unpanty pantyhose,' a spoon-size cereal, or spiced-up chicken wings have been defined as the results of progress. Similarly, a department store like Eaton's could apply a futuristic aura to hype its women's wear (B8051) and a furniture outlet like IKEA could tout its new catalogue (B8841) in an ad that featured a robot. Such Bessies merely give voice to the vulgar belief that things are getting better bit by bit.

At another level, however, the narrative celebrates technology, which it advances as the motive force of all that is Modern. The most energetic champions of technology have been the advertisers of assorted appliances, home entertainment products, business equipment, and automobiles who strove to outfit the family and business with the most up-to-date gadgets available. Right from the beginning, their ads encouraged what can only be called the worship of the machine. A succession of early Bessies, for example, touted the macho virtue of toughness: a cut-up Ford Pinto revealed its strong frame (B7301), a skiddoo proved durability on a roller-coaster (B7345), a Bell telephone was 'tortured' (B7341), a Toyota underwent the most rigorous winter testing possible (B7704). Not that this exhausted the imagination of ad-makers: an ever-expanding series of connections demonstrated how Bell linked people together (B7342), a hair-dryer proved it could manage a lion's mane (B7701), a steam iron blasted off (B8001) to show its effectiveness, talking food praised the cooking mechanism of one special microwave (B8202), and so on. All admirable, but hardly very exciting.

That changed roughly in the mid-1980s when ad-makers wedded the new vogue of High Tech with the old credo of individualism. First car ads, soon the rest worked to show how their marvel enhanced the worth, the status, and above all the power of the owner. One of the pioneers was the 1984 Gold Bessie *Electronics* (B8401) for General Motors of Canada, which combined a high gloss finish, an array of striking visuals, a rising crescendo of electronic music, and computer-generated numbers and letters to give the impression that here was the embodiment of style, beauty, and potency. Other Bessies drew a more direct link between machine and (usually) man: you literally disappeared off the road (B8310); you provoked awe (B8405); you conquered the countryside (B8507);

Figure 4.3: *Chunky Challenge*. Douglas the hacker challenges a know-it-all computer to determine whether it is better to eat Chunky Soup with a spoon or a fork. Computers, robots, and their imagery became commonplace in the ads of the 1980s. They might serve as objects of fun, means of enhancing personal power, symbols of High Tech, or (as in this case) rivals to humans. Douglas, of course, wins this contest of wills. (Courtesy of Campbell Soup Company Ltd.)

you entered a state of ecstasy (B8924). Not to be outdone there was a computer that gave you the competitive edge (B8720); a video camera that became the extension of your eye (B9107); a cordless vacuum cleaner that enabled you to escalate the assault on dirt (B8908/9); a cordless phone that ensured your message got through (B8910); a set of appliances that enhanced your senses (B8735). There was even a lawnmower that made your day (B9101), which mocked the argument of such ads.

By far the best spoof, however, was sponsored by Campbell's Soup. Called *Chunky Challenge* (B8808), this 1988 Silver Bessie winner pits an unkempt Douglas the hacker against a talking computer, with a soundtrack full of electronic noises and a woman singing a sad love song in the background. Irritated by the computer's arrogance, Douglas sets it the task of deciding whether it's better to eat Chunky soup with a spoon or a fork (that refers to the wider campaign in which the soup was positioned as a meal in itself, so suited to the fork). The test sends the computer into a tizzy and it ultimately crashes, filling the screen with a kaleidescope of images. Man triumphs over machine: the ad exploited that vague fear about the glorification of the machine, and most especially the computer, which was the darling of the 1980s, because this might portend the eclipse of human predominance in the near future. The ad, as ads normally do, reassured in a witty fashion – no fear: man still has the edge.

The other dimension of Modernity was expressed in a barrage of corporate ads financed by the country's largest corporations. Such Bessies usually emphasized how the corporation in question was a good corporate citizen: perhaps it helped youth (B8244), sponsored an Olympic team (B8301), or aided the disabled (B9028). Back in the 1970s, London Life financed a fine campaign (created by Goodis, Goldberg, Soren) called 'The Human Journey' where it linked its past to aspects of the Canadian experience: growing up Canadian (B7429), the family reunions right after the Second World War (B7643), the workingman as hero (B7940), and the fact of multiculturalism (B7847). Just recently, a car ad entitled *Manifesto* (B9232) has voiced the newest twist to this old theme, namely to represent Nissan Canada as a socially conscious company. The Bessie offers a series of panoramic views of natural marvels, the prairies and its towns, even the big city, enhanced with some striking special effects, another collection of medium shots of life in and outside the cities, and the occasional close-up, all to cover the variety of the Canadian experience. The announcer explains that Nissan believes in a host of good things, including 'the right to rest, and especially to leisure,' as well as companies' 'responsibility for the products they sell.' Nissan Canada has tailored its image to suit the unease and the doubts of the early 1990s.

Putting fashion aside, though, there is one message that has remained constant over the years: the corporations are the masters of capital, expertise, and technology, and so the leaders of Modernity. The Bank of Montreal used to tell Canadians (B7315 and B7427) how it worked with entrepreneurs to make Canada a land of winners. Oil companies like Gulf Canada (B7614) and Imperial Oil (B8240) explained how they were striving to develop new energy resources. In one orgy of self-congratulation, the CN Group (B8538) boasted of its pioneering role as an agent of progress in the field of telecommunications. More sophisticated was Northern Telecom's presentation of its technological wizardry (B8816), where it advanced a claim to world leadership in 'fully digital telecommunications.'

But the most amazing, and to my mind sinister, of these ads was Shell Canada's display of its new refinery and petrochemical plant in Alberta,

Scotford (B8535). The purpose of the ad was simply to proclaim just how advanced the 'massive' facility was ('technology of the future') and how lots of Canadian companies had benefited through their participation in the project. The mood was set by some dramatic, indeed pretentious music, and a very male announcer, clearly the voice of authority. What I found most striking were the array of pictures: huge structures, complex machines, banks of computer equipment, anonymous and uniformed personnel, a totally sterile environment (dirt couldn't be allowed here, of course). What was being celebrated was the gigantic and the technological, dwarfing humanity and reducing people to servitors of the god machine. It amounted to a cold, forbidding vision of an engineered future. However unintentional, that message seemed to fit all too well the narrative of Modernity.

In the last few years, the predominance of Modernity has receded somewhat, no doubt one signal among many that the enthusiasms of the 1980s are giving way to different kinds of concerns. A few more of the Bessies employ the narrative of Tradition to organize their meanings; even more make reference to Nature, which shouldn't surprise given the new zeal for Green marketing and the general popularity of environmentalism. But it is too early to tell whether this change in fashion marks a major shift in the balance among the three narratives. In any case, for the foreseeable future, the expression of both Tradition and Nature will likely work best as a reaction against the vulgar belief in progress and all that implies.

The Gospel of Consumption

At the 1989 Bessies, the Campaign First went to an extraordinary series of commercials for Black Label beer – one of which, *Bodypaint*, won the Silver Bessie in its own right – and the following year two more commercials were awarded certificates of merit. The campaign was designed by Bruce McCallum, listed as the creative director in 1989, and Paul Hains, listed as the art director in 1989 and the creative director in 1990, both employed by Palmer Bonner. In my opinion, these seven commercials are the most innovative and imaginative Bessies in the whole of the collection. They sparked a surge of public interest in central Canada and likely assisted a miniboom in Black Label sales, though the campaign disappeared outside of Quebec (where Black Label sales remained strong) shortly after Molson's took over Carling O'Keefe and thus the Black Label brand.

The seven commercials shared a number of attributes. They all used the slogan 'The Legend Is Black,' a play on words which referred in part to the fact that Black Label had been a languishing brand of the 1960s, only revived when

Figure 4.4: *Bodypaint*. This was one of the most familiar and striking images from a commercial Carling O'Keefe used to emphasize the fact that the brand label was not painted on the bottle. This image, like the commercial itself, was ambiguous, inviting the viewer to make up her or his mind about just what was being celebrated here. (Courtesy of Molson Breweries)

it caught the fancy of trendy youth in Toronto's Queen Street zone. They all had a common visual signature: they were shown in black and white but for a couple of colour shots of the beer's label. And they all lacked a voice-over, depending instead upon music, sometimes sounds, in one case a song to supply added meaning to the sequence of pictures.

Beyond that, it might seem the seven shared nothing but a studied ambiguity. The surreal *Images* offered a selection of white-on-black pictures of people, who might be off to a party in the city somewhere, accompanied by a hard-driving electronic sound. The essentialist *Eight Ball* flashed close-ups and angle shots of a game of pool, along with a jazz soundtrack. The two naturalist commercials, *Rooftop* and *Boxer*, portrayed life on a hot summer night in the city, to a jazz tune, and a woman's hunt for a young boxer, its mood heightened by a female singing a torch song. That left the three mannerist ads: *Bodypaint*,

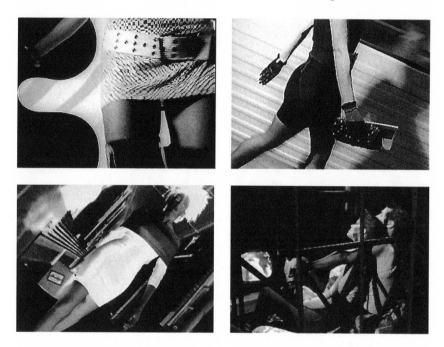

Figure 4.5: The 'Black Label' Campaign. These images are taken from *Bodypaint*, *Belt Buckle*, *Images*, and *Rooftop*, part of the initial wave of commercials shown in central Canada. They illustrate the taste for the bizarre, the element of sexual display, and the focus on the female body that characterized the campaign. (Courtesy of Molson Breweries)

where male and female dancers gyrate to a rock melody; *Belt Buckle*, which follows the actions of a beautiful woman in the city, accompanied by heavy drum music; and *Berlin*, named after the Toronto nightclub, where young people are shown at play, again to the sounds of a strong beat. You can find here shadows of the forties (*Boxer*), of the fifties (*Rooftop*), or of the eighties (*Berlin*); signs of the bizarre (*Images*), the cool (*Belt Buckle*), the frenzied (*Bodypaint*), or the mellow (*Rooftop*).

But, in fact, nearly all these ads can be read as a celebration of youth and play, even more of sensuality. *Images* gives pictures of female breasts, bums, legs, and backs; *Belt Buckle* flashes shots of the woman's mouth, legs, lips, breasts, or back; and both focus on the sensual movement, the body language, of women in tight clothes. Hungry looks, the sexy walk of the temptress, the body of the young man, all are on display in *Boxer*. There's a bit of sexual innuendo in some of the scenes of *Rooftop*, and a lot in *Berlin*, where performers glory in black leather, patrons in their special 'look,' and both strike poses. But it's *Bodypaint* that tops the list: here there are not only shots of sensual dancing, the female shape, a painted midriff and a moving crotch, lots of ovals and circles and wet radiant waves, but a brush that seemingly licks a phallus, the Black Label bottle, as it applies the colours of the label. In short, the campaign was emphatically 'dirty,' both in the moral sense of that word, since some ads have undertones of soft porn, but even more in the symbolic sense: it wallowed in images of the brazen sensuality of the (largely) female body that were normally kept hidden from sight. The very ambiguity, the fact there was no direct sales pitch, that a viewer could play with the images to concoct his or her own fantasy, was just further evidence of this 'dirtyness.'

The campaign was evidence of the increasingly sophisticated way in which ad-makers have worked to seduce the public. The aura created by 'The Black Label Campaign' might be startlingly different from that of other campaigns, whether for beer or more prosaic goods – but what's significant here is that the effort to create an aura is commonplace, and that's been true for many years. The world of the Bessies is full of meanings, meanings tied to commodities, and these are what the public is supposed to consume to realize fantasies or build identities. Again, this gospel of consumption can be reduced to a form of binary logic, and in this case the contrasts are virtually opposites:

Possession	Deprivation
individual	fool
enriched	impoverished
satisfaction	want
empowered	impotent
status	obscurity
excessive	constrained

There's something inherently ironic about this gospel. On the surface the Bessies are continually hyping 'you' or the cult of individualism. A perfume ad (B7617) tells women there are three varieties available, 'as individual as you are.' A motorcycle ad (B8309) explains 'you' don't own a suit, a lawnmower, or designer jeans, just the Midnight bike, which means 'nobody owns you.' Bell Canada (B9225) exclaims, 'Because everyone's individual, we offer a natural selection of calling options.' Two ads for Amstel beer (B9252 and B9253) celebrate people with an independent mind or an unusual style – notably a man who tosses out his answering machine – equating Amstel and individuality.

The rhetoric of individualism can even inform representations of big business. I counted eighty-five Bessies, mostly corporate, financial, and public utilities commercials, where the most obvious motif was the friendly corporation. Questions of who makes what profit, who really is the master, just how the goods reach market, and so on are rarely addressed. Rather, the aim is to put a human face on capitalism. The Bessies show time and again that the chief concern of the corporation is to serve 'you,' the consumer: a bank (B7316) talks about 'you and the Commerce'; Union Gas (B7715) tells how it always prefers the 'little guy' to the 'big guy'; a newspaper (B8585) provides Joe Citizen with the necessary knowledge to understand politics; another bank (B9266) recounts the story of the elderly Mrs McIlquham, who is so well served by her teller. The occasional Bessie that admits service isn't always as great as the hype suggests, such as one campaign (B9264 and B9265) where the poor consumer must suffer all kinds of callous mistreatment, also promises a solution: 'At National Trust, we believe that we're there for your convenience, not the other way round.' The consumer, it seems, is queen or king.

But one can find a more unpleasant undertone to that National Trust campaign, namely that if 'you' don't patronize this financial institution, then you're the fool. Since irony became common, and particularly with the rise of deadpan humour, the Bessies have portrayed consumers, not 'you' of course, who are misguided, ignorant, or even stupid. Witness the half-awake nerd (B8501) who's only saved from making another mistake by a Moulinex coffeemaker that allows him to pour before all the coffee's made. What do you think of the father (B8646) who is so uninformed about the low cost of Bell Canada's rates that he rushes the family through a long-distance call? Or the male rookie (B8637) who needs instruction from the washing machine to do his laundry right? Then there's all those silly people (B9168) who have foolishly tried to solve the problem of car breakdown on their own, using cranes and inflatable dummies, when the emergency road service of the British Columbia Auto Association is so readily available.

The fact is 'you' only prove your individuality by purchasing the good in question, not by refusing to buy something. Such people suffer all manner of dire consequences. A man is reduced to a whining fool (B7321) as he tries to get his ancient water heater to generate sufficient hot water for a shower; another (B7912) tears his face up with a safety razor, unlike his happy compatriot who uses an electric shaver, during a train ride; a man (B9024) and a woman (B9023) have their faces hideously transformed by a 'hack attack,' since they didn't take the precaution of using Delsym Cough Remedy. Contrast those sad tales with the happy stories of possession. An attractive Louise Bonneau (B8812) recalls one joyous Christmas of her childhood when she received a treasured gift from

Eaton's. Similarly, a man (B9029) looks back on his youth when his dad bought him a marvellous red bike featured in the Canadian Tire catalogue. That's one reason why those who possess the favoured good are enriched: they have gained in experience.

But, and this is crucial, they have also gained in meaning. Why that's so emerges from the way the Bessies talk about commodities. Consider again the 'Black Label Campaign': the commercials presumed that this beer embodies the people and the lifestyle portrayed, that Black Label is outrageous, scandalous, youthful, avant-garde, etc. Drinking that brew symbolized, to yourself and to others, that you share the same meanings, you enjoy the same persona and lifestyle. This semiotic process whereby commodities appear to embody, symbolize, and transfer meanings works on an enormous range of different products. Like most national and international advertising, the Bessies try to create a parallel economy, a cultural economy of meanings and pleasures, where consumers may select those products that suit their perceptions of self-image, the looking-glass self (what others see), or the ideal self.

Allow me to briefly cite a couple of examples. A lowly battery takes on the properties of both masculinity and potency: the commercial (B7947) features sharp sounds, the flash of lightning, a luminous glow, a battery that thrusts upwards out of a desert, and a deep echoing male voice-over. Levi's Red Tab jeans evoke the legend of the Old West: the ad (B8325) makes clear these are jeans with a history and the young user casts the shadows of a miner, a cowboy, and a gunslinger. Some personal stereos from General Electric become emblematic of the teenage style: the campaign (B8981/2/3) uses a collage of still photos of the stereos in unusual colours, one with coloured pins, and a female narrator speaking breathlessly in teen lingo about what you can do with these marvels. Hellmann's mayonnaise acquires the aura of distinction: this campaign (B8901/4/5) borrowed the then trendy pink flamingo, the fabled characters the Walrus and the Carpenter, and the style of Art Deco, in each case using these images to grace what looked like a still life painting where the mayonnaise was the centrepiece. One of my personal favourites, a surreal ad for the Pontiac Grand Prix SE (B8820), borrows from imagery of Hieronymus Bosch to create a postapocalyptic setting where a man, symbolically the explorer and the hunter, dives into space and discovers the car, which promptly awakens as a machine/creature (that's ambiguous) representing glamour and power. The voice-over intones, 'Unleash Your Senses.'

As that imperative suggests, the semiotic process can have a more obviously utilitarian purpose. So the telephone company (B7441) envisages the long distance call as a smiling, stuffed telephone, and an elderly lady happily displays her collection of these memories to a young visitor: the telephone call is an act of love. The clear implication of one Camay ad (B7840) is that the soap will make your man want to caress your soft skin: the ad presents a woman in an upscale setting, soaking in a bath and lathering her skin, until the man eventually strokes her back with the soap. Playtex (B8247) calls upon women to 'make your fantasy a reality' by showing a number of beautiful women aggressively displaying their charms while wearing the company's undergarments. A succession of campaigns for milk and eggs have suggested their products embody Nature, and can make you healthy and vigorous, maybe even beautiful, just like the folks in the commercial. William Neilson sponsored a marvellous spoof (B9201) of such reasoning: it shows two teenagers, one short and one tall, separated by seven inches, which just happens to be the size of a Mr. Big chocolate bar – and it turns out that while the tall teen had regularly eaten this bar, the short teen hadn't. What was so clever about the ad, and more generally the campaign, was that it closely associated the bar with the insecurities of teenage males about their height and left the ironic impression Mr. Big was a source of power.

There's one promise that became particularly noticeable during the 1980s. All kinds of Bessies began to suggest that the commodity in question would transform what was routine into a form of play. An early effort involved milk, which suffered from the reputation of being merely a kid's beverage: instead, so the ads had it, milk was a fun drink (B7607) that had its own special excitement (B7925) – 'you drink milk 'cause it tastes soooo Wow.' Corning Corelle borrowed from the fable of Snow White (B7905) to depict the lovable dwarfs playing with the dishes while washing up. Honda's all-terrain vehicles (B8604) made working on a farm a lot of fun. A father and his child go crazy with the excitement of taking their car through a car wash (B8607) – just like a ride at an amusement park. Christie Brown (B8557) told kids it's 'okay to play with an Oreo' because people of all ages were doing just that at a party. Two different ads presented men in a shower having loads of fun, one singing (B8723) and the other making music (B8938). This fun ethos reflected the enhanced importance of play in everyday life. Ad-makers showed how you could gain new pleasure out of doing chores, cleansing your body, eating, driving, whatever.

The man in the shower who happily banged away at the walls, the soap dish, and so on to make his music was, to say the least, a bit manic. This display of excess was also a feature much more prominent in the last decade than before. Earlier, people had usually been presented acting in a more restrained fashion: the craftsman's eyes light up with joy when he takes his first sip of Black Label beer (B7303). My survey of Bessie contenders in the late 1960s and 1970s found outlandish actions, whether by people or products, were largely confined to ads for, say, a cereal (Post's Alphabits) or a toothpaste (UltraBrite) directed at kids or teens. During the 1970s ads for candies, chips, gum, and other snacks led the way, perhaps because they were already identified as fun foods. In 1976 alone, three such Bessies (B7612, B7613, B7640) were loud, frenzied portrayals of wacky people apparently suffering from a terminal addiction: one of these sported a mad general on a rocking horse (the adult as fool again) who was totally consumed by his passion for Smarties. Since then, there has been animated bubble gum (B7802), bouncing popcorn (B7824), singing lunch-boxes (B8621), some mad teddy bears busting up the kitchen (B9122), a taste that blows a crazed professor's mind (B8431), another that turns a boy into a rock singer (B8438), and so on. One marvellous Bessie (B8532) shows a young man flipping through the TV channels: he chances upon an ad for Coffee Crisp, which grabs his attention (wishful thinking?); he records it on his VCR, replays to isolate the candy bar and pauses the action; then he reaches through the screen to seize the prize. 'You can't resist,' so the ad claims. Indulge yourself.

The infection soon spread to other types of advertising. A jaundiced observer might even conclude that ad-makers had decided to celebrate the infantile. Household products: getting a new Teledyne Water Pic transforms a grumpy Uncle Edgar into a jolly soul who plays merrily in the shower (B8348). Fast foods: a man is so joyful over the low prices at Swiss Chalet that he keeps repeating 'so little' with heartfelt surprise throughout the ad (B8471). Retail: first the farmer and then his wife join a host of crazed bargain hunters rushing (the action is speeded up) to a Canadian Tire sale (B8730). Health products: a medieval bellman relieved of his headache by Headstart swings totally around on his huge bell (B8825). Leisure: an upscale family get so taken with their card-game that they begin to act out the images inscribed on the cards (B8951). The 'Huggamugga' campaign of Maxwell House (B8614/5, B8702, B8842/5) was chock full of bizarre images of people overcome with the pleasures of drinking the coffee: dancing, frenzied, floating, and the like. Recall, as well, the surge of youth ads that often indulged in a similar display of excess.

I can't help feeling that some of the craziness results from letting the imagination of ad-makers run wild. But that's not the whole story: advertising has always had a justified reputation for exaggeration, and the display of excess represents the visual expression of that tradition. Indeed, the spectacle of excited products, fevered shoppers, or ecstatic users signifies much more than either print or even still pictures could do previously. It symbolizes things and people out of control, liberated from what's routine, normal, expected.

Consider just one of the commercials in Molson's rock video campaign of the late 1980s, namely *Hard Day's Night Twist* (B8718), which features the Beatles' high-energy song 'A Hard Day's Night' throughout. It's made up of a series of vignettes taken from modern life: on one level the ad exploits the contrast between work and play; on another, it infuses all of the scenes with humour and even frenzy. So, in the first half of the ad, there are two shots of life at a neighbourhood restaurant, the kind that once was called a 'greasy spoon,' where the head cook fires a burger into the air; a brief focus on three female flight attendants plus their baggage running, almost out of control, for a plane; and three workmen playing basketball with some bags at a loading dock. In the last half, the flight attendants let their hair down at home, one dancing around the kitchen; the three workmen rush joyously from work; and a load of people let off steam at a frenzied dance party where the Molson's Canadian is very prominent. The ad ends with a parody of the Beatles' cover from the album *Abbey Road*, except here the look-alikes are carrying twelve-packs of Molson's Canadian.

Hard Day's Night Twist overflows with meaning: about the frustrations of work, about making do and having fun, about female and male bonding, about partying and the good times, about rock and specifically the Beatles, about Molson's Canadian as the brand of these good times, to name but the most obvious. All that excess conveys the impression of both power and pleasure – these folks have found a way to enjoy life to the fullest. The ad exceeds the bounds of common sense, denies the boredom and the drabness of the ordinary, and portrays the liberation of the body from the constraints of everyday life. Here is evidence of that cultural economy of meanings and pleasures I mentioned earlier. This ad appropriates the signs of resistance and evasion, the desire to escape social controls. So the gospel of consumption becomes once more a gospel of personal liberation.

5

The Cannes Lions, Etc. (1984–92)

'Think globally, act locally' is the VISA philosophy ...
                                    – Cited in *Marketing* (2 March 1992)

By 1990 TV advertising expenditures worldwide had reached around $65 billion U.S., according to Les Brown's *Encyclopedia of Television*. Although this statistic doesn't count cinema advertising, never mind the cost of actually making the ads, it can serve as a rough guide to the sway of the commercial. What's clear is that television advertising, as distinct from advertising in general, is not yet a truly global phenomenon. The bulk of the $65 billion was spent in North America (47 per cent), what was then noncommunist Europe (25 per cent), and the capitalist states of the Asia/Pacific region (23 per cent). Expenditures in Central and South America only amounted to some 4 per cent of the grand total. The percentages spent in Africa, outside of South Africa, and in the Middle East were negligible. And there were wide differences even in the First World: per capita expenditures in American dollars for the top ten countries ranged from a whopping $117 (United States) and $89.6 (Japan) to $50.8 (Canada) and $41 (France). Elsewhere the figures fell to $27.5 (West Germany), $19.7 (South Korea), $13.9 (Venezuela), $6.7 (South Africa), and $3.3 (Saudi Arabia, 1989 figures). The overall rate for Latin America and the Caribbean was well under $10 per person.

Statistics like these only tell a small part of the tale, however. Written into television advertising is evidence of an emerging global community. Commercials, like advertising in general, form part of a Superculture, a common repertoire of images, spectacles, meanings, strategies, and pleasures that seems destined to become everyone's other culture. I say 'other' because the Superculture usually overlays and informs, rather than supplants or replaces whatever is local or particular. It is still possible for the mariachi bands in

Mexico City, samba music and dance in Rio de Janeiro, or the world-famous tango in Buenos Aires to coexist with the hard rock of Los Angeles or London. (I experienced that very kind of disjuncture when I visited one of the birthplaces of tango, where the store sold tango cassettes and its café played rock.) Nor does this Superculture negate local expression: it comes in the form of commodities that people may choose to fill with some special meaning. A book like Pico Iyer's *Video Night in Kathmandu* has demonstrated how the old worry about cultural imperialism was too alarmist: Rambo in the East is not necessarily the same as Rambo in the West.

Which doesn't mean that the charge of cultural imperialism lacks substance. You could point to the North American fame of that Japanese creation Godzilla or the more recent frenzy over Brazil's lambada as proof of how open this Superculture is to innovations throughout the world. But these examples are really exceptions. By and large, the Superculture is the global extension of a pop culture made in English by Americans for domestic consumption, with a little help from the British. Hollywood is, to borrow the phrase of Peter Dunnett, the 'world provider' of movies and television to a host of clients in western Europe, Asia, Africa, and Latin America. The Terminator succeeds Rambo, rap succeeds heavy metal, Madonna and Michael Jackson become world stars, and American dominance persists.

That American dominance is not so apparent in the realm of advertising, where Madison Avenue has powerful rivals like the Japanese giants Dentsu and Hakuhodo, France's Eurocom group, and the British conglomerates Saatchi & Saatchi and WPP, which rose to the top of the list of world billings by buying leading American agencies. Even so, Madison Avenue remains the most influential player on the global scene, its practices and styles echoing around the world – Armand Mattelart claims that what was once American has 'metabolized' into 'world-modernity.'

Television advertising worldwide bears the marks of this history, and thus of privilege. It involves the spread of American images that may well be alien to the local milieu. This is most obvious on the level of trivia. A Chilean ad for Firestone Tires (IS8758), for instance, used an image of the North American Indian, complete with the head feather and the fringed garb, which was never the dress of that country's aborigines. Although *War Dance* (C89046), a spot designed to sell Bata shoes in Zimbabwe, employed traditional dancers, it turned these men and women into objects of fun whose sore feet could only be remedied by buying the world brand, which enabled them to return to their ancient ritual full of vigour and joy. Watching television commercials in Ecuador a few years ago, I detected a distinct preference for the very whitest of white women in a land full of people of colour. More serious are charges like those of John Sinclair, that advertising has worked to transfer the tastes of North America to Mexico, which has had a sad effect upon the dietary habits of the poor. There's sufficient cause to doubt whether the global advance of television advertising, whether into the Third World or the old Soviet empire, will be wholly benign.

There is a much less sinister side to this story, however. Images born in one place or time have been appropriated to suit the needs of ad-makers in a very different context. Consider the case of three commercials made in Japan in the late 1980s to sell drinks owned by Coca-Cola. In the first two ads, Dentsu borrowed from the pre-Colombian art of ancient America – the step-pyramid, a calendar disk, stone reliefs – to picture how a beautiful white woman (maybe an archaeologist?) provoked a can of the soft drink Aquarius to rise up, which releases a flood of liquid that spreads down the sides of the pyramid before it freezes into an icy blue glaze. This imagery served to give Aquarius a mysterious, exotic, even numinous character (emphasized in one ad with the addition of radiant beams that came down from the heavens to bathe woman and can in a golden light). Another ad touting Georgia, a canned coffee drink, focused upon a very American male who arrives home to some country town, presumably in Georgia: he is tall and handsome, dressed in business clothes, walks or rather strides in a slow and powerful fashion, gets a ride in a pick-up truck, meets friends at a restaurant and a garage, and of course keeps drinking the marvellous brew. Throughout, someone who sounds like Ray Charles sings 'Georgia On My Mind' – only the Japanese voice-over plus the on-screen text at the end registers this isn't made in America. The imagery evokes ersatz memories of the American South that might establish the authenticity of the coffee. Both examples are modest evidence of that 'common repertoire' of images, etc., that I mentioned earlier. Dentsu had found settings and symbols familiar to audiences who 'knew' the world through television or movies and that it hoped would confer special meanings upon its client's brands. Whether such activities serve to enrich the recipient's culture or to debase the images is immaterial – they do make clear how television advertising breaks down the supposed 'purity' of national cultures.

But even the most enthusiastic fans of global marketing must sometimes take the local milieu into account. In an excellent chapter on transnational advertising, John Sinclair noted how in times past there have been only a few examples of a successful world brands strategy, such as those of Coca-Cola or Marlboro, and many more instances of an effective 'multidomestic' approach, notably those of Nestlé or Procter & Gamble. The cover story in *Marketing* (2 March 1992) found that global marketing could mean different things to different sellers: if Coca-Cola, Kodak, or British Airways felt comfortable advertising their brand in much the same way almost everywhere, some multinationals like VISA or Kellogg often employed 'different creative' based on a common set of motifs for various markets. Ironically Coca-Cola itself has exempted Quebec from its one-world approach: a story in the *Toronto Star* (21 January 1992) noted how a forthcoming Coke campaign there would feature the local singing sensation 'Celine Dion, family gatherings and hockey players in distinctly Quebecois settings,' instead of Elton John, Katerina Witt, and the resurrected Jimmy Cagney. French Canadians were so proud and so parochial that Quebec had to be treated as a distinct society in the ad world. Will there always be exceptions?

Apple's *1984*

The year 1984 had a special meaning for all kinds of people throughout the world: it was one of those shared metaphors embedded in the Superculture. *Nineteen Eighty-Four* is the title of the novel by George Orwell, in which he had fashioned the totalitarian dystopia of Oceania ruled by a brutal Inner Party and its titular master Big Brother. Orwell's was a story of the defiance of two souls, Winston and Julia, who fall in love and challenge authority. Eventually they are arrested and broken, betraying each other – at the end Winston discovers he has learned to love Big Brother. First published in 1949, it was taken as prophecy, warning, or satire, whether directed against Stalinism or socialism wasn't altogether clear, but certainly against all forms of authoritarianism. The tragedy became one of those modern classics, made into a movie in 1956, because it so suited the temper of the times. If the actual story was soon largely forgotten, the notion of 1984 as a sinister year and 'Big Brother' as the ultimate tyrant was kept before the public by scholars and journalists. Indeed, as the actual year dawned, both groups offered weighty discussions about Orwell's meaning and his power of prophecy (and a new movie was released). Some critics like Mark Crispin Miller found evidence of Orwell's feared authoritarianism in the power of the mass media, including the siren songs of worldwide advertising.

So powerful a metaphor as 1984 was unlikely to escape the attention of ad-makers. As things turned out, it met the needs of Apple Computer. During the late 1970s and early 1980s, Apple had been a leader in the so-called computer revolution that made microcomputers a powerful business tool. But the company's preeminence was swiftly undone when the giant International Business Machines introduced a personal computer that found favour with American business. Steve Jobs, Apple's cofounder, and John Sculley, the new executive hired from Pepsi-Cola, hoped to recapture public favour and regain momentum with the introduction of the Macintosh, a new kind of computer that would be both powerful and easy to use. Apple needed to create a sensation: the fact that the Macintosh was due out early in 1984 suggested a way to position the product as a revolutionary innovation.

The rest of the story has been told by Sculley in his reminiscences. Chiat/Day, Apple's hotshot agency, developed the notion into a script, hired the acclaimed movie director Ridley Scott, and shot the sixty-second spot at Shepperton Studios in London using some local skinheads, a bunch of amateurs, and a female hammer thrower. The result was a highly unusual commercial: no list of technical features, no display of what the Macintosh could do, not even a shot of the product itself. Only after the story ended, did the voice-over and on-screen text deliver an oblique message.

Storyline: *1984*   Big Brother's words in *Italic*

Video	Audio
Camera moves in on a glass tube entering a large, dark tower numbered 14, itself in an enormous greyish cylinder.	(Low background roar. A siren-like sound which will continue off and on.)
A row of men, their heads shaved, dressed alike in grey, baggy fatigues, march through the tube. The leading zombie wears a gas mask. On one wall are regularly spaced television sets.	*Today we celebrate,* announced a commanding voice, full of authority, *the first, glorious anniversary of the Information Purification Directives.* (Siren)
Flash of upper body of young, tanned, buxom, blonde woman running through a hallway. She wears a T-shirt, decorated with a Macintosh logo, red shorts and sneakers, and carries a large hammer.	
Close-ups of the expressionless faces of the marching zombies .	
Flash of four guards, dressed in black uniforms with silver face helmets and carrying truncheons, who also run through the hallway.	*We have created, for the first time in all history,*
Shot from below of the zombies marching, cutting off their feet and heads.	*a Garden of Pure Ideology, where each worker may*

Video	Audio
Shot of marching feet. Flash of running woman.	(Siren)
Long shot in sepia tones of a huge assembly hall, where zombies enter to sit in rows. At the far end is a large TV screen on which is the face of a bespectacled Big Brother, his words appearing beneath his image.	*bloom,* *secure from the pests*
Near full body shot of running woman. Pan of the rows of zombies, bathed in blue light, staring inertly at the screen. Then a back shot of their heads and Big Brother's image. Return to pan.	(Siren) *purveying contradictory force.* *Our unification of thought is more powerful a weapon than any fleet or army on earth. We are*
Distance shot of running woman as she enters the room, slowed motion. Cut to close-up of guards. Front shot of Big Brother harangue.	*one people.* (Siren) *With one will. One resolve. One cause. Our enemies shall talk*
Woman twirls hammer. Guards arrive. Woman twirls more. Big Brother continues to harangue. Woman releases hammer. Hammer flies through the air.	(Sounds of the hammer twirling) *themselves to death. And we will bury them with their own confusion* (Woman's yell)
Shot of the screen as the hammer flies towards it. Burst of light when hammer hits. Back shot of zombies heads.	*We shall prevail.* (Explosion)
Front shot of zombies, their mouths open, as a huge wind blows over them. They slowly fade from view.	(Sound of wind and a long 'aaaaaaaah')

Video and Audio
On January 24th,
Apple Computer will introduce
Macintosh.
And you'll see why 1984
won't be like '1984.'

What Chiat/Day had made was a surreal fantasy, full of drama and symbolism, which turned Orwell on his head. The action was loosely based on a passage early in *Nineteen Eighty-Four* where Winston Smith attends the compulsory 'Two Minute Hate' in a huge hall dominated by a giant telescreen. But the agency had wedded this to an imagery and a style drawn from recent sci-fi hits, which presumably would be much more familiar to an American audience. Indeed Ridley Scott employed some of the same techniques of lighting he'd used previously, notably in *Alien* (1979) but also in *Blade Runner* (1982), to establish a sinister mood. The running woman was reminiscent of the role played by Sigourney Weaver, the tough heroine of *Alien* who outwitted her foes. The men acted more like dehumanized automatons, a type of person who had appeared in many a TV show over the years, rather than the civil servants of Orwell's novel. The helmeted guards might easily evoke the memory of Darth Vader, the masked villain of the famous *Star Wars* film. The words of Big Brother weren't cast in the jargon of Orwell's Newspeak, but rather represented an expression of arrogance that also recalls the rhetoric of Vader. The climactic scene in the assembly hall reminds me of many an act of destruction, complete with special effects, where villainy is undone in a paroxysm of violence.

1984 rested first upon a stark contrast between the colourful woman and the grey zombies, a contrast that suggested a range of further oppositions – individual/mass, rebel/followers, alive/dead. It played on that old celebration of the iconoclast common in so many forms of popular culture. The other opposition was between the woman, who stood for Apple, and Big Brother, meaning IBM – here the contrasts were new/old, underdog/oppressor, freedom/tyranny, even good/evil. In this context, the thrown hammer represents the Macintosh, the tool that will end IBM's dominance. The smashing of the telescreen released the zombies from their thraldom: the blast of wind and the sound of relief signified the freeing of America from its subservience to that giant corporation.

Where *Nineteen Eighty-Four* ended on a note of defeat and hopelessness, *1984* ended on a note of triumph and promise. Chiat/Day and Ridley Scott had produced a masterpiece of the ad-maker's art, applying a small dose of imagination to create a dramatic message out of a mix of inherited ideas and styles. And the result suited the mood of exuberance and aggressiveness of the mid-1980s, just as Orwell's tale of woe and depression had suited the sombre mood of the late 1940s.

1984 almost didn't get on the air. Jobs and Sculley planned to make their splash by running the ad during the 1984 Super Bowl, on Sunday, 22 January, two days before the official launch, when the largest number of males (who were the chief buyers of computers) would be glued to their TV sets to watch the annual football championship. The trouble was that using the sixty seconds of reserved airtime would cost around $1 million, and Apple's board of directors was shocked by the expense. Good sales in the pre-Christmas season, though, allowed Apple to run the commercial in the third quarter of the game, which had an average audience of 38.8 million viewers.

It caused exactly the sensation Apple hoped for. According to Sculley, even one of the jaded sports announcers exclaimed, 'Wow, what was that?' The press and TV treated the commercial as a news event in its own right, giving Apple an enormous amount of free publicity for its launch: large numbers of potential buyers were excited by the prospect of seeing the Macintosh. Ironically, *1984* became one of the most effective and famous unseen ads of all time, since Apple only paid to run the blockbuster once. (The attempt to replicate this sensation a year later with a more downbeat ad called *Lemmings* was in Sculley's mind a terrible 'flop' that only underlined how difficult it was to predict audience response.)

The World's Best Commercials?

1984 won a total of thirty-five national and international awards, the most significant being the Grand Prix of the International Advertising Film Festival (IAFF) in Cannes.

This competition, known as the *other* Cannes festival, brings together people and ads (for both TV and cinema) from all over the world. Here creativity reigns supreme: 'It's the art of advertising not whether you sold anything,' Ayer chairman Jerry Siano claimed (*USA Today*, 19 June 1991). The festival awards Bronze, Silver, and Gold Lions as well as a grand prize to one, sometimes two commercials. Its activities have achieved sufficient fame to win notice in newspapers and magazines: the thirty-eighth IAFF of 1991, for example, was written up in *Time* (15 July), where the ads were used to 'reveal a world of cultural differences.' That particular gathering attracted around 4,500 ad people and 3,778 entries, from forty-eight countries. But in fact the representation of national advertising is very unequal: the United States submitted most ads at 781, Britain came second with 387, followed by Spain (336), Japan (318), and Brazil (273), while Canada was well down the list with seventy-two entries. Besides, the twenty-three member jury was biased towards the eight countries that were allowed to select two judges: Brazil, France, Germany, Great Britain, Italy, Japan, Spain, and the United States. In the past, there've been charges of 'vote-trading,' where countries agree to vote for each other's commercials, and unofficial quotas, where prizes are awarded proportionate to entries, so Dianne

Allen reported in the *Toronto Star* (6 July 1991). One former judge, Marcio Moreira of McCann-Erickson, complained to *USA Today* (19 June 1991) of 'rampant nationalism ... like World Cup Soccer.'

You might well question whether the Lions are the best in the world. I have found award-winners in all years that lacked either originality or skill. Yet the fact that a commercial has won an accolade from the jury does give it stature as a work of art. I have chosen to analyse the 942 award winners from the festivals 1984 through 1991: these cover the gamut of products and services, and include seventy-eight public service announcements (PSAs), though over one-quarter of the ads are devoted to touting the virtues of food and beverages. I have also surveyed 405 commercials found in what's now called the Kodak International Showcase (1987–92), which includes samples of award-winning or notable commercials (some of which also appear on the Lions tapes) from outside Canada. This latter collection is much more parochial than the Cannes Lions, though: two-thirds of the ads come from Great Britain (43 per cent) or Australia (25 per cent). One cardinal virtue of both the Lions and the International Showcase is that many of the commercials have been dubbed into English or given English subtitles.

Who made the 'best' commercials? Top honours in the eight years of Cannes competition were shared among the British and the Americans. Altogether, juries gave out the Grand Prix to eleven ads, four of which were American, three British, two Spanish, one Japanese, and one French. For the record, I have provided a ranked list of the origin of the 823 Lions, excluding Runners-Up and Diplomas, which could be readily identified (out of 826). This provides a rough indicator of where one collection of veteran ad-makers think the most creative work is coming from. The big winners are either the Europeans (including the British) at 473 awards or the Anglophones (including Canada and South Africa) at 447, depending on how you want to tally the results.

Margot Hornblower, the *Time* writer, pointed out that the work honoured at the 1991 Cannes bared 'the psyche of a nation.' More apt, if less poetic, would be the claim that the ad-makers in each country fashioned a particular idiom that slants the language of advertising to suit the tastes of their audiences. European ads boast many more allusions to sex than their North American counterparts. The British remain the masters of wit. There's a charming softness to Spanish ads, which as a group became more sophisticated when new television channels began to appear on the scene after the mid-1980s. Brazilian spots sometimes boast an extraordinarily sensual quality that is reminiscent of the look and the body language of sun worshippers in Rio: thus *Mother & Daughter* (C88119) features two naked females, a young mother who strokes her body with lotion and a daughter who pretends the same actions. The French

Cannes Lions, 1984–91

Country	#s	%s	Country	#s	%s
1. Britain	202	25%	15. Denmark	7	1%
2. United States	193	23%	16. New Zealand	7	1%
3. France	84	10%	17. Switzerland	4	
4. Spain	68	8%	18. Belgium	3	
5. Japan	51	6%	19. South Africa	3	
6. Brazil	38	5%	20. Singapore	2	
7. Germany	32	4%	21. Israel	2	
8. Australia	32.	4%	22. Korea	2	
9. Italy	22	3%	23. Austria	1	
10. Norway	21	3%	24. Finland	1	
11. Sweden	17	2%	25. Chile	1	
12. Canada	12	1%	26. Ecuador	1	
13. Holland	10	1%	27. Soviet Union	1	
14. Argentina	7	1%	28. Zimbabwe	1	

offer up large doses of peculiar and even baffling advertising: frankly, there are times when it is difficult for a foreigner to see just what the point of a commercial may be. A Citroën spot (C85044) featured a collection of lively wild horses rushing through the streets of an empty city, across a bridge, and eventually onto a plain where they made the pattern of two open Vs. Australian commercials, by contrast, often justify the notion that the Land of Oz is in love with the ultramasculine. Witness a macho spot for Kellogg's Nutri Grain (IS8908) where a rugged, muscular male virtually snarls at the viewer as he punishes his body with all kinds of exercise – weightlifting, swimming, boating, running, riding, surfing – this guy does it all.

The Americans are notorious at Cannes for their romantic ads, 'schmaltz' in the words of one ad-maker quoted in the *Time* story. Typical of this genre was *Reunion* (C84054), a Kodak commercial, where people of all ages, both sexes, black and white, are shown in slowed motion getting together to renew old memories of friendships. Likewise, U.S. ad-makers are well known for their wide assortment of hard-sell ads, which confront and sometimes bludgeon the viewer with their message. So one loud toothpaste spot (C85070), appropriately called *Battle*, featured a poor sot whose mouth was agitated because it was under assault from plaque, an assault emphasized by the sounds of gunfire and the like, which could only be resisted by purchasing Check-Up.

But what isn't so widely recognized is just how the aggressiveness and competitive zeal of Americans find a particular expression in their penchant for comparative advertising. No matter what the brand, ad-makers manage to assert its superiority by denigrating the opposition: Avis car rental (C84126), Alaska Airlines (C85016), Businessland computers (C85092/3), Sprint long-distance (C89053), Beneficial loans (C89095), Glad-Lock Zipper Bags (90012), the portable Macintosh (C90033), Red Roof Inns (C90068), Nature's Course Dog Food (C91082), IKEA USA (C91094/5), and on and on. One of the best of this style was *Operators* (C91045), made for Southern Bell's Charge Card, which portrayed a consumer's nightmare. In a busy airport, a succession of people try to make a long distance call from a pay phone, using a rival's charge card. Each consumer runs into a real nest of vipers: we see the operators fail to connect the poor souls, lecture them, and take glee in their plight. They constantly end the conversation with the lie 'This is a recording.' Their happiness turns to frustration, though, when a man with the Southern Bell charge card comes to the phone – apparently this magic card compels them to deal properly with the call. But back we go to scenes of an operator having fun with another consumer, for he dialed with the wrong finger. All the time the voice-over is nattering on about the advantages of Southern Bell. Yes, ad-makers in other countries do occasionally employ the comparative style, notably for British and Australian banks. Yet the Americans clearly remain the masters of this kind of advertising, which often positions the consumer as a fool.

Japanese advertising, according to Hornblower, continually puzzles West-erners. 'The cultural gap is so great that it is almost impossible for the West to appreciate Japanese commercials,' noted the president of the 1991 Cannes '91 jury, Allen Rosenshine of BBDO Worldwide. That's a bit of an exaggeration. It's true that some ads seem to mystify more than they explain: for example, the assorted minidramas and dream sequences for which Shiseido has become famous in its efforts to sell make-up. But being different doesn't necessarily mean indecipherable. Many Japanese spots evince a naive enthusiasm for high technology. So *Mischief* (C86034) features two polished male and female robots that perform a variety of delicate tasks at a simulated dinner party – indeed, the male lifts the female's skirt and gets slapped with a pie. A corporate ad for Toshiba, *Voice Recognition* (C91054), celebrates technological advance in general, ending with the claim 'The twenty-first century is going to be truly amazing.' None of this should surprise, given the way the Japanese have won fame as the manufacturers of High Tech.

No wonder Japanese ad-makers appear to be in love with product demonstra-tions. *Wherever You Go* (C89085) compares the spherical Hitachi vacuum cleaner to beads of water racing playfully around on leaves. A beautiful ad for the Canon colour copier (C91044) compares the fidelity of its pictures to the real thing by presenting a flawless composite arrangement of real and copied flowers. Such ads draw upon the narrative of Nature as well as Modernity to construct charming images of the beneficence of High Tech. In a different vein, the Japanese carry out a wide assortment of exaggerated or just plain phony product tests. A steam iron calms a sea of wrinkles on a gigantic blue cloth, while Wagner's music plays in the background (C86098); a battery-powered boat competes on the open sea with human rowers (C87067); extreme close-ups and slow motion show how quickly Superset Glue seals a balloon (C90053); a copier works so fast that a policeman comes along and gives it a ticket (C91077); flour transforms other foods or itself into all sorts of delicacies before our eyes (IS9215). Indeed an Italian ad-maker spoofed this style in *Japanese Demonstration* (C91062) in which a Japanese tester tries to show the potency of 'Super Fix' by trying unsuccessfully to glue together two pieces of oven paper – 'The paper that never sticks.' Apparently, if the Japanese couldn't stick the paper, then nobody could.

Even more striking, however, is the Japanese skill in cinematography. Nearly one-third of all Japanese Lions (fifty-nine) fall into the mannerist camp, a far greater proportion than the work of any other country. Their ad-makers take great pains to ensure that the colours, shape, and positioning of objects and settings and people fulfils some aesthetic purpose. So a camera ad (C84104) displays an extraordinary series of moving and still shots of animals entering or leaving what appears to be a cavern. *Blooming Light Bulbs* (C85108) places bulbs in flowers or arranges these bulbs into flowers, to create works of art. Shiseido borrows the imagery of African legend and dress to hype its Inoui colours (C87070), just as Suntory Whiskey borrows the imagery of the American South to sell Jack Daniels (C88078) – the latter seems a faithful rendering of the history, ease, and calm that's associated with this place in legend, if not in fact. Gekkeikan Sake (IS9021) marries scenes out of Tradition and Nature: the opening of a flower, a bird landing on a rock, leaves blowing in the wind, a rust-coloured field, three herons on a lake, and two people in traditional costume. These are but a few of the exquisite commercials coming out of Japan.

Perhaps the Japanese will supplant the British during the 1990s as the recognized leaders in world advertising. The reason? The Japanese style embodies a growing international tendency to create striking images. That taste for special effects (so apparent even in the first Clios) found a new lease on life when the computer, among other kinds of electronic wizardry, became one of the tools of ad-making during the early and mid-1980s. Outside of the PSAs, which are a special case, the on-screen announcer or the voice-over plays a much less crucial role than in the past as the guide to understanding in North America and much of Europe, where audiences are so well trained in the logic of television. Ad-makers can use a bevy of other signs – special soundtracks, popular or classical music, on-screen text, mixes of colour, and above all pictures – to drive home the message.

This is expressed in the same display of excess so evident in the Bessies, where people are shown overcome by their lust or their joy. Everywhere there are images of obsessed consumers: the Inuit with kayak and spear who travels through London in search of his beer (C84007), the throngs of people who adore new Coke (C86019), the dinner guests with an unnatural and definitely sinful passion for Juliette's cooking (C86031), or a nasty mom who deprives her hungry child of the last morsel of food (C90079). Everywhere there are portraits of overreaction: an Australian cuckoo (yes, in a cuckoo clock) that goes mad with joy over the arrival of odour-eating Glad Garbage Bags (C87016), an Englishman whose overindulgence turns him into a liquorice all-sort (C88011), or a Japanese family worshipping their new answering machine (C89106). In *Chain Reaction* (IS8719), drinking America's Hawaiian Punch energizes first robots and later youth who eventually engage in a dancing frenzy – there the promise of liberation, the body freed from restraint, is blatant. Equally explicit is *Dirty Words* (IS9029), in which a group of attractive, sometimes stylish Brazilian women vent their frustration and anger – we don't hear what they say, but the camera focuses on their lips, which is appropriate because this is a lipstick ad.

One brand of advertising has become addicted to chilling images: the PSAs. During the 1980s a wide array of government agencies, private organizations, and special interest groups took to the airwaves to advance their causes – against drunk driving and spousal abuse; the war on smoking, drugs, and AIDs; animal rights and environmentalism; Third World assistance, and so on. Many of these advocacy commercials from all over the world have tried to shock the public out of its torpor with menacing pictures. They use metaphors of death or corruption as well as drama or actual footage of some horror or another: thus the images of the Grim Reaper (IS8927), skulls (C88120), corrupted faces (C87049), maggots and flies (IS8826), guns (IS9126) and shootings (C84119), famine victims (C89112), domestic violence (C88040), blood and anguish (IS9243), the Holocaust (C90098), animal slaughter (C89066), burning rain-forest (C91050), or nuclear disaster (C87041). Watching all this is like entering a nightmare. What a contrast to the normal happy face of advertising.

Some of this fearful imagery is extremely weird. Indeed, the most intriguing evidence of the visual emphasis in all forms of advertising is an extraordinary passion for the bizarre. Consider the 1991 Grand Prix winner: a remarkable spot for Perrier, *The Lion & Lioness*, made by Ogilvy & Mather and directed by the acclaimed Jean-Paul Goude. This thirty-second minidrama can be given a feminist reading: it represents a struggle between a woman and a lion for the ultimate in refreshment, which is at the top of a hill. The dominant colour is a golden yellow and the overall texture is grainy, all to suggest a jungle setting. Both characters are shown moving on all fours through tall grass, both spy the Perrier, and both climb the hill from opposite sides. They meet at the top. The camera gives us close-ups of their battle: the lion's grand roar is more than matched by the woman's shriek of hate, which is so enhanced that it sounds like the scream of a banshee. She throws out her arm pointing down the hill, the soundtrack blaring some words from an American pop song, 'I'll put a spell on you.' Outclassed, the king of the beasts turns and flees. She takes the Perrier and drinks lustily, the water spilling down her chin. Eventually, standing as queen of the hill, the wind blowing in her hair, she salutes the Perrier name that appears in the sky. What a marvellous demonstration of that old cliché, the yearning for the product. Indeed the ad is full of references – to animal lusts, the struggle for dominance, the male/female contrast, the joy of triumph, the sins of indulgence.

Perrier has long been known for its sophisticated and weird ads. In fact, a taste for bizarrerie is an attribute of many French ads. A Kodachrome spot follows a family through an assortment of impossible adventures on land and sea (C84124); vultures launch a vicious assault upon a dying car, first in the desert (C84105) and later in the city (C86010), all to hype the virtues of Hertz rent-a-car; a long ad for a magazine takes the viewer through an Egyptian pyramid (C87002); beautiful women yell wildly out the windows of a plush hotel, signifying their anger and frustration at the man (only his hairy arm is shown) who uses the potent Egoïste (C90086). Other spots have featured a waitress who strips off her uniform and dances madly (C84095), a bevy of grey adults who self-destruct (C84129), a black man who drives a grand piano through the streets (C84131), a partially nude black woman who sticks her head in a cannon and emerges blonde (IS8769), a white male overrun by weeds (C86049), roses that grow out of a compressed car (C88079), and so on. It's the plethora of such images that makes French advertising so exciting and elusive.

If the bizarre remains a French speciality, the British are close rivals. Advertising regulations so restricted what could be said about cigarettes that Winston offered a nonsense commercial (C84083) in which an eagle steals a pack of smokes and suffers a vicious attack by fake biplanes! Radio Rentals has won a number of awards for its efforts to show the advantage of renting a TV, including a TV movie entitled 'The Incredible Seven' that's eventually reduced to 'The Lone Ranger' to match the modest size of an owner's screen (C87112). But it is the makers of beer commercials who have proven the most consistent

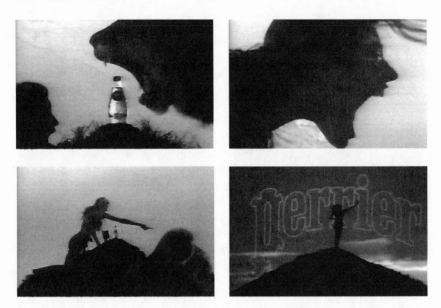

Figure 5.1: *Le lion et la lionne*. Images of conflict, triumph, and celebration. This commercial borrows from the mythologies of sexism and feminism to craft an imaginative story of a woman's victory in the so-called battle of the sexes. (Courtesy of Source Perrier)

fans of the bizarre, probably because they feel they must entertain since they cannot sell beer on its merits. McEwan's Lager (IS8714) mixed the imagery of horror movies and Escher's prints to portray a bleak building where people were slaves to their jobs. Tuborg Lager (IS8761) announced the arrival of its import with a weird train of men and women dressed in green who move forward in a jerky motion. And Bass Brewers Ltd. has had actors kick around poor Yorick's skull in a mock performance of Hamlet (C86056), presumably to reinforce the image of Carling Black Label as an unusual brand.

Nor is that the end of the list. The Australians, who often mimic British styles (just as the Canadians mimic American ways), have had their share of poster people who come to life (C91012), dieting cows to hype low-fat milk (C91014), and even talking camels who come across the skeleton of a driver who foolishly didn't use genuine Toyota car parts (IS9226). One stunning and novel commercial, *Spot the Lizard* (IS9039), portrayed the manufacture of a series of artificial humans in some kind of special birthing factory where hard rock filled the air.

A sudden spurt of energy sets everything off, and we move into a world of mad symbolism – a cloven hoof, musical notes mixed in a cauldron, an assembly line of eggs, a machine composed of angry-faced males who bash the eggs, a bevy of beautiful women who collect ears, the cracking and energizing of the eggs, the emergence of winged metallic males, and so on until a radio explodes, leaving behind the logo and the whisper 'Triple M.' In an American existential ad for Honda (C88019), questions philosophical ('Who am I?') and trivial ('Is there any pizza left?') are thrown on the screen before a dry voice says, 'If it's not the answer, at least it's not another question.' In a surreal Japanese spot for Suntory (C85107), a white rabbit and a North American male in a blue suit watch a series of armadillo-like creatures dance out of a TV set with whiskey and a Perrier. A German commercial shows a man in a bow-tie, fondling himself, who actually opens his coat to reveal what looks like an extended member, provoking the beautiful woman to laugh and offer him a West cigarette (IS9125). A supposedly Spanish ad for Kattus Sparkling Wine (IS9237) (that is the claim, though the ad is wholly in German) is reminiscent of the artistic style of René Magritte, in which darkened figures of men slowly fall in unison from a deep blue sky.

In short, everyone's caught the French fever. No doubt the prominence of all this bizarrerie, in the Cannes collection anyway, has something to do with the fact that the jurors are veteran ad-makers: their jaded eyes are more likely to be captivated by something unusual or weird. Besides, such images cross linguistic boundaries and thus better suit an international competition. But the spread of the bizarre is also related to that postmodern taste which relishes the play of signs: a visual extravaganza, unusual images and weird juxtapositions, ambiguity or scandal serve to intrigue and titillate the palate. They offer an escape from the ordinary, an invitation to join a new kind of game, to discover the mix of meanings embedded in a particular spectacle.

My emphasis on the spread of the bizarre, though, might leave the impression that the Cannes Lions have broken with the past. Not so: you can still find product demonstrations, testimonials, straight talk, sentimental spots, and others that recall the first Clios. But exemplars of these old-fashioned formats have been dressed up – an ironic treatment or some special effects can turn even the most clichéd spiel into something novel, perhaps startling. The whole intent is to provide viewers with an immediate jolt of pleasure, to mask the sell as a form of entertainment, whether this means recognizing a celebrity or a situation, working out a puzzle, laughing at a person or a style, thrilling to some sign of excess, or whatever. The ads may seek to educate, but first they must divert.

Sex, Laughs, and Rock 'n' Roll

That's why these commercials often borrow from the other realms of the Superculture. American and British stars of past and present abound, whether for real or as look-alikes: Joan Collins of *Dallas* fame (C84138), the comedian John Cleese (C90004), the tough-looking and tough-talking Grace Jones (IS8704), George Burns playing God (C90005), the blues musician Miles Davis (IS9275), a Sikh Elvis Presley sound-alike (IS8968), a Roger Moore look-alike (C89002), both Marilyn Monroe (C88003) and Cary Grant (C91021) in cuts from old movies. Even the superstar Arnold Schwarzenegger crops up in *Mah-Jong* (IS9276), a Japanese spot for the vitamin beverage Alinamin. Drinking the marvel turns Schwarzenegger into a powerhouse who can overawe some obstreperous rival players in this spoof of Superman and other cartoon heroes.

Most celebrities and their doubles, as in the case of Schwarzenegger, play out their persona in some sort of a spoof. The spoof, in fact, has become common-place among commercials of distinction. Innumerable ads appropriate the look and feel of movies: James Bond sells cars in France (C84024) and shoes in Germany (C84038); *Tootsie* is recalled for Brazil's TAM Airline (C84051), as is *Close Encounters of the Third Kind* for Coke in the United States (C86019); Leslie Nielsen plays out his persona of the dumb inspector from *Naked Gun* for Britain's Red Rock Cider (C91003/4). Bass went to a favourite of the past with its mockery of *The Dam Busters*, a 1954 hit which celebrated the British bombers that destroyed Germany's Ruhr dam during the Second World War, except that in *Dambusters* (C90077), the German guard plays catch with the British bombs, not only saving the dam but proving he must drink Carling Black Label.

Sometimes ad-makers reached even further back to the well-loved legends and the High Culture of Europe. A toothpaste ad from Ecuador (IS8869) adopts the style and story of Sleeping Beauty; a German ad touting Ajax Window Cleaner (IS8916) does the same with Snow White. In *La Soirée* (C90062), it's a male Cinderella who leaves behind the shoe: when the woman who picks up the shoe (with an address inside) arrives at the apartment, she discovers a long line of women and one man waiting at the door. A spot for Catalonia's railway system (C89007) uses Richard Wagner's 'Die Walküre' to underscore one old woman's mad rush to the train station. Guess Jeans' *Picture Show* (IS8726) combines scenes from Texas 1958, youth at play, and *Madame Butterfly* in one confusing effort to sell to British consumers.

Music plays a special role here because familiarity breeds rapport in the world of commercials. Once ad-makers commissioned a special tune or designed a jingle to suit their sell, but that practice has increasingly given way to the use of bits and pieces from the general musical repertoire. Usually the use of classical music connotes quality and class, whether to hype a brand of clothes in Brazil (C84039) or the achievements of graphite technology in Japan (C84120). The ecstasy a beautiful woman experiences after eating Nestlé's chocolate bar is accompanied by the powerful sounds of Carl Orff's 'Carmina Burana' (Holland's IS9265). Perhaps most striking, though, is the way the Japanese have assimilated the classical music of Europe: one spot for Suntory whiskey amounts to a disquisition on Gustav Mahler (C86009), while another beverage ad uses scenes from the lavish opera *La Traviata* (C87097).

Naturally there's much greater use of popular music in Japan and every-where else because this music has become a lingua franca across the globe in the past generation. Even old favourites have been called in to help sell: you can find the dulcet tones of Nat King Cole in an ad for Japanese robotics (C85021), something from the oh-so-smooth Frank Sinatra for a Spanish yoghurt (C87101), even Fats Domino's lively 'I'm Walkin'' for British diapers (C85081). But that's modest compared to the amount of play given to rock 'n' roll, especially the hits of the 1950s and 1960s. Often the songs are used to provoke a laugh. The Beach Boys' 'Barbara Ann' accompanies scenes of a bouncing baby in one Italian ad (C84028) and bouncing men in a Dutch spot (IS8931); a modified version of the Guess Who's 'Shakin' All Over' turns up in a British commercial for Rowntree's jelly dessert (C84134); we hear 'La Bamba' in another British ad (C86059), where a compact Vauxhall Nova drives over the top of cars caught in a traffic jam; the twist enlivens a Brazilian spot for Ajax (C90014), where people slip and slide on a greasy patch on the kitchen floor.

Even the recent emergence of American rap has been used for advertising. So a very clever *M.C. Hammer: Switch* (C91081), one of the 'New Generation' series, has that rap superstar turn into a romantic singer under the influence of Coke until a worried fan gives him the Pepsi, which brings back his high-energy self. Here, at least, the connotations of insolence and rebellion that are so much a part of rap echo. Not so in other contexts, where rap becomes merely the most recent novelty on the music scene. A vitamin ad (IS9034) actually assembles a man before our eyes, who sings rap-style the virtues of Britain's Complan as he is 'made.' A postal officer becomes a rap singer, complete with the requisite jerky motions, when he's asked to wrap a parcel – Australia Post wants you to 'postpak' this kind of mail (IS9002). Here's appropriation with a vengeance: both singers are white, both parody the rap style, and both serve to provoke laughter.

But rock has also been used to establish a variety of different moods. Nostalgia: late sixties music is one of a series of overlapping signs that serve to recall memories of the Austin Mini in its heyday (IS9024). Loss: the Everly

Brothers' 'Bye Bye Love' conveys a sense of sadness in a wicked Brazilian spot, where the voice-over tells prospective dieters to spend some time indulging at Dunkin Donuts before taking the plunge (C91037). Expectancy: Phil Collins's 1981 hit 'In the Air Tonight' runs through a surreal spot for Michelob beer, where night people search for company and pleasure in Big City, U.S.A. – this comes in two versions: C87050 and IS8763. Isolation and entrapment: Pink Floyd's 'Is There Anybody Out There,' from the 1979 megahit album 'The Wall,' accompanies a visual where some lost soul is trying desperately to break through what looks like a huge piece of blue plastic – we see the outline of hands and a face (C86110).

Even more effective, though, is the way Levi Strauss, more properly its agency, Bartie Bogie Hegarty, has used hits from the 1950s and 1960s to push 501s in Britain. These jeans are associated with images of masculinity, romance, youth, sometimes rebellion, and above all America. Through each commercial runs one song, which nicely accentuates whatever story is played out on the screen: Eddie Cochran's lively 'C'mon Everybody' (C88093) – crashing a party (*Eddie Cochran*); Percy Sledge's poignant 'When a Man Loves a Woman' (C87108) – a sad separation (*Parting*); Marvin Gaye's 'I Heard It Through the Grapevine' (C86117) – insolent male display (*Laundrette*); the Ronettes' 'Be My Baby' (C89092) – stealing a girl (*Pick-Up*); and Spencer Davis's throbbing R&B song 'I'm a Man' (C88020) – aggressive male display (*Climate*). The most famous of these, *Laundrette*, features a sexy young Latino who strips down to his underpants to put his clothes in a washing machine at a laundromat, much to the astonishment of onlookers. Altogether the commercials give the impression that 501s are 'the real McCoy,' a badge of status, a sign of belonging to some wider community of free-spirited men and women.

The campaign was an unquestioned success. In *The Discourse of Advertising* Guy Cook reports that the chief actor in *Laundrette*, Nick Kamen, 'became a major star in his own right.' Cook adds that rereleases of the 1960s song appeared once more on the hit parade, and that sales figures for 501s exploded, rising 'from 80,000 pairs to around 650,000 in one year.'

It's often claimed that rock 'n' roll and especially rock videos, movies, and TV shows, as well as popular fiction, are suffused with sex. Extending such a claim to these commercials of distinction would be an exaggeration. That said, a lot of this advertising is full of sexual imagery, often masked, sometimes blatant. Not surprisingly, romance figures in many different kinds of ads. Two strangers meet over a Campari (C87005) in Belgium or a Serkova Vodka (IS8874) in Greece – indeed men and women are forever getting together over drinks, that great social mixer all over the world. Woman pursues man: Levi's *Eddie Cochran* told the story of how a woman's jeans won her the attention of the rock star. Man pursues woman: the classic *Apartment 10E* (C87098) showed just how far a young male, in this case Michael J. Fox, would go to please his new neighbour, a ravishing blonde. He climbs down an outside staircase in a rainstorm, braves the heavy traffic, and even makes his way through some motorcycle toughs, all to get a can of Diet Pepsi from a street dispenser. Man gets woman: a plumpish young man in Paris beats out a fast mover to win the favour of an English beauty, simply because our hero has taken the Berlitz course in English (C86014). Woman leaves man: the brilliant *Changes* (C88063) depicts a woman, reminiscent of Princess Diana, who forsakes all the tribute gained from a past love except, that is, for the Volkswagen. Love won, love lost, such subjects draw upon a wealth of references from the Superculture.

That's just the beginning, though. There are plenty of examples of dirty talk to capture the attention of the casual viewer. 'Guess wha' I got?' a plumber asks Marilyn Monroe in a Holsten Pils spot (C88003). 'The biggest thing since the Graf Zeppelin,' she replies hopefully. Asked if he likes turkey legs, a Brazilian male says they're fine, but he prefers breasts, referring to a young woman at his side in a tight outfit that emphasizes her bosom (C85030). A devilish French ad, *La Femme* (C89090), gives us an attractive, well-dressed, young woman who goes into some detail about just what she's wearing underneath, only to announce she has no intention of showing us these items – what a 'Scandale,' declares a male voice-over, thus naming the product. A controversial Australian ad, *Stiff Cheddar* (IS9202), opens on a shot of a very handsome man, with a cloth over his midriff, the cloth raised as if to suggest an erection. A woman's hand removes the cloth, only to reveal the erection is no more than his raised finger. A female voice-over says, 'A good unmarried man is really *hard* to find but not in this month's *Cleo*,' where you can read the list of Australia's fifty most eligible bachelors. Both *La Femme* and *Stiff Cheddar* are a mild form of tease for the man and the woman with the tastes of a voyeur.

Indeed teasing is commonplace, especially in the ads from Europe and South America. The final scene in *Busy Day* (C84080) has the Lee Jeans sigh with pleasure because their owners are under the sheets. The extraordinary and unusual Levi's *Climate* seethes with passion: a strikingly handsome young man, his body freely displayed, stuns both a beautiful waitress and the patrons of a restaurant with his extravagant masculinity – one brief shot of his crotch, sheathed in tight-fitting boxer shorts, is especially suggestive. An upscale Jamaican couple play with silk and Smirnoff in a cool and classy commercial subtly entitled *Good Friends* (IS8847). Two spots for Durex contraceptives use a woman's giggle, plus a rocking car (C85012) and the sounds of bedsprings (C88042), to suggest sexual intercourse. The act of eating gets folded into sexual play in *9 1/2 Weeks* (IS8809), a Venezuelan spot where a man feeds, teases, and caresses a woman with little tidbits of food. A Spanish couple shed shoes, socks, and nylons before they're shown making love to each other's feet, a display made possible only because of Pie Pik, a foot deodorant (C90055). The most explicit ad in a continuing campaign for Freixenet, *Sueno* (C89014), depicts a couple drinking, dropping clothes, and enjoying each other – we see the kiss, the stroke, a woman's bare breasts, the clenched hands (a sign of orgasm), though all in silhouette. In one ad for Langnese (C85061), that German iced treat rises up like a penis between a woman's partially covered breasts; in another (IS8812), a woman sucks on the same treat in a fashion that is positively sensual. Yamaha's *Pleasure* (C87074), also German, combines the sounds of a motorcycle with pictures of the body of a naked woman: we get the illusion of driving over her curves, and at the end a woman says 'Yamaha' in a way that suggests extraordinary pleasure.

By far the best examples of sexual innuendo, though, can be found in the French work, confirming that hackneyed cliché about the French and sex. Perrier's *The Dream* (C86050) is a superb short story of mutual seduction, full of bizarre imagery, wherein a man and a woman end their drama in bed – with a Perrier. A man becomes amorous in *Embraceable* (C86051) and everything in the house, from umbrellas to the hands of a clock, follow suit: the action ends when the newly awakened TV displays a train rushing into a tunnel. Then there's the aptly named *Le Tube* (C85112) for a rock radio station. A woman massages a phallic object, a tuning device, which agitates a group of sweating men who are waiting in cars; her stroking awakens their antennae, which rise up, makes one man suck in his lips, tunes their radios till they reach 100.6, when loud music breaks forth and the cars rock happily. The promise? 'She goes all the way.' All this is titillation with style.

On occasion, ad-makers borrow from the repertoire of erotica to present viewers with appealing and even sensational images of beautiful women (though rarely of handsome men). There's many an ad that focuses upon exercising, dressing and undressing, the swimsuit, or some state of dishabille, all of which put female sexuality on display. We might well call this the peek-a-boo effect. That can be fairly mild as in *Behind the Scene* (C84036), a Brazilian spot modelled on the movie *Flashdance* where we see young females dancing their hearts out. Or it can be humorous as in the American *Rituals* (C87076), which features slim and attractive young women struggling to get their legs into tight jeans. But *Bollé Protection* (C90061), though spoofing the cult of safe sex – in order to sell Australian sunglasses – actually presents images of a beautiful woman in a tight-fitting swimsuit engaged in foreplay. Similarly, the risqué *Surfen* (C85061) is full of women in bikinis, including three nuns who lift up their habits to reveal their sexy bodies, all to please the watchful eyes of males on the beach and at home.

Another ploy is to turn the sexual spotlight on some aspect of a woman's body. *Different Strokes* (C87035) celebrates the extraordinary mane of reddish brown hair of the female 'beauty' who first rests, then plays in the calm waters of a tropical paradise. *The Film* (C87030) pauses for a close-up of a woman's bum in tight-fitting jeans. A gust of wind whips up a woman's skirt to reveal her thighs, clothed in the classic garters of pornography (C85076). Many more ads give us lingering shots of women's legs, whether they're walking (IS8953), running (C84041), sitting (C86008), or standing (C87094), all of which suggest grace, desire, and beauty.

Special attention is given to women's breasts, which represent the acme of desire and beauty in the eyes of the male voyeur. Sometimes the sexual spotlight is on swelling or partly bare breasts, ripe with sexual promise, broadcasting availability if not passion: that can be seen in ads for Peugeot (C84024), Barilla pasta (C84032), even a telephone (C87065). One variation on this theme is Brazil's *First Brassiere* (C87107), which portrays the excitement of a teenager who gets her first Valisère, signifying her femininity, and the look the new display provokes from a young male, which merely confirms that femininity. Sometimes the spotlight focuses on breasts in motion, symbolizing the freed, even wanton body: a man dreams that a luscious blonde, clad in a swimsuit, is rushing towards him (C84027); an attractive woman dances and jiggles her pleasure (C86045); women dressed in bras and panties play soccer (C88041). And there are times when the spotlight shows the naked breast, its immodesty scandalizing. This image is often presented as an invasion of privacy caused by, for example, a suddenly transparent parasol (C86016), a spying photographer (IS8811), or a satellite camera (C89001).

Finally, there's the display of the naked body. Here the mark of history is very apparent: a naked woman remains an object of beauty, of male desire and female admiration, in guises that nearly always suggest patriarchy. The motif can be played out in many different ways, of course. Spain's *A Way of Life* (C89015) presents an image of purity and innocence, a naked woman and her baby (sex indefinite), to celebrate the qualities of Evian. Another Spanish effort, *Desnudos* (IS9054), makes naked bodies of a man and women objects of art that recall the statues of the ancient Greeks. Great Britain's *Blue Velvet* (C91020) portrays the playful nymph, a naked woman who loses herself in the pleasures of creaming her legs, arm, upper chest, and face. By contrast, Denmark's *Sauna* (C87088) offers us woman as sex incarnate, a collection of naked beauties, their lush bodies on display for a peeping Tom who, not surprisingly, acquires an erection. (Strange as it seems, this was an ad for a newspaper – the newspaper is used to cover his extended penis!) And France's *Crystal Statue* (C87023) depicts the aggressive temptress: a drop of perfume first energizes and then shatters a statue, which becomes a stunningly beautiful nude woman, her breasts prominent, who glories in her power to excite males. I caution that the meanings above come out of the preferred reading of each commercial; it would be quite possible to give every one of these examples, not just the last two, an erotic reading.

Largely missing from the world of advertising (outside of the PSAs) is violence, that great staple of cinema and television entertainment. There are some exceptions, of course: witness the destruction of Big Brother in *1984* and the screaming match in *The Lion & Lioness*. But however entertaining, violence rarely suits the happy face of consumption, especially if that violence is serious rather than playful (though, as we shall see, advertising in Scandinavia is a partial exception). What more than fills the void is comedy: just over two-thirds of the Cannes winners use some form of humour, and four out of ten fall into the absurdist camp.

Humour comes in many shapes and forms. I've already said enough about the British and their assorted spoofs. The French style of bizarrerie usually has a humorous twist. American ad-makers pioneered the deadpan approach to humour, notably for Alaska Airlines and Bartles & James Wine Cooler, where expressionless folk reflect on their own merits or portray the flaws of rivals. Some kinds of products, notably glue, seem to strike ad-makers as a fit subject for mirth, whether the market is France (C87064), Germany (C89032), Japan (C85066), or Chile (C90084). Mild versions of ethnic and sexist jokes are common right across the ad world. Witness the three fat Italian women who sing and dance to tout the authenticity of a spaghetti sauce (Brazil, C84012); a Latin American policeman who can only say 'manana' to a distressed European tourist (Holland, C84044); a black boy who turns white when he eats the wrong marmalade (Great Britain, C84088); a drab fashion show in the Soviet Union, featuring an obese and dowdy matron, used to highlight the virtues of choice (United States, C85045); or an uptight schoolmistress, the classic old maid, who covers up the private parts displayed in works of art (Germany, C89028). The long-running British campaign for Castlemaine XXXX (C84115, C91001, and C91002), a brand of beer, amounts to an extended ethnic joke, with sexist undertones, because it mocks Australian manners, mores, and lingo. Look hard enough and you're likely to find an ad somewhere exploiting some hoary old cliché about a person's race, nationality, or sex.

What I find more disturbing is the large number of commercials that ask viewers to laugh at other people's stupidity or misfortune, whether an electrocuted man (Germany, C89060), a vain fat lady (France, C89061), the dupes of a phony insurance school (United States, C88089), or a man in a wheelchair who loses his brakes as he flies down a hospital ramp (Great Britain, IS8772). The deadpan style is especially prone to this kind of a reading. So *Sisters* (IS8832) presents two always friendly bankers who explain to some nice but naive old ladies how the interest on their savings becomes the bank's money. Likewise *Blimp I* (C90003), one of the Bartles & James series, offers up some homespun folks who've rented a blimp to advertise their new Cherry Wine Cooler at the football game, only to discover the stadium is covered. Slightly more sophisticated are two clever spots for Hawaiian Tourism, *Don Juan* (C91091) and *Bob & Ellen* (C91092). Each contrasts scenes of what people say about Bob and Ellen with what the couple is doing on their vacation. Their neighbours, Ellen's music teacher and her mother, as well as Bob's boss, emerge as a bunch of constricted folk who, in one way or another, denigrate Bob as a workaholic, Ellen as shy, both as dull. But instead shots of the couple show them being excessive, enjoying life and their bodies, bike-riding, running on the beach, swimming or lounging in the water, dancing and displaying, and smooching. 'Come to life in Hawaii,' the ad urges the slaves of routine throughout America.

Scandinavian ads carry this taste in humour to an extreme. Two ads for the Swedish Lottery (C86084 and C87046) feature a scene where an angry male gives the ear of an offending senior a nasty twist. In *Prickar* (C89019), a greedy doctor making his rounds eats all the treats of one patient who, swathed in bandages, can only babble incoherently; he then smashes a second patient who is in traction and who screams; and finally he swipes the candy of a third. A little old lady and a big young hunk trade insults and blows – for example, she knees him in the crotch – while a patient voice-over explains how one should be friendly in traffic (C90036). A bus driver laughs gleefully as he smashes into the convertible of a young punk who's done him wrong (C89097). An old woman in *The Thief* (C90009) thrashes another young punk who has stolen her purse, then returns to her knitting and her milk – 'Milk fortifies,' we're told. Fed up with the antics of a male driver who has been making all kinds of obscene gestures and remarks to other drivers, the female passenger hits him hard across the face with her purse (IS9263). There's some special pleasure in showing life's little accidents: a man is splashed by the droppings of seagulls (Norwegian Book Club, C85097–9); a dog pees on a woman's boots (Nokia Boots, C87078); an apartment is blown up by a faulty stove (VG Newspaper, C86048); a stove is dumped on a car (Storebrand Insurance, C91030); a car turns over and crashes (Swedish Rail, C86101); a woman twice burns her wash (Norwegian insurance, C89005). Is this just compensation for a style of television entertainment that has long been considered the most boring on the continent? But, in fact, many of these ads must have appeared in theatres, since public television, especially in Sweden, has strongly resisted advertising. I can't speculate otherwise about why this convention has emerged, only that it suggests a morbid sense of humour.

One type of satire has occasioned much comment, though it isn't really 'new' in the annals of advertising: I'm referring to the ad spoof where the commercial mocks the hype or the style of advertising itself. (One of the best, by the way, is from the mid-1970s, a Bell Canada spoof of the hard sell called *Inflation* (B7630), which used the Second City comedy troupe.) The previously mentioned *Japanese Demonstration* for an Italian oven paper was an example of this genre. In a similar vein is a Brazilian effort entitled *Cans* (C89083), where a Pepsi and a Coke can are glued together – 'Just to demonstrate once again that Araldite Glue joins even what seems impossible.' Much of the French bizarrerie is so excessive that it mocks the very nature of hype. *La Cave* (C85094), for example, wildly exaggerates the contrasts so dear to ad-makers: it displays first a dingy, dark, unpleasant restaurant, where the food falls on the customer's clothes, and then a plushy Freetime, spotlessly clean and decorated with plants, where a customer in a white suit not only enjoys his hamburger but gets the beautiful Natasha as well.

The British and the Americans employ a more direct kind of satire. The famous Isuzu campaign (C87106, C88086, C89041) in the United States featured 'Joe Isuzu,' a very smooth operator who was forever exaggerating the virtues of the car beyond belief, on one occasion at the cost of his 'mum' who gets struck by a bolt of lightning, while on-screen text corrected his lies. Energizer batteries created commercials within commercials: we view scenes from a movie promo (C91063), a telephone ad (C91064), and a forthcoming crime drama (C91065), each of which is upset by the pink bunny and his drum, powered by the Energizer, who just keeps on 'going and going.' (So familiar is this campaign to American audiences that in *Hot Shots: Part Deux*, a 1993 satire of the action/adventure genre of movies, both the star Charlie Sheen and one of his foes pause in the midst of a shoot-out to train their submachine guns on a replica of the energetic bunny – when it blows up, they exchange signals of triumph before resuming their fight.) A spot for Irn Bru (C91057) parodied American-style ads for soft drinks, full of happy folks, beautiful people, romantic moments, except this Scottish brew bestowed so much strength that the joy of the drinkers wreaked havoc around them. Likewise Slice Soda offered a satire of the hard sell (IS9088): not only did the consumer get the drink, that person could have a marvellous can, a special flip-top can-opener, and a plastic carrying case if a six-pack is purchased – all for free, enthused the spokesman. And Rover Cars sponsored *Balloon* (IS9109), which told viewers the ingre-

Figure 5.2: *Laundromat*. In *Laundrette* Levi Strauss celebrated the brazen sensuality of a young Latino who stripped in public down to his undershorts so that he could wash his jeans. A few years later, WCRS (the agency for Bass Brewers) used the same story-line, except this time the ad ended with an image of two blokes who were completely naked. What was the point? That these two men were drinkers of Black Label Beer, the brew for men who were truly unusual. This was just one spoof of many in a campaign in which Shakespeare's *Hamlet*, the movie *Dambusters*, and so on were mocked to extol the virtues of Black Label. (Courtesy of Bass Brewers Ltd.)

dients needed for 'the complete car commercial': a rugged landscape (to 'show nippy handling'), 'a rugged driver' (who displays himself), a 'famous old rock track' (a bit of Steppenwolf), 'a sudden landslide' (to 'demonstrate the brakes nicely'), a 'grand finale' (car carried away by balloon). 'It's easy you see – you just need the right car.'

Indeed agencies have taken to spoofing campaigns that have earned some stature as popular art. So Heineken's *VW* (IS8857) exploits the Volkswagen image and style; Carling Black Label's *Laundromat* (IS8861) steals the look and feel of Levi's *Laundrette*; and Slice Soda has its *Pink Rabbits* (IS9087), where the bunnies are powered by assorted soft drinks. The next step, of course, is self-parody. One Heineken ad (C88098) opens with an attractive, proper young lady who questions the good taste of the forthcoming minidrama. *Nonsense* (IS9210) makes fun of the magazine campaigns waged so successfully for years to hype Absolut Vodka. Those advertisements had turned the bottle itself into a work of art to suggest, among much else, the distinctiveness of this beverage. *Nonsense* shows a traditional still-life painting of a table, on which are the bottle and a glass. Magic balls of light touch aspects of the painting, bringing them to activity: a violin, a statue, candles, the maid dancing in a picture. But then comes the text: 'Absolut Nonsense' – and the violin knocks the statue, which topples the bottle, which hits the picture, and the painting as a whole falls to one side. You could count all this as evidence of the confidence and sophistication of both ad-makers and clients. Certainly it is a clever ploy to escape the discount viewers give to hype. Beyond that, such parody and derision mark the spirit of the age when a self-conscious irony enjoys so much play in the realm of literature and the fine arts.

Images of Products

This parody has a further significance: it represents the ad-makers playing with their own images rather than those designed by Hollywood and the other centres of mass culture. I suggested earlier that agencies worked to repeat and refashion songs, styles, and stars from the entertainment industries. Another way agencies contribute to the global Superculture is by associating clusters of meanings with particular products. No less than Hollywood, Madison Avenue and its cousins across the world are dream factories, which fashion images that enter the realm of popular culture as part of the shared repertoire of symbols and clichés. It would take another book to outline the meanings of the whole range of products represented in these commercials of distinction, so I'll confine myself to a discussion of clothing, automobiles, and cosmetics.

Why clothing? Recall the old saying 'Clothes make the man.' Clothing is a personal item, sold to both men and women, which is treated as a sign of the consumer's persona. Take the case of K Shoes, which gave two of its ads a feminist twist. In *Creaks* (C88067), a woman dressed in black leather, a subtle sign of allure and mystery, takes revenge on her cheating lover: she quietly enters his apartment, where she surprises him at a private dinner, dumps what looks like linguine on his head, crushes out the woman's cigarette on the floor, and closes the woman's mouth (chin up) with her finger – then leaves. The point is that K Shoes are made of the softest leather and never creak, a claim that is spelled out in interspersed words throughout the commercial. The especially clever *Great Idea* (89045) portrays the triumph of a wronged woman:

Figure 5.3: *Creaks* & *Great Idea*. Beautiful women of the sort pictured in these two ads for K Shoes have always been commonplace in the ad world. But during the 1980s such women appeared more and more as people with agency – 'empowered' in the jargon of the times – as well as objects of desire. Here C. & J. Clark employed the ideal of the liberated woman in two minidramas where self-possessed women exact revenge against the men who have 'done them wrong.' (Courtesy of C. & J. Clark Ltd.)

whatever the cause of her upset, she marches into the boss's office, clips her resignation to his tie, cuts the balls(!) on his desk ornament (which makes another man cross his legs), and withdraws with grace, even though her heel gets caught in a grate – for the heels of K Shoes will never break off. Need I add that both women are stylish, upscale, beautiful, and thus desirable?

The two ads employ the image of today's woman, who is self-possessed and indeed aggressive, no longer anyone's patsy. Her K Shoes are a sign of her liberation from the past. That same kind of message is spelled out in two American commercials from Maidenform Lingerie, one of which shows the array of confining undergarments once in fashion (C91067) and the other portrays the assorted images of women, from chick to cat to fox, once popular

(C91068). 'Isn't it nice to live in a time when women aren't being pushed around so much anymore?' asks a female voice-over.

But not only women are liberated by the clothes they wear. One Brazilian ad (C84039) shows a group of preteens and teens in assorted clothes from Hering (makers of the 'most natural and enjoyable fashion in this country'), swimming gently and happily underwater, free from all constraint. The zany French ad *Life's Too Short* (C84129) contrasts a collection of fat, dusty, sullen, and grey adults, who in a variety of ways self-destruct or disappear, with colourfully dressed and knowing youngsters who go about their play, thrilled by their freedom from the dull and the routine. The American *Higher & Higher* (C88002), sponsored by Arrow Shirts, portrays the transformation of a solemn church choir, full of males in white shirts and ties singing an old-fashioned hymn, into a happy crew of smiling, gyrating souls in all manner of colourful casuals, singing the modernized version of the same hymn. Nike won two awards for separate portrayals of the San Onofre Senior Surfers, one slow and even romantic (C91024) and the other wild and zany (C91025), but both showing active, engaged people who'd broken free from the debilitating stereotype of old age.

These ads were part of the 'Just Do It' campaign, which has urged people in a variety of different ways to liberate their souls and free their bodies from whatever's normal. One of the more famous of these spots, *Bo Diddley* (C90063), has the star athlete Bo Jackson demonstrating how he can do just about anything, including play a guitar. A response to this campaign was Reebok's *Head for Heights* (C91066), which was actually banned from British TV because it seemed to encourage a dangerous practice. It features a Mohawk Indian in his Reeboks, who runs up an unfinished Atlanta skyscraper, at one point making a death-defying leap across a gap, to end his feat by looking down on the city. Slogans like 'Reebok the Edge' or 'Just Do It' are ambiguous, but they plug into this wider mythology of liberation wherein the right clothes come to symbolize the freedom of body and soul.

No single overriding set of meanings serves to hype the automobile. Sometimes the car is presented as a work of art, where its styling and spirit suggests beauty: that message comes through in *White Car in the Garden* (C85109), a Japanese ad for Toyota. Sometimes the car becomes the embodiment of High Tech, which merely updates an association between the automobile and modernity that goes back to the 1920s: that claim is made in different ways by Britain's *Elite* (C87025), where an industrial spy reports on the marvellous BMW Seven series, and by Spain's *Like Father* (C89006), which compares the Renault Espace to a superfast train. One romantic spot for Porsche in America (C90059) manages to celebrate this prestige item as both a work of art and technological wizardry, the product of individual genius rather than (sneer, sneer) 'committees.' Indeed the pretentious ad asserted a third meaning, the car as a mark of status, which also has a long history in the annals of automobile advertising.

But I find much more intriguing two quite different representations of the car, one associated with fun and the other with security. The first identifies the automobile as a toy, chiefly a boy's toy. The toy rarely appears in the city or stuck in traffic, the latter an image that is much more common in train ads. No, the toy is usually found in more exotic settings where it's shown performing all kinds of marvellous stunts. A Fiat Uno (C85079) twists and turns over what looks like a snowy plain (though this is a Brazilian ad) to avoid being lassooed by a gas hose. Some madman drives a Citroën (C85011) off a French aircraft carrier whence it's saved from drowning by a submarine. A James Bond look-alike manoeuvres the rival Peugeot across an arid landscape (C84024) and over ice (C87073), all the while pursued by villains firing assorted weapons. A British Land Rover (C87026) bashes through the wild and even scales a dam, albeit assisted by a pully – 'Nothing, but nothing gets in the way.' Although some Japanese ad-makers did put the Isuzu in the city, they showed two cars waltzing together in one spot (IS8702), then leaping into the air like ballet dancers in a second commercial (IS9082).

These scenes of mad driving connote fun, excitement, adventure, in other words they display excess. No wonder Grace Jones (C86090) yells her defiance and pleasure at the viewer after she's sped her Citroën over the desert. Likewise British office workers cheer and applaud a businessman who engages in some wild and impossible driving to secure a parking space for his Montego (IS8955). The speeding car offers us escape into a world of play where we can show our derring-do, our skills, and perhaps find again the pleasures of being a child.

The other cluster of meanings is quite different. Imagine you're a successful British businessman leaving work. There's some classical music playing gently in the background. You signal your Peugeot 605 and the door unlocks, only for you. You settle in and lean back. Already the day's cares are slipping off your tired shoulders. As you calmly drive through the city streets, which are strangely empty of traffic, you see on the sidewalk hordes of pedestrians rushing crazily by. Indeed, everything else is speeded-up: above you cranes twirl, beneath a bridge trains shoot by, around you factories belch smoke – but nothing touches you, and when you hit the highway, you simply raise the window to isolate yourself from the traffic. You can even set your own temperature by pressing a button. Eventually you reach your mansion in the countryside, well rested by this peaceful drive. A voice-over tells you, 'Relax as the world flies by.' You've just experienced the life celebrated in *Relax* (C91022).

Here the car is not a toy but a womb, a warm, comforting, safe refuge against the turmoil of the world outside. The most advanced engineering, we're promised, has been assigned the task of protecting you, the driver or passenger. Volvo has become a bit notorious around the world for its demonstrations of how tough its design is, so much so that in an Australian (C84079) and an American (C88016) ad it spoofs its own reputation. Mercedes-Benz makes a similar but more serious claim in two separate ads, one South African and the other Australian. What purports to be a reenactment, *Chapmans Peak* (C90087), shows how one Christopher White dropped 100 metres off a highway and lived, thanks to his seat-belt and his car. Another 'true story,' *Safety Car Crash* (C91086), tells how a family survived a head-on collision because of the safety devices built into the Mercedes-Benz; the camera, meanwhile, circles around the car to display its front destroyed but the rest of the car largely intact. 'Engineered like no other car in the world,' able to protect you against your mistakes or those of others.

Unchanging reliability has been the continuing theme of an imaginative Volkswagen campaign in Britain. In *Casino* (C86046), we see a handsome, well-off, but clearly unfortunate playboy who has made a lot of mistakes in his life: he lost 'a million' on black, he married 'a sex kitten just as she turned into a cat,' he 'moved into gold just as the clever money moved out.' But he does drive a Volkswagen Golf – 'Everyone must have something in life he can rely on.' The analogy of the womb, however, best suits a moody, black-and-white spot entitled *God Bless the Child* (IS9111) where a little girl walks with her dad through the big city. She witnesses a harangue by a street preacher, a man cursing his stalled car, a police arrest, she hears the hustle and bustle around her, she looks up at the tall buildings – all images of a world of turmoil, even of threat. Then mom arrives in a gleaming Volkswagen Passat, and the girl gets in safe and sound, happy in her place of comfort. 'If only everything in life was as reliable as Volkswagen,' laments the on-screen text. Here the car has become one solution to a world gone awry, a source of security in times when little else can be counted upon.

If cars are often 'boy's toys,' then cosmetics are 'a girl's best friend.' Consider *Don't Cry Baby* (C87022), an Israeli ad for Helena Rubinstein's cosmetics, which gives expression to what's been called the beauty myth. It is a story of transformation without any voice-over but instead a woman's song, presumably Etta James's hit 'Don't Cry, Baby,' playing throughout. The initial scenes are in black and white, showing a young woman in her slip, sitting in front of a mirror, obviously distraught. Attached to the mirror is a photograph of a handsome, smiling man, looking out at her, a sign of her man and of the male gaze. She opens a small bottle of cream and, lo and behold, colour begins to enter the picture. We watch her apply facial cream, eye shadow, mascara, lipstick, until she emerges looking poised, self-confident, and beautiful. She expresses her new mood by using the lipstick to doodle on the photograph of her man. We see her finally in an evening dress, her earrings in place, her hair perfect, spraying on perfume, ready to conquer her world.

Implicit in *Don't Cry Baby* is the presumption that a woman's face can become a work of art. That's represented best in ads from Shiseido (Japan) and Anaïs Anaïs (France). *Night Blue* (C87070) surrounds a heavily made-up woman with the sounds and masks of Africa, creating as it were a portrait of beauty. *Images* (C84085) displays a collection of faces that are apparently withdrawn from reality, caught up in a trance, perhaps, an image heightened by classical music, softened pictures, and the way the women touch themselves. *Secrets* (C88039) gives us close-ups of women in a world of their own, sharing some sort of knowledge that's never specified. Running through each of the commercials are signs that speak of delicacy (the flowers in *Secrets*), wonder (the wide-eyed look of one woman in *Images*), and serenity (the static pose of the woman in *Night Blue*). You get the feeling, especially in *Secrets* and *Night Blue*, that these women know, indeed relish, their beauty, and their glance beckons the female viewer to join them in this enchanted place where Art reigns.

Much more obvious in *Don't Cry Baby* is the motif of transformation, where a woman's look is changed for the better. That too is played out in different ways. Sometimes the woman's face is a canvas on which someone creates images of beauty. So in *Changes 'Makeup'* (C85007) and *Skincare* (C85008), two British ads, we see only the face of a young woman upon whom changes in colour, shape, and look are registered magically by some unseen hand. Another Shiseido ad, *White Make-Up* (C85036), shows a man making up the woman, presumably for some theatrical performance. But more often the woman is active, able to transform her own image. Yet a third Shiseido winner (C86114) stations its woman at a richly embellished cosmetic table, rococo in style (signifying art), where she gently and slowly enhances the beauty of her face. That same sort of representation is given a much more joyous cast in a Brazilian spot for Max Factor (C88085), where a supposedly ugly woman (she's not, by the way) turns herself cute. And the ever-witty British give a humorous twist to the motif in *Identikit* (C88061), where a woman changes her appearance constantly to fool a male pursuer. Nothing's impossible: the right cosmetics allow any woman to adopt whatever mask she wishes to present to the world.

Why she would do so, of course, is to win the admiration of others, notably of men. This motif of feminine power is apparent but muted in *Don't Cry Baby*. Typically Shiseido's *Perspective* (C89039) cloaks the promise in a fantasy: a fully transformed woman, demure yet confident, wanders into a room full of male Greek statues, which awaken to her presence – they look, they turn, they reach out, and she smiles. In more obvious commercials a woman excites the desire of a street urchin (Italian, S8961), destroys the composure of a male interviewer (German, C86058), and turns men into her worshippers (French, C87105). But by far the best presentation I found is *Monument* (C87069), a story of infidelity sponsored by none other than Chanel No. 5. Here, Carole Bouquet ('Je suis Chanel Numero Cinq') is apparently the possession of a tycoon, obviously an older man of wealth and power, stationed in his office atop a skyscraper, who has showered her with gifts; her looks and charms excite the desire of a young, handsome gas station attendant, left pondering his hopeless passion; and she travels into what looks like the American West to meet a mature, rugged lover who delivers the kiss of admiration upon her perfect lips. Carole Bouquet is a lot more than beauty personified: she is a woman of class, quality, style, the mistress of her own destiny because she is able to command the desires of all men.

Whether it's Chanel, Shiseido, Rimmel, Max Factor, Cacharel, whoever the sponsor, these celebrations of cosmetics embody motifs that cut across the boundaries of nation and language. Multiply their efforts a thousandfold and you get the full impact of international advertising on television. It is a source of meanings, an aspect of the Superculture, an agent of capitalism that is spreading an enticing embrace across an increasingly larger expanse of the globe.

6

The Captivated Viewer and Other Tales

'I shop therefore I am.'
'Buy me, I'll change your life.'

— Barbara Kruger, 1984 and 1987

Commentators are forever trying to work up a sense of wonder and sometimes horror at the sheer amount of time we spend with television commercials. The listing of great numbers is usually prologue to an argument about the awesome power of commercials, the way advertising has taken over the culture, or the increasing discontent of the consumer. We are told by NBC's 'Sex, Buys & Advertising' that the 'average American' (whoever that is) is 'bombarded' by 1,000 commercials a week, and by writer Martin Mayer that altogether the American networks air over 6,000 commercials a week. In *The Independent* (6 March 1991), Winston Fletcher, an English advertising man, claims 'average' Britons watch between two and a half and three hours of commercials a week. The *New York Times* (31 March 1991) cites the American ad-maker Gary Goldsmith, who asserts that some 13,000 commercials – most 'stultifyingly boring' – will be 'forced' on the 'average' American viewer each year; the Canadian journalist Jim Bawden, writing in Toronto's *StarWeek* (13–20 April 1991), worries that his neighbour's kid sees around 20,000 TV spots a year; and critic Mark Dery for the journal *Adbusters Quarterly* (vol. 2, no. 1) laments the fact that the 'average citizen' of the United States watches 32,000 ads. So we should hardly be surprised by Kalle Lasn's claim, also in *Adbusters Quarterly* (vol. 1, no. 4), that the 'brain' of the 'typical' high school graduate in North America is 'shot' by viewing 350,000 commercials. This person will have seen one million commercials by the age of forty, according to Neil Postman, with another million to look forward to before the first pension cheque arrives.

Making sense of these statistics is not easy. First, they measure only exposure, not consumption: a count of viewing hours will allow an observer to guess how many commercials a person might see, but not how many he or she actually watches or listens to. Second, they presume there is such a creature as the average viewer: forgotten is the import of gender, age, class, and so on. Third, they employ variations of the myth of the Captivated Viewer and its opposites, the Bored or Angry Viewer: we are asked to accept that audiences have a common response to the wave of commercials that engulf them. It isn't that simple.

(Inserted throughout the chapter are anonymous opinions of various students. I teach a lecture course on the history of advertising at the University of Toronto. In January of 1991 and again in 1992, just as the course began, I carried out surveys of students' opinions about advertising, particularly television commercials – in short, before they'd been influenced by my views about advertising. These students are mostly in their early twenties, divided about equally between women and men, all enjoying at least two years of university experience, but coming from a variety of ethnic backgrounds that reflects the multicultural character of the city. I make no claims about these students being representative of the wider society. But their opinions mirror views here and abroad about advertising.)

A Marketing Tool?

'What I want to know is how many cameras is that commercial going to sell?' So said Doug Harvey, general manager of the U.S. and Canadian Photographic Division of Kodak in 1980, just after he had finished reviewing three commercials. Listeners only chuckled. But storyteller Roger Morrison thought Harvey's question could soon be answered, that before long research could indicate which commercial would sell 150,000 or 200,000 cameras.

The purpose of any advertising, as Martin Mayer has emphasized, is to give a brand name 'added value,' to convince consumers *this* garbage bag really is stronger than its rivals or *that* hair shampoo makes its users sexy. 'The president of Revlon is reputed to have said,' claimed William Thorsell in the *Globe and Mail* (19 October 1991), '"We manufacture perfume, but our customers buy hope."' Advertisers like television because of its ability to add glamour and excitement to their message, its broad reach into the homes of the nation, and above all the way it can engage an audience. Studies have confirmed the common sense view that watching TV can be 'almost physically compelling,' note researchers Patrick Barwise and Andrew Ehrenberg: 'If we are in a room with a television set on, our eyes are almost continually drawn to the screen. We are so made that we are attracted by a moving picture with sound.'

Though seeing isn't necessarily believing, pictures do enjoy a greater credibility than words. Not only do we 'lack the ability to argue with pictures,' claims advertising historian Roland Marchand, we do not 'approach' pictures with the same 'feelings of insecurity and distrust' that affect our response to words. 'If you have a story that isn't a story, if you have to deal in clouds like perfumes and stuff, if you have an emotional story to tell,' mused Marty Myers, a Canadian ad-maker, cited in *Social Communication in Advertising*, 'your best bet is probably the right-brain medium, which is clearly television.' That way you are more likely to leave an imprint on the consumer's mind.

The task of making that impact has become enormously expensive. Back in the days of black and white television, it was still possible to create an effective commercial cheaply: McCann-Erickson's *Obsession*, a 1965 ad for Rose Brand Pickles, won both a Bessie and Canada's first international award, and cost about $6,000. Since then, the increased sophistication of television programming, plus the clutter of competing ads, has meant agencies must spend much larger sums to produce commercials that will stand out. By the mid-1980s average costs were roughly $200,000 in the United States, £50,000 in Britain, and $100,000 in Canada, reaching $150,000 by 1992. The estimated costs of the most famous commercials could be much higher. According to Eric Clark, £600,000 was spent for British Airways' *Manhattan Landing*. When the Beer Wars heated up in Canada's big Ontario market in the mid-1980s, rumour had it that production costs for the new style of music video spots were over $400,000. Overall, the result has been advertisements boasting production values and a look and feel that are sometimes far superior to those of the host program, especially outside North America. Even there, audiences have often told investigators that the most polished ads are better than the regular fare of sitcoms and cop stories.

Once the agency has made the commercial, it has to spend a lot more of the advertiser's money to buy airtime. Bulova Watches only had to pay $9 for the first spot ever broadcast on NBC's fledgling New York station in 1941. Things soon changed. Annual grumbling about escalating costs has long been a ritual in agency circles. Nowadays television networks sell the agency a small portion of the audience's 'watching time' (in the words of Sut Jhally) at the highest possible profit, which varies according to the time of day, audience size, and at times the demographic make-up of this audience. So in 1990, reported the *New York Times Magazine* (25 November 1990), NBC charged buyers $400,000 for each of eight thirty-second spots on its top-ranked 'The Cosby Show.' And CBS, according to the *New York Times* (19 January 1992), was looking for $850,000 for a similar spot on its 1992 Super Bowl broadcast, traditionally the single most watched show in the television year.

Agencies find they must pay to saturate the airwaves with their message to ensure it will reach the evasive viewer. All of this can mount up when the advertiser plans a major campaign. Eric Clark guessed that Pepsi-Cola spent around $65 million, commencing in the spring of 1986, to air its two Michael Jackson commercials worldwide: $15 million for Jackson, $2 million apiece for the commercials, and close to $50 million for TV time. The making and placing of commercials for any national or international campaign has become a rich person's game.

This whole process produces a series of commercial clusters that in the case of North America, and at times in Britain, break the flow of an evening's viewing. On Sunday, 2 December 1990 viewers glued to London ITV between 6 and 11 PM could have seen almost thirty-eight minutes of commercial time, composed of eighty-three separate messages, many for products or companies familiar to North Americans: Volkswagen, Heineken Lager and Miller Lite, Seiko watches, Esso, Estée Lauder, Eternity and Obsession for Men, Rowntree's Black Magic, Atari Computers – though the tobacco ads for Hamlet and Grandee Cigars would have seemed very strange. Putting your commercial in a cluster with six or seven other ads is far from ideal. Still most of these commercials were run only once, a few twice, which is a contrast with North American practice, where it is all too possible for a viewer to see the same commercial four times in the course of watching a movie. 'I'm convinced the biggest reason people tune out during commercial breaks is that they're fed up with seeing the same @*%! ad for the umpteenth time,' claimed business journalist Jim McElgunn in *Marketing* (10 June 1991).

Ironically, the companies willing to pay the huge sums necessary find that there is a lot they cannot say on television. Even though surveys demonstrate that people think advertisers can get away with murder – one Canadian investigation found half of the respondents believed the ad-makers could 'say or show almost anything they like' – in fact television advertising is the most regulated brand of commercial speech. In December 1990, Britain's Independent Television Commission issued an updated 'Code of Advertising Standards and Practices,' which ran to forty-one pages of bans, warnings, and guidelines, plus an appendix with the titles of forty-three separate laws regulating ad content. Some kinds of advertising are banned altogether in many countries: cigarettes disappeared early from the airwaves in Britain (1965), the United States (1971), and Canada (1972). Others are very severely restricted: ads for kids are often limited to a certain time, prevented from using certain techniques or testimonials and, in the case of Quebec, banned if aimed at children under thirteen. A range of government agencies and network boards subject ads to a system of preclearance: NBC's own documentary 'Sex, Buys & Advertising' (1990) claimed that seven people at the network reviewed 45,000 scripts and storyboards each year. In Britain a Philips 1987 Softone ad, *Windows*, was recut because it included some frightening scenes of a woman menaced at night, as was Peugeot's 1988 *Cane*, which originally used a sequence showing a man who intentionally sets fire to a cane field. The diversity of advertising codes in the countries of western Europe is the chief reason why ad-makers feel that community-wide television campaigns will remain more an ideal than a reality in the newly integrated European market.

The general rule, stated in the British guidelines, may seem straightforward: 'Television advertising should be legal, decent, honest and truthful.' When advertising isn't, the offender can be hauled before the courts in Britain and elsewhere. The *Globe and Mail* (12 February 1991) reported that early in 1991, the Provincial Division of the Ontario Court fined Remington $75,000 for 1988 ads claiming one of their shavers shaved closer than rivals, something it had not proved.

The emphasis upon truth in advertising has pushed some ad-makers away from making commercials laden with facts towards image advertising. In short Pepsi could not say Coke will make you old, a proposition that is impossible to prove; but Pepsi did offer *Shady Acres*, which showed seniors gyrating to rock music when they drank Pepsi, while students at a fraternity house played bingo and slept when they consumed the Coke meant for the retirement home.

The Acceptance of Advertising

Advertising is a necessary evil. It is is the price of watching television which is otherwise free. It also subsidizes newspapers and magazines. It is an irritant as even the most entertaining advertising becomes stale through overexposure. But when one considers that the option of turning the page or changing the channel is always available, it is difficult to be more than slightly irritated over the interruption of one's reading, listening, or viewing enjoyment.   Male, 1991

It seems that advertising has become firmly entrenched in our society, so that while we may not at times appreciate being told to buy, buy, buy, at other times we make use of the information we get from them.   Female, 1991

But no amount of money and creativity can guarantee the ad will have the desired effect. An extensive survey of the attitudes and behaviours of over 3,000 Canadians in 1976, sponsored by the Canadian Radio-television and Telecommunications Commission (CRTC), revealed much about how people say they handle television and commercials. The researchers decided that the use made of television was 'more casual than purposive in nature.' Indeed, 21 per cent of the people often ate meals in front of the little screen, nearly half fell asleep when it was on, and fully six out of ten occasionally or often did 'other things' while watching. Although most were willing to accept commercials because they paid for the programming, they were annoyed by the number of ad clusters, the way they interrupted programs, the loudness of the voices and the music, and the supposed insults they offered to the intelligence or the sensibilities of viewers. (If this seems familiar, that's not surprising – look back to the Steiner survey of 1960.) Just as important, they were wont to avoid commercials: 86 per cent claimed they occasionally or often left the room during a commercial break, about the same proportion might do something other than watch TV, and a third often flipped to another channel.

The Allergic Response

Certainly I object to the presence of advertisements on radio or television; they interrupt the continuity of programming with a frequency that annoys. Thank God for CBC Radio.   Male, 1991

Because advertising is so manipulative, it is hard to watch without feeling oneself either consciously succumbing to or resisting the manipulation.   Female, 1992

A final word on why certain jingles particularly annoy me. Many of the same jingles that I hate are the ones I find myself humming.   Male, 1991

Most ads on TV and radio insult my intelligence. I find them more irritating than enjoyable to watch and try to avoid them whenever possible.   Male, 1992

Much the same kind of aversion may now afflict Europeans, who in the past decade have been exposed to increasing levels of TV advertising. According to Armand Mattelart, a 1988 poll revealed that the numbers of French viewers who admitted to watching commercials attentively had fallen, compared to results collected five years earlier. Not only were viewers upset by too much advertising, and the interruption of news and films, but they were more likely to switch channels, leave the room, or cut the volume.

These findings, like the CRTC data, are probably exaggerated, since the survey measured what people said, not what they did. Even so, they do fit the results uncovered by other investigations in Britain and the United States. Usually people turn to TV to relax and escape, not to concentrate. They become increasingly passive the more they watch, Robert Kubey and Mihaly Csikszentmihalyi found. Barwise and Ehrenberg linked their comment on how TV can captivate with the paradoxical statement that viewing is normally a casual, undemanding activity, so easy it requires little concern or involvement. They added that roughly 60 per cent of the audience turns away from the TV at a commercial break. Little wonder that the coming of the remote control device in the 1980s provoked widespread concern among ad-makers over zapping – 'I watch my teenagers,' claimed Laurel Cutler of FCB/Lever Katz Partners in the *New York Times Magazine* (19 May 1991), 'and they watch with their thumb.' But in fact her teenagers may be unusual, since in American households with remote controls, only about 6 per cent actually 'zap' during breaks in ongoing programs, according to W. Russell Neuman. Apparently, the television experience is so 'passive' that 'even the simplest intervention of changing the channel has thus far been a curiously seldom-used capacity.'

Maybe no more than one out four viewers actually watches the commercials, reasoned Michael Schudson. And he went on to recount statistics that suggest only a quarter of the audience can recall a commercial seen the day before, even when given clues, and less than 10 per cent can perform this feat unaided when a market researcher calls them away from the TV. A more recent and favourable survey of day-after recalls by Cramer-Krasselt Inc., cited in the *New York Times* (6 January 1991), estimated the average primetime commercial was remembered by 23 per cent of viewers and the average Super Bowl commercial by 52 per cent. Even more revealing is the difference between high and low scores: 'Some commercials are recalled by as few as 2% of the people who saw them whereas others are recalled by 77% of the viewing audience,' wrote Neuman.

The Distaste for Advertising

I tend to have a negative view of advertising as it promotes the capitalist myth of increasing production consumption.   Female, 1991

Because advertising appeals to the lowest common denominator re sexual fantasies, material acquisition, etc., it promotes conformity rather than unique individualism, intellect, positive values, etc.   Female, 1991

I feel manipulated by advertising and resent the ways in which it directs our culture and lifestyles. It stimulates commercialization of all aspects in our lives.   Female, 1992

Recall does not measure believability. A variety of surveys, claimed historian

Daniel Pope, have found around half of the public believes advertising is dishonest. Raymond Bauer and Stephen Greyser noted that 'it's just advertising' is a commonplace bit of cynicism in America. Similarly in the CRTC poll people discounted advertising of all kinds as a form of licensed lying. Nearly three out of four agreed with the statement 'You can't believe most of the things they tell you in advertisements.' The old image of the ad-maker as huckster lingers on. A Gallup Poll that surveyed Canadians' views of 'the honesty and ethical standards' of assorted professions ranked advertising executives at the bottom, just slightly above the much maligned members of Parliament (*Toronto Star*, 3 August 1992). That's one reason for the popularity of ironic appeals that offered ad-makers a way to get around the automatic discount: since 1984 roughly one-third of the Bessies have used irony, more than double the proportion from 1973 through 1983.

There is a wealth of research data to assist the advertiser and the agency in planning a campaign to seduce the consumer. In 1989 Backer Spielvogel Bates Worldwide Inc. offered its 'Global Scan Fact Sheet,' the results of a questionnaire answered by over 15,000 people in fourteen countries with 'over 250 readings on values, attitudes, lifestyles and media behavior,' pertinent to both the global and local markets. The agency employed a variant of the very common Values and Life Styles system to classify global consumers into six segments: Strivers (26 per cent), Achievers (22 per cent), Pressured (13 per cent), Traditionals (16 per cent), Adaptors (18 per cent), and Unassigned (5 per cent). Its press release listed a number of sample predictions about the 1990s: that a world cuisine will emerge, that light foods will gain new popularity, that consumers will become more materialistic, that marketers should emphasize how products will 'enable consumers to control their lives.' Presumably buying the service (this fact sheet was in the Campbell Soup Oral History and Documentation Project in Washington) would offer clients more precise data.

Advertisers conduct or contract studies specific to their particular brands or campaigns. Psychologists and even anthropologists are hired to investigate the habits, tastes, and attitudes of the target group. In 1988 Sunkist launched its first set of animated TV spots in North America aimed specifically at children because the organization had learned, *Marketing* (7 January 1991) claimed, that 'people in households with children tend to eat more oranges.' Early in 1991 Canadian Airlines mounted a new television campaign which addressed the fact that most frequent fliers found air travel unpleasant by promising 'a more thoughtful and responsive business travel service,' claimed Ira Matathia of Chiat/Day/Mojo in a *Toronto Star* report (21 February 1991). Ironically market research led Canada's banks to plan quite different ways to attract customers in 1991, according to the *Financial Times of Canada* (20 May 1991):

the Bank of Montreal, Scotiabank, and Toronto Dominion intended 'the warm and cuddly approach' to suggest their concern for people, whereas the CIBC and the Royal Bank were framing a 'hard-line' promotion of their array of different services.

Advertisers hire agencies or special research firms to analyse just how consumers respond to commercials, before and after they have aired. In 1982 ASI Research, Inc. examined five Federal Express commercials, in part to learn whether two entries with a different 'tonality – relatively straight-sell, presenter dialogue' – were as effective as the normal humorous sell (they weren't). Recently the *Toronto Star* (22 April 1991) discovered that Research Systems Corp., an American firm, had extended its operations to Canada to test whether made-in-America commercials 'that sizzle south of the border' would 'fizzle when they reach the Great White North.' In both cases the investigators employed fairly standard techniques of questionnaires and discussion to discover how people felt. In *The Want Makers*, however, Eric Clark outlined a range of more bizarre efforts to measure brain-wave activity or physical responses (eye dilation, sweating, even saliva production!) via an assortment of electronic devices. In a different vein, researchers have recently begun to link exposure to ads with supermarket purchases, aided by the sophistication of TV monitoring devices, the spread of scanners, and the arrival of the universal product code.

Does any of this research really work? Some observers have their doubts. 'I don't think you'll ever discover whether you have a really great advertising idea,' the creative director of Ogilvy & Mather in Toronto told *Marketing* (14 July 1980). 'There's no way you can test that. You just have to believe somebody, and hope for the best.' After reviewing the literature on market research, William Leiss, Stephen Kline, and Sut Jhally admitted they were tempted to believe 'that in no other domain has so much effort yielded so little insight.' The three academics could not find much hard data on what kinds of advertising would move which group of consumers, or why viewers did or did not respond to commercials. Such claims strike me as excessive, and certainly are not widely accepted in the industry, but they do highlight the inability of market research to turn advertising into a predictable science.

Ultimately the effectiveness of television advertising must be judged by how eagerly the public accepts its messages, which normally means how the ads contribute to sales. There have always been success stories where, with reasonable confidence, one can accept that advertising has had either a short-term or a long-term effect on sales. Short-term: in June 1990, the Dairy Bureau of Canada ran in Ontario the remarkably imaginative series of animated spots, designed by Graham Watt and Jim Burt, which used dance music (especially the lambada) and sexual innuendo to make butter appear sensual. Later the president of the bureau informed the *Toronto Star* (4 October 1990) that butter sales in Ontario in July had shot up over 10 per cent, compared with monthly totals a year earlier. Long-term: in the late 1980s Slim-Fast began to use baseball manager Tommy Lasorda, in print and on television across North America, to testify to the miraculous ability of the company's diet aids to take off the fat. By 1991 Slim-Fast reported an increase in users from roughly thirteen million to twenty-nine million, and was able to claim a 76 per cent share of the diet aids business in the United States, according to the *Toronto Star* (22 August 1991).

Such stories are not confined to the hyperactive markets of North America. Peter Dunnett recounts the impact of the advertising associated with one of the first Brazilian telenovelas, *Simplemente Maria*, in the 1960s which focused on the rise of a 'girl from the slums' who eventually became 'a famous fashion designer.' The advertising slots before and after the show had been purchased by Singer. Much to the company's delight, there was 'a dramatic rise in the sales of Singer sewing machines' and when the telenovela was exported to other South American countries, sales soared again.

It is more of a problem to assign blame when sales do not respond to advertising. A 1983 review of the results of Campbell Soup's 'Project Goodness' campaign to boost Red & White Soup shows why. The purpose of the national campaign, begun in fall 1981, was to raise consumer awareness of the nutritional value of soup as well as to increase sales by 2 per cent a year and per capita consumption from 10.9 to 11.9 cans a year. The bright spot was that consumer awareness had increased (though that had also probably peaked), and TV exposure was the key to that. By contrast, sales had fallen far short of the objective.

There are short- and long-term dimensions to this story as well. What the review does not explain is the efforts of the competition, or the importance of price and promotions, or the visibility of the product on supermarket shelves, all of which could affect sales. It is extremely difficult to isolate one element in the marketing mix to determine the reason for failure. Thus a front-page story in *Marketing* (11 February 1991) noted how American attitudes towards holidaying in Canada had sharply improved since the launch of 'The World Next Door' campaign (print and television) in 1985 – but, unaccountably, this had not yet translated into more visits. Long-term: Red & White Soup sales had been suffering a slow decline for fifteen years, so perhaps the fact that shipments were up 0.8 per cent was a good sign. Advertising of any kind has little chance of reversing a decided trend in consumer tastes, no matter how energetic the campaign. According to Michael Schudson, the consumption of coffee in the United States dropped 22 per cent, while ad expenditures by the industry quadrupled in the 1970s.

The prospect that Doug Harvey's question can be answered convincingly in the near future isn't good. 'Half the money I spend on advertising is wasted,' goes an old lament by an advertiser, 'and the trouble is I don't know which half.' Because television advertising has been so common and so expensive, the debate over its effectiveness has always been especially heated inside and outside the ad industry. Much of the debate has revolved around the issue of whether commercials are noticed and what approach works best.

There is one camp of experts – call them the TV-philes – who extol the virtues of television. One of the best known and most accomplished of these is Dr Herbert Krugman, whose research in the 1960s demonstrated to his satisfaction that commercials for many kinds of goods could bypass a consumer's 'perceptual defence' and teach a message that stayed in the mind – 'learning without involvement' was what he called the process. This applied especially to trivial commodities that didn't excite the individual or threaten the pocketbook. 'The public comes closer to forgetting *nothing* it has seen on TV,' he told Eric Clark in an interview in which Krugman argued that people unknowingly stored the information which could trigger a buying decision when in a store. Certainly a lot of research has demonstrated that TV advertising can be 'effective in proselytizing children,' the most vulnerable and impressionable of consumers, asserted the psychologist George Comstock. He cited one study in which the 'toy preferences' of several hundred boys were 'shifted in the direction of advertised items' by TV between November and late December. That helps to explain why advertisers interested in the children's market in the United States spent $500 million on broadcast time in 1990–1. In a different vein, two investigators, David Stewart and David Furse, carried out an elaborate test on 1,000 commercials, a test which purportedly indicated that a single exposure to what they considered a good commercial could give a brand a '15 percent advantage' in the marketplace. *USA Today* (7 March 1984) reported on two studies that indicated irritating commercials, such as the ads featuring Palmolive's Madge, Wisk's 'ring around the collar,' and Charmin's Mr Whipple, had a greater impact than most spots. But another researcher, Russ Haley of the University of New Hampshire, supervised an extensive experiment (financed by the industry and published in 1990) that demonstrated, he told Martin Mayer, 'if you like the product and you like the commercial, you buy it.'

The rival camp of doubters can, of course, come up with their own research to question the impact of TV advertising. Patrick Barwise and Andrew Ehrenberg were so impressed with the evasive tactics and the disdain of viewers that they concluded commercials have only 'a *weak* influence' on sales. 'We note that people see a great many advertisements but rarely buy the items in question, let alone rush out immediately to do so.' Similarly, Michael Schudson questioned the effectiveness of all advertising, especially television commercials, which he believed (using in part data from press-funded studies) had largely lost their ability to command consumers' attention, because of increased ad clutter since the 1960s. A recent study from Video Storyboard Tests, mentioned in the *Globe and Mail* (1 June 1991), found that Americans' ability to name their favourite television campaigns had fallen from 64 per cent (1986) to 48 per cent (1990). Winston Fletcher, by contrast, felt television advertising was no longer so effective because it had become too entertaining, thus pursuing a line of argument that has found favour with some ad-makers since the mid-1950s.

It may well be that the balance of opinion among big advertisers in North America has begun to edge over to the camp of the doubters. Martin Mayer has shown how during the 1980s American business, especially manufacturers of packaged goods, began to lose faith in national advertising and put more trust in direct mail, price wars, and in-store promotions to generate immediate sales. In Canada TV's share of advertising dollars, according to Statistics Canada, has fallen slightly from a high of roughly 17 per cent in 1983 to 15.5 per cent in 1990. Ken Auletta has noted how since the mid-1980s ABC, CBS, and NBC suffered because the decline of the audiences for their programming led advertisers to shift dollars to cable television and even out of TV altogether. The onset of a severe recession in 1989 has had a further dismal effect on TV ad revenues in the United States and Great Britain, though this must also have a lot to do with the overall slump in the ad industry. And talk about the coming of the multichannel universe (with up to 500 or more options available to the consumer) and the multidisplay set (eight or more channel services resident on the screen) has fostered new concerns about the reach and import of commercials in the future. The former threatens a dramatic fragmentation of the mass audience; the latter threatens to enhance the practice of inattentive viewing and what's been called 'channel surfing.' In short, the prospects for television advertising in North America are shadowed by both economic and technological change. Even so, it's too soon to suggest that the commercial's heyday as the great marketing tool is ending.

Making Popular Culture

Mass culture is what 'they' make; popular culture is what 'we' do with it. The audience for newspapers, movies, newscasts, sitcoms, records, sports, leisure parks, and the like is not passive. Madonna and Michael Jackson mean different things to different people. Whatever meanings a communicator may build into his or her message, the consumer may accept or alter this preferred reading, less often resist that reading, or, occasionally, even manufacture a totally eccentric meaning. This act of repossession occurs not only with television news and entertainment but with commercials as well. That is why the cultural signif-icance of television advertising in everyday life is greater than its importance as a marketing device.

What Does Advertising Show?

For the most part, advertising portrays a larger-than-life image. To this extent they don't really explore 'the way we are,' rather 'the way we want to be.'   Male, 1991

I don't think that commercials present reasonable impressions of social reality because most of the ads are glamorized. But I do think advertising explores 'the way we are' since they cater to our desires and wants.   Female, 1991

It presents an image of that which is rewarded in our society: prestige from the possession of objects, a beautiful mate, or countless friends.   Female, 1991

There are signs that people look upon certain kinds of television commercials with favour. The Toronto restaurant The Groaning Board has regularly shown tapes of Cannes Lions to attract a clientele. At least by the late 1980s, these reels also went on a tour of art movie theatres in other Canadian cities. In 1982 NBC ran a special 'Television's Greatest Commercials,' which catered to the viewers' sense of nostalgia and won number-one standing in the Nielsen weekly ratings. Since then, collections of commercials have occasionally turned up on network schedules or as segments in public affairs shows. In 1992 the six-hour film *Night of the Ad Eaters*, composed of 500 commercials, was showing to sell-out audiences on the Champs-Elysées in Paris. In Canada the Watt and Burt butter campaign, claimed *Marketing* (10 June 1990), actually generated fan mail: the Dairy Bureau was pleased and astonished by the number of thank-you letters from across the country. The *Observer* (16 June 1991) reported that a video of Britain's Hamlet cigar commercials, running since 1964 to the acclaim of ad-makers and the public, would be released for rent or sale at the end of 1991. During 1991 the Saturday *Toronto Star*, the city's most popular daily news-paper, regularly employed Dianne Allen, a former advertising copywriter and creative director, to review ads and especially television commercials as though these were plays, movies, or TV shows.

Creativity

I enjoy ads as long as they are creative. Often advertising is boring for me and I wish that it would change in some way or another so that it would be more interesting. In other words, I find myself recreating ads.   Female, 1991

What offends me is the lack of intelligence used in ads. It is an art form, and no one likes bad art.   Male, 1992

I appreciate the innovativeness and the creativity of European commercials. They seem to have more humour and yet are simple, not overdone.   Female, 1992

These signs, of course, are noteworthy simply because they are unusual. But there is less dramatic evidence that commercials can play another, unintended role in people's lives. Surveys of viewing attitudes and habits in North America, going back to Gary Steiner's in 1960, suggest that viewers always have been on the lookout for entertaining ads. People have been ready to say that some commercials are better than the programs, and willing to admit that they actually make a point of watching a commercial they like. Indeed the Index in *Harper's Magazine* (December 1991) mentioned that 45 per cent of Americans over the age of sixty claimed that they almost never switched channels during commercials. What people especially prefer is diversion and stimulation, rather than information, though there remains a lingering view that commercials should be informative. Market research in Britain, noted Winston Fletcher, has apparently demonstrated much the same phenomenon, a desire for amusement, a chance to laugh. Viewers have remained distressed by ordinary commercials, though, convinced that most are in poor taste, boring, insulting, or annoying. Put another way, experience makes people more discriminating in their appraisal and appreciation of television advertising.

Likings I

Ads I like – most beer commercials. In particular, the commercial when the guys are attempting to 'pick up' a woman in a bar and after they show how it's done they do instant replays. I like this commercial because I feel that I can relate to picking up women in bars.   Male, 1992

British Airways commercial where all the people come together to make a face and the world – great commercial! Makes you feel warm, happy. [The reference is to a British ad entitled *Global,* a Cannes award winner in 1990, which was also shown in Canada.]

Female, 1991

What do we like? Some men like allusions to sport in beer ads, and some women like the glamour of perfume ads. You'll find people who enjoy seeing dogs, cats, babies, or for that matter 'babes' in their ads. Many kids seem to like cartoon characters such as Kellogg's Tony the Tiger (the longest-running character on American TV), Charlie the Starkist Tuna, 7–Up's Fido Dido, so much so that Kraft Foods reportedly wants to produce 'children's shows using their advertising critters' (*Toronto Star,* 6 August 1992). Certain adults respond well to the romantic style of advertising, a commercial that leaves a warm feeling. More fancy humour, though whether they actually like the commercial depends on the object and the type of humour – the Scandinavian brand, for example, would probably cause offence in Toronto, just as the deadpan style irritates many people today. Youth is more likely to derive pleasure from fast cuts and heavy rock, which create the illusion of high energy; these are exactly the kind of gimmicks that distress older viewers, who find the excess of imagery too confusing.

Likings II

I find the Sprite, Coke, Pepsi ones humorous, witty, and very clever. They're almost like minimovies.

Female, 1991

These ads [Club Med] have a constant theme of relaxation, fun, exceptional service, and beautiful scenery that captivates the eye. In winter these ads seem like a wonderful escape.

Male, 1992

I like the Black Label commercials because I find them aesthetically pleasing & contemporary. The music helps too.

Female, 1991

Consider some of the findings of Video Storyboard Tests Inc. (taken from the Federal Express collection), which carried out surveys to discover the commercials and campaigns that Americans considered the most outstanding. In the early 1980s the best-liked campaigns were for Miller Lite and the two soft-drink giants, Coca-Cola and Pepsi-Cola. The Backer & Spielvogel spots for Miller Lite took the top ranking in 1981, 1982, and 1983: they featured a series of ex-athletes, and sometimes a sexy blonde, in an assortment of humorous spots. In 1984 Miller Lite was knocked off its pedestal by a down-to-earth grandmother asking, 'Where's the beef?' for Wendy's. Humour seemed the surest way to win the favour of viewers: the Federal Express campaign starring a 'motormouth salesman' scored number three and number four in 1982 and 1983. But there were other ways to please. Poignancy: Coke's number one standing in 1980 owed much to *Mean Joe Greene*. The spot was so popular that it inspired a year later an NBC made-for-TV movie, 'The Steeler and the Pittsburgh Kid.' Celebrity: Pepsi-Cola ranked number two in 1984 on the strength of its spots displaying the new superstar Michael Jackson. Sex: one memorable ad for Diet Pepsi in 1983 showed three women trying on sexy silk dresses ('Sip into something irresistible, sip into Diet Pepsi'). The spectacular: British Airway's *Manhattan Landing* and Apple's *1984* were considered so striking that people didn't think they were commercials. The crucial element, commented a one-time creative director, was breaking with 'the formula,' presenting something that was extraordinary.

An Eccentric Response

A number of years ago, there was a TV spot for Dici brassieres, in which an animated brassiere floated out of its box and metamorphosed into a bird. This was all done in romantic soft focus. It took itself so seriously that it seemed oblivious to the absurdity of it all. For that reason, I found it to be the funniest thing I'd ever seen.   Female, 1991

Winning accolades, though, doesn't necessarily translate into a sales boost. People often enjoy the ad and remember its cleverness without recalling or even caring about the product. David Vadehra, president of Video Storyboard Tests, pointed out that one-third of the people cheering what they thought was the Kodak campaign in 1980 said that they liked James Garner and Mariette Hartley, who played out humorous skits as husband and wife (people actually thought they were married). The trouble, from the standpoint of Doyle Dane Bernbach, who made the commercials, was that these two performers actually touted the virtues of Polaroid's cameras. Nissan's 1989 campaign for its new Infiniti luxury auto featured a spot that was full of beautiful pictures of nature, though not of the car itself, which, according to Gallup, was 'the best-recalled commercial on U.S. television.' Though interest was piqued, sales lagged – by contrast, reported *Time* (22 June 1990), comedian Jay Leno joked, 'sales of trees and rocks are up over 300%.' The *Wall Street Journal* (cited in *Globe and Mail*, 3 August 1990) recently published news of a U.S. study which showed that Eveready's very popular and entertaining spots for Energizer batteries might well be boosting Duracell sales! 'Many respondents in the survey remember the pink bunny in the battery commercials, but mistakenly thought the commercials were for Duracell.' Just as frustrating to the advertiser is a British report, referred to by Winston Fletcher, that kids say they enjoy beer ads, not toy commercials – 'they like zany ads, which are both clever and funny.' The children, like the adults, are treating ads as art.

Dislikes

Eno Commercial – bubbly bubbly Eno! Hate it! Actors look and act stupid – song is stupid!   Female, 1991

Club Med buys fifteen-second ads at the beginning and end of commercial breaks. In every commercial they play a few bars of *Hands Up, Baby Hands Up*. I have heard this ditty so often that it makes my flesh crawl.   Male, 1991

I also dislike car advertisements where the car races up and down hills and zigzags etc. These advertisements just encourage the crazy Toronto drivers to drive even worse.
                                                                                                    Female, 1991

No less revealing are the stories of what people dislike. Britain's Independent Broadcasting Authority (IBA) publishes a monthly summary of all complaints received and the replies sent regarding both radio and television advertising. The September 1990 report listed a total of 125 letters and calls, the majority directed against offensive ads (seventy) rather than misleading ads (twenty-five). There were twelve objections to the line in one Cadbury's Fingers commercial, 'Only the lowest forms of life have no fingers' – eight of the people apparently had children born with fingers missing. The IBA apologized and Cadbury's changed the claim. Eleven complaints took issue with a Carling Black Label parody of the famous Dam Busters Raid of the Second World War, though the IBA noted that the spot had been checked with veterans and war widows. There were objections to a scene where a bald person was de-wigged and another where a fat boy was mocked (insensitivity), to a dog chasing its tail (animal rights), close-ups of 'the female anatomy' (sexism), a demanding child (bad manners), sexual innuendo (bad taste), and stereotypical presentations of blacks (racist). Thirteen people found evidence of harmful ads – one encouraging debt, another promoting an unhealthy interest in black magic, and still a third demonstrating how to break through a patio door. One poor viewer complained the flashing lights on a girl's face provoked an epileptic fit, though to no avail since the IBA could only offer sympathy. A story in *Marketing* (23 February 1981) reported the same kind of response to an Australian commercial for a rock radio station; the ad was removed.

Feminine Products

I am frightened to say I also enjoyed a tampon ad this week.   Female, 1992

They often connote female stereotypes that I don't identify with or appreciate. There are few intimate subjects dealing with males to be viewed by the female mass on TV.

Female, 1991

They're becoming increasingly more graphic in their description of the product and its function. My mind shudders at the prospect of what these ads will be like in a few more years.   Male, 1992

I often find myself squeamish in the presence of a female during these ads. You rarely see ads on jock-itch.   Male, 1992

These complaints were largely idiosyncratic. But there is evidence that certain kinds of commercials, even some specific campaigns, do provoke a more widespread reaction. Women are often upset with ads that insult the intelligence of the housewife or tout the virtues of feminine hygiene. Nor do they care for ads that employ the female body to sell unrelated products, an issue which excited a feminist assault on beer advertising in print and on television in Ontario in 1990. Canadians object to commercials that are blatantly American – there was a small outcry early in 1991 over the use of Steve Landesberg, one-time star of the sitcom 'Barney Miller,' in a Canadian Airlines spot. According to *StarWeek* (21–8 April 1990), Toronto parents phoned the Global network about a Delsym 'hack attack' ad (where the features of the man or woman are contorted by uncontrolled coughing) to complain that 'their kids have seen it and can't sleep at night.' Local residents in the Alberta hometown of k.d. lang, a country singer, got very exercised over the news she had made an antimeat commercial – that was just too much of an affront in ranching country. Then there was the uproar in the United States over a rigged commercial which showed that a Volvo was the only automobile left relatively intact after a monster truck ran over a line of cars. The ad was pulled, and Scali, McCabe, Sloves resigned the account. In Philadelphia the Hot Rod Association took revenge when it arranged for Bearfoot, Predator, and Black Stallion, all monster trucks, to drive over a row of Volvos for the TV cameras. Indeed the rising tide of what is called political correctness in North America (a sensitivity to words and images that employ stereotypes or victimize groups of people or cause offence) has brought a much closer scrutiny of all kinds of ads since 1989.

A Special Peeve

I dislike ... the 'Bud Man' ones. They are so flagrantly sexist and degrading, I can't believe they are on the air. Men should be just as insulted as women. If I was a man I sure wouldn't want to be a Bud man. These commercials try to have authentic looking men but they still have the requisite number of babes on them.   Female, 1992

It is safe to say that most viewers greet most commercials most of the time with indifference, even when they notice them. Usually they are not in the market for the goods advertised. But there are times when the consumer says, in effect, 'I like that' or 'I find that unpleasant.' Back in 1973 the ad-maker Tony Schwartz made famous his principle of resonance in his aptly named book, *The Responsive Chord*. Commercials, he argued, were best seen as packages of stimuli which attempted to 'evoke *meaning*' in the individual. The effect depended upon what the viewer '*gets out* of his experience' with the commercial, what that person believes the message is all about.

Schwartz demonstrated resonance by recounting the story of the *Daisy* spot that he had created for Lyndon Johnson's campaign in 1964. The black and white commercial displayed a picture of innocence and vulnerability (a girl in a field counting the petals from a daisy); an image of impending disaster (when she reached ten, the visuals were frozen and a countdown began); and a sense of horror and relief (at the count of zero, on the screen flashes the image of a nuclear explosion and Johnson's voice explained what was at stake). Although only shown once, the spot provoked a lot of anger and comment, especially among Republicans, because the ad conjured up the image of a trigger-happy Senator Barry Goldwater, the other presidential candidate. Nowhere in the ad, though, was Goldwater mentioned or featured. But he had stated his willingness to make use of tactical weapons in the nation's nuclear arsenal. This was the time of the Cuban missile crisis, the gathering Vietnam mess, and Stanley Kubrick's movie *Dr. Strangelove*. The spot worked upon the public's existing anxiety, evoking a widespread distrust of Goldwater's intentions, if not his stability. In fact, later on, people came to think that the ad had made direct reference to Goldwater.

Resonance can cause ad-makers lots of trouble. In 1982 Nicholas Research International carried out four focus group investigations for Federal Express and its agency, Ally & Gargano. The purpose was to discover what business people, both 'generators' (those who produced letters and packages) as well as 'implementors' (those who selected overnight carriers), thought about the television advertising in the highly competitive field of courier delivery. The research indicated that the respondents were pleased by Federal Express's humourous approach, that the commercials were 'entertaining and memorable.' But there were also negative responses growing out of the satirical treatment of business people. Concern was expressed over the humiliation of some characters, plus the 'implicit put-down or slight' of 'implementors' who did not know what to do until Federal Express saved them. The attack on the competition evoked the charge that such ads told people they were fools to believe the claims of rivals. 'There is a feeling that "everyone comes off looking bad" in Federal Express commercials,' warned the report, 'so that ads could be interpreted as a "slam" both at "corporate America" and at the whole overnight business.' Unintentionally, some commercials had tapped into personal concerns about status and insecurity as well as a sensitivity about the reputation of business.

Viewers interpret what they see and hear on the basis of their own experiences and character: their gender, age, class, race, career, beliefs or expectations, mood, or situation, etc. Commercials that excite one viewer can often upset another: Dianne Allen of the *Toronto Star* noted in her survey of likes and dislikes (18 April 1992) that a number of leading Canadian commercials made it onto both lists. One of the IBA complainers was shocked by an apparent slight against blacks because he/she misheard the word 'dawg' as 'wog.' One of the poorest participants in a study of audience responses to 'The Cosby Show,' according to Justin Lewis, expressed her disgust with its commercials because they embodied a version of the good life totally beyond her means. A man watching an antidrinking and driving ad produced for Ontario's attorney-general thought the surreal presentation suggested that the culprit was about to be electrocuted for his sins – in fact he was already a victim, appearing in a wheelchair. Boeing received a host of thank-yous and praise after it aired on CNN a commercial saluting the armed forces just after the Gulf War broke out. In fact, the ad was finished long before the conflict exploded, and its initial intent was to 'celebrate peace.' But in the new context of war, the spot connected with the surge of patriotism in the country: 'One [caller], a soldier's mother, said she cried tears of joy instead of sadness after seeing it,' noted *Marketing* (11 February 1991). In *Fear of Falling*, Barbara Ehrenreich retold the story of the Webster family, Christian fundamentalists who objected strenuously to all signs of immorality and materialism. During a dinner conversation, the family got exercised over a Dole commercial in which the act of eating pineapple was made oh so sensuous. 'It wasn't selling pineapple!' claimed the mother. 'It was selling sex!' There was some controversy over the highly successful Nike campaign, which employed the ambiguous slogan 'Just Do It' (*New York Times Magazine*, 11 November 1990). It was intentionally open-ended: 'The line, written by Dan Wieden, is a call to action, though the viewer is left to decide what, exactly, should be done.' A journalist rather arrogantly filled out the script by suggesting the ad told the middle class to get 'in shape' and the ghetto class to 'do whatever' (steal, mug?) to get your way.

Different readings, one might expect, would be especially common among viewers living in places not yet a part of the consumer society. So Umberto Eco speculated that a television ad could become a call to revolution in a different setting: while the 'Milanese bank clerk' might see a refrigerator ad as 'a stimulus to buy,' the 'unemployed peasant in Calabria' could take it to mean 'the confirmation of a world of prosperity that doesn't belong to him and that he must conquer.' Actual tests of the responses of young, affluent Muscovites revealed that their experience with propaganda made them very sceptical about television advertising. 'Their interpretations were often quite sophisticated,' noted the item in the *Globe and Mail* (13 May 1991): 'a spot for Listerine mouthwash was seen as a morality play where evil (bad breath) was conquered by good (the product).'

John Sinclair carried out an intriguing experiment in Mexico involving one group of young, affluent students (male and female) and another group of young *campesinos* (male only). The students recognized the rules of the game, judging commercials 'by aesthetic and moral criteria' or whether they were entertaining, and were sceptical about some of the claims made. The *campesinos*, by contrast, showed more 'awe of consumer goods,' responded 'in terms of product types rather than brand names,' and looked for information about 'new kinds of products which they either liked or disliked.' Some even advanced their own contrary readings, 'one asserting, for example, that advertising was an imposition by "*gringo*" campaigns.' Although a fifth expressed a general dislike because the ads 'show things which I can't have,' Sinclair could not tell whether this amounted to 'passive resignation, revolutionary resentment, or resolve to strive for such things.' Indeed, he decided nearly all students and *campesinos* accepted the ads' invitation 'to join the democracy of consumption.' And he concluded that both groups displayed an ability to read the commercials according to their own presumptions about life.

All of which helps to explain how the slogans, sayings, and images of television advertising become part of the wider popular culture. 'Day after day we're engulfed by a tide of commercial imagery, and some of it washes right into our reflexes,' wrote Janice Tyrwhitt in Canada's *Maclean's* (1 January 1966). 'We catch ourselves whistling, or at least recognizing, "Things go better with Coca-Cola," and "Come alive! You're the Pepsi generation!"' In the 1950s Clairol's marvellous question 'Does She Or Doesn't She?' acquired a double meaning, referring not only to a woman's hair but also to her sexual behaviour.

Later American Express's long-standing warning, 'Don't Leave Home Without It,' became a humorous aside that you might direct to any accoutrement a traveller would need. Coca-Cola's 'It's the real thing' came to signify true authenticity: a personal ad in the *Globe and Mail* (22 June 1991) told prospective readers, 'I'm looking for COKE the real thing – not diet Pepsi or any other substitute.'

Remembered Slogans, 1991

That's why the trend today is to Du Maurier [Cigarettes]	Male, age 44
You'll wonder where the yellow went when you brush your teeth with Pepsodent [Toothpaste]	Male, age 32
Coke Is It!	Female, age 23
Lets UBU [Reebok]	Female, age 23
It's the real thing [Coca-Cola]	Female, age 22
Just Do It [Nike]	Female, age 21
Get Crackin' [Eggs]	Female, age 21
Have It Your Way [Burger King]	Male, age 21

In the American experience, at least, such commercialese soon infected politics. Stephen Fox recalled that George McGovern, winner at the Democratic convention in 1972, transformed a famous line from Alka-Seltzer's advertising into his own statement of astonishment: 'I can't believe I won the whole thing.' Years later, Walter Mondale made Wendy's slogan 'Where's the beef?' part of the Democratic campaign. And George Bush became briefly 'the Eveready President,' his tireless energy convincing one journalist in the *New York Times* (2 June 1991) that he 'seemed for all the world like the mechanical bunny with the bass drum on the battery commercials.'

Youth has shown a special propensity for the playful appropriation of the metaphors and meanings of ads. The ease with which kids pick up and parrot ad slogans has often been a cause of comment and concern, but that does not mean they have been programmed. John Fiske noted how children in Sydney, Australia, in 1982 turned a beer commercial into a profane little ditty: 'How do you feel when you're having a fuck, under a truck, and the truck rolls off? I feel like a Tooheys, I feel like a Tooheys, I feel like a Tooheys or two.' Early in 1991, Toronto students took a fancy to a spot from Buffalo where an anxious senior proclaims plaintively, 'I've fallen and I can't get up.' The ad promoted a special device that would enable people in trouble to immediately call for help. Suddenly it became the in thing to say. The slogan was used to name a pub evening at St Michael's College at the University of Toronto. It appeared in an ad for a local clothing store on a rock radio station where the announcer greeted a (fake) call from his mother with the comment, 'I know, you've fallen and you can't get up.' Young people wore T-shirts sporting variations like 'I'm choking and I can't spit up.' The slogan and the image had become a way to mock the aged, an expression of the distance between the generations.

The British author Martin Davidson elaborated an even more bizarre tale of repossession. During the mid-1980s the government used posters and commercials to warn people that 'Heroin screws you up.' Its agency, Yellowhammer, once employed 'the idiom of the cosmetics ad' to show how the drug ravished the appearance of its victims. But the irony was apparently lost on some people, who saw the campaign as a celebration of the forbidden lifestyle of heroin addiction. It apparently conjured up images of self-indulgence, alienation, difference, giving a certain sinister glamour to the face of the junkie. Vandals even stole the posters to hang them in their quarters. What was supposed to caution people against drugs had, in fact, come to promote drug use. The conclusion? Yellowhammer 'had actually managed to brand heroin!'

The Influence of Advertising I

Other people must be influenced by ads or else there wouldn't be such a huge advertising industry.   Female, 1991

Overall, I feel that advertising is generally aimed at the vast majority of the public, which is not very difficult to trick or mislead.   Male, 1992

Children are particularly vulnerable. Recently friends brought their eleven-month-old baby to visit. I was amazed at how totally engrossed the child became in the TV when ads were on.   Female, 1991

Whether people like or dislike a particular commercial, they do believe TV ads influence attitudes and conduct. This presumed cultural power explains why all sorts of groups take such a deep interest in how they or their causes are represented. The Royal Canadian Mounted Police, for example, have taken issue with a humorous Labatt's campaign in Britain using 'Malcolm the Mountie,' who 'always gets his can.' The RCMP called this 'a tasteless image,' and wanted him 'stopped,' noted the *Toronto Star* (21 July 1992). Labatt claimed the campaign had been a great success in generating new sales. Organizations that work for the mentally ill have gotten upset with print and TV ads, asserted the *New York Times* (23 April 1992), which use terms like 'crazy,' 'nuts,' 'cuckoo,' and 'wacky.' Such flippancy, the critics charged, merely accentuated the stigma under which the mentally ill suffer. In Canada, Media Watch continued to wage war on sexism, whether against Quebec's jean commercials, called 'little porn movies' (*Globe and Mail*, 14 April 1992) by one spokesperson, or against Ontario's 'booze ads,' where care should be taken to honour 'the individuality of women' (*Toronto Star*, 9 April 1992) according to another. Change the ad and you change society?

The Influence of Advertising II

I like to think that I am individual enough to not be influenced by advertisements. Sometimes I will joke about it. For example, if I drink Molson at a bar, I will joke about the fact that it is supposed to be 'the way beer's supposed to be.'   Male, 1991

Advertisements do not really affect my life that much because I don't have money at the present to spend on a lot of things that advertising pushes. However, I would buy a thousand things that I have seen in ads if I had the money.   Female, 1991

   Any relationship between cause and effect is bound to be more complicated. The image advertising so common on television works its magic because it draws upon what people believe. That fact inspired one lament by Michelle Barker, a freelance writer who published an opinion piece in the *Globe and Mail* (13 March 1992). 'What has the woman's movement really accomplished,' she asked, 'when an 11-year-old girl watches Cindy Crawford on the new Pepsi commercial and decides that, instead of becoming a dentist, she wants to be a model?' Was the girl just another victim of advertising, which tells us 'appearance – the superficial – is what counts'? Not quite: the fault really lay with her elder sisters. The host of commercials for cosmetics and diet aids prey upon the self-doubt, insecurities, even the misery of adult women, Barker argued. The solution lay with women, who must break free from the wretched traditions of the past, set a better example that would free girls to dream of being a dentist or whatever (but not, apparently, a top model).
   There's certainly merit to this lament: the messages and images of TV

advertising embody the aspirations, the dreams, and in some measure the fears of the throngs of people who consume goods. Even so, Barker was much too hard upon her sisters. Everywhere gender is the single most important resource ad-makers use to give meanings to commodities. The Pepsi campaign Barker mentioned involved an ad that features two boys who watch an astonishingly sensual Cindy Crawford languidly select a can of Pepsi. It appears they're ogling the woman; in fact what's caught their eye is the new style of the Pepsi can. The humour lies in recognizing this incongruity. But was there any necessary reason to employ sexual display to announce Pepsi's change? No more and no less than in some automobile or beer ads: the ad-makers assume that gender differences lie at the core of our dream worlds. Little wonder commercials so often make a fetish of femininity, presenting us with compelling images of female perfection that help to perpetuate what feminists now call sexism. That's why I find the appealing analogy of the mirror dangerous. What advertising selects it also reworks, accentuates, oft-times glamorizes. Recall the slogan 'making the ordinary extraordinary.' This is as much an act of creation as it is an example of reflection.

In fact, the cultural significance of advertising extends well beyond its ability to fashion images of our ideal selves. Ads, and particularly commercials, have become the most obvious emblem of the way of life that prevails in North America and other parts of the First World. The January/February 1992 issue of the *Utne Reader*, a digest of the alternate press in America, published a cover story entitled 'Commercial Break.' All but one of the abbreviated essays cried alarm: how the 'hard sell' was impossible to escape; how advertising was transforming museums, invading the news, and taking over children's television; how target marketing threatened a new onslaught of manipulation. One short piece, an excerpt from *The Christian Science Monitor*, feared that the power of advertising was so great it imperilled the psychological well-being and the traditional values of the United States – 'Unchecked commercialism has the potential to destroy America.' The answer? Avoidance, outcry, boycotts, and above all censorship. The only exception to this litany of paranoia was by Michael Schudson, who doubted the power of advertising (it was not 'an institution of social control'). He emphasized that so much of advertising was utilitarian ('Quaker' and 'Puritan' he called it), and pointed out that the longing for consumer goods was deeply rooted in American history, even before the onset of modern advertising. What he desired was a reappraisal of consumption, 'recognizing a certain dignity and rationality in the desire for material goods.'

The issue of materialism still underlies this controversy, then. It all recalls the debate of the mid and late 1950s, during that first decade of television advertising. How a person reacts to commercials often reflects how she or he feels about the acquisitive urge. Nowadays the critics have been strengthened by the surging popularity of a Green philosophy that champions environmental priorities at odds with a rampant consumption. But the villain has also gained in strength, though its power works through seduction and not coercion. Television advertising is an especially potent agent (how potent remains a matter of dispute) of the gospel of consumption, which preaches that you can buy satisfaction. It's a common piece of sophistry for advertisers, notably cigarette and beer makers, to explain to the news media and politicians that their only desire is to increase the market share for a brand, not to expand the market itself, say by winning over teenagers. More believable would be the claim that they do not intend to increase the grip of consumerism over the public mind. This effect is the result of the unceasing waves of advertising imagery that lap over the collective minds of all generations, whether they are children or adult, rich or poor, First World or, increasingly, Third World. So Sinclair noted that at times nearly two-thirds of total advertising expenditures in Mexico has gone to TV, and much of this is spent by multinationals. You might call commercials a kind of accidental propaganda for the consumer society. According to Peter Dunnett, the charge that 'they created consumerism and unreasonable expectations' was used to justify Indonesia's ban on television commercials in 1981.

One reason for the potency of commercials lies in television's conquest of leisure time. Of course the extent of this conquest varies. Using 1986 figures, cited in *1990 Canada Facts*, the United States had 813 television sets per 1,000 people, Japan 585, Canada 546, France 402, and Italy just 255. Americans now watch slightly more than four hours a day, the Japanese slightly less, whereas the averages are only three hours in Spain and under two hours in Scandinavia. But television is the privileged mode of communication throughout the First World and fast gaining that stature elsewhere.

Another reason lies in the spread of commercial television, where entertainment is fashioned to bring in the largest audiences. Right across Europe the old bastions of public broadcasting gave way after France privatized much of its airwaves in the middle of the 1980s. Perhaps critics like Mark Crispin Miller have made a bit too much of the way the imperatives of commerce have determined what we see on our screens in North America and, consequently, what many others see everywhere else. But TV entertainment does offer advertising a marvellous place to tell its 'beautiful lies,' largely free, as Miller puts it, of 'all threatening juxtaposition' – meaning any contrary evidence of the disorder outside the home. That argument applies with even greater force to Latin America's telenovelas, which offer lush spectacles of glamorous lifestyles, than to Hollywood's creations.

The last reason, and I think the most important, is that ad-makers have turned the commercial into a highly sophisticated form of art. Looking at the ads of the 1950s provokes laughter in present-day audiences because their primitive visuals, simple-mindedness, and earnest enthusiasm so often make them seem camp. All this changed during the 'creative revolution' of the 1960s, and the commercials of that period have a more contemporary look and feel. Since then, not only have ad-makers exploited the ever-improving technology of video, they have mastered the power of the metaphor, the play of contrasts, the motif of transformation, and the strategy of irony. What I've called the commercials of distinction are among the most ingenious, compact, and effective means of communication around. Is it any wonder that governments, political parties, and advocacy groups have come to rely upon the commercial to influence the public mind? Or that some recent consumer ads in the United States, notably those indulging in Japan-bashing or claiming social responsibility, have begun to invade the domain of public affairs? All of which brings me back to the presumption that the commercials of distinction are 'the art of our times.'

The Active Viewer

Recently Rick Groen, a columnist with the *Globe and Mail* (17 October 1991), sheepishly admitted that he had even begun to enjoy some spots. 'More than enjoy – I find myself looking forward to them. Gee, will those yapping L.A. lawyers finally shut up so we can break for an intriguing word from our sponsor.' He was particularly struck by the artistry and the skill of a Taster's Choice commercial, the lush Egoïste ad, and a very moody spot for Coca-Cola ('shot through a burnt-amber filter'). The point is, Groen was taking pleasure from these commercials in a fashion reminiscent of the way we view what tradition sanctions are works of art.

Viewing commercials rarely matches the highs – that is, the emotional intensity and the ability to transport the observer – of what is called 'the aesthetic experience.' But there are interesting parallels. In *The Art of Seeing* Mihaly Csikszentmihalyi and Rick Robinson use Csikszentmihalyi's theory of 'flow,' where an individual experiences 'a heightened state of consciousness,' to outline a model of the encounter with art. Of crucial importance is that the encounter take the viewer out of the everyday routine, that it offer 'vivid experiences' and some concrete rewards. It assumes the shape of a dialogue between the piece of art and the mind of the individual. 'The aesthetic experience occurs when information coming from the artwork interacts with information already stored in the viewer's mind,' they wrote. 'The result of this conjunction might be a sudden expansion, recombination, or ordering of previously accumulated information which in turn produces a variety of emotions such as delight, joy, or awe.' I would add annoyance, disgust, or outrage as well. The authors identify four dimensions to this encounter that, with some licence, can be applied to viewing commercials: the 'perceptual,' a response to the form of the ad; the 'emotional,' a reaction to its content and to personal associations; the 'intellectual,' where the viewer fits the ad's information into her/his knowledge of the product or product type; and the 'communicative,' where our archetypical viewer links the message to notions about the culture.

Do You Ever Talk Back to Commercials?

If something strikes me as odd, I oftentimes remark about it. I usually object. For example, 'Product X can take 10 pounds off your buttocks in ten days!' To this I'd reply 'Bull S ...!'
Male, 1991

Yes, usually only when I have something *extremely* negative or *extremely* positive to say.
Female, 1991

Of course! That's what makes commercials interesting and fun.   Female, 1991

I live in a house with eleven other girls and we often comment, sing along, or talk back to commercials.
Female, 1991

A few years ago Quaker State Motor Oil had a slogan 'Quaker State helps cars last.' I consistently responded with 'helps its stockholders first' both alone and in public.
Male, 1991

This argument will only carry us a certain distance, though. The encounter with the TV ad is chancy and fleeting, even after two or three hasty readings, quite unlike the more leisurely viewing of paintings in a gallery. Besides, we approach ads as we do news, songs, or horoscopes, claims historian Roger Chartier, with 'an oblique or distracted attention that reads or understands them with pleasure and suspicion, at once fascinated and distanced. Belief and disbelief go together.' We gain pleasure or relief from enjoying the beautiful imagery, recognizing the situation or the character, completing the story or catching the humour, evading or denying the message – anger over an unpleasant commercial was one of the most oft-cited reasons for talking back to the TV or radio in the Goldfarb survey of Canadian habits in 1969. Experience has taught us that ads 'play with truth,' that they excerpt from reality and condense that reality to focus our attention on some situation or claim that mixes the true and the false. Advertising is treated as 'a kind of ironic game,' in the words of Northrop Frye, for we know 'it says what it does not wholly mean' and 'nobody is obliged to believe its statements literally.'

Do You Notice Advertisements?

I generally am aware of them, but I 'tune them out.' On rare occasions, however, I encounter one that is so brilliant (such as the 'lambada' butter spot on TV) that I lie in wait for it, with my VCR at the ready, to capture it on tape for my permanent collection.

Female, 1991

Like other works of art, the ad can offer audiences, as Freud among others believed (according Ellen Handler Spitz), 'a safe realm in which boundaries may be crossed.' That is why TV ads can function as a kind of daydream, or better yet supply the visual images that are so important to 'reverie and fantasy,' as Roland Marchand put it. Janice Tyrwhitt presented one such example of this magic at work:

An acquaintance of mine once figured as a happy drinker at a beach party in a beer advertisement. Months later, driving to the airport, the taxi driver insisted that they'd met at a barbecue. The cabbie swore he could remember a fire, hot dogs and songs (but no beer).

'We had a ball that night, didn't we?' he said wistfully. 'Let's do it again sometime.'

The cabbie had appropriated the part of the commercial that caught his eye, making of the encounter an ersatz experience, a false memory. He had used that unknown beer commercial as a piece of art to construct his own reality.

Afterword: Travels in Europe
(October 1992)

Setting: a modern city, somewhere in the world. Protagonists: the mighty Godzilla and a huge basketball player. Story: Godzilla goes one-on-one with the black star who breaks through the lizard's defence and drops the ball in the basket. Then they walk off together down the street, while the victor asks Godzilla if he has ever thought about the type of shoes he wears. The commercial neatly mixes the imagery of the Japanese horror movie and American basketball: we are treated to an amusing juxtaposition of two mythic figures, locked in a contest of wits and strength. The images had been ripped free of their original contexts, though they retained their initial meanings in the new, ersatz context created by the ad-maker. The sponsor of this little piece of postmodern irony was none other than Nike, that famed leader in the Sneaker Wars. Back in the fall of 1992, the commercial was running in at least Paris, Toronto, and Buffalo to my knowledge. The language might be slightly different in the French version, but the visuals were the same, and so was the preferred reading: be a winner, buy Nike. Such are the ways of global marketing.

We understand our lives and our world according to a few grand narratives that explain what is happening to us, whether for good or ill. One of the most compelling of these narratives in the early 1990s is the story of how the world is fast becoming a single community where shared technology, common ideas, and the culture of consumption shape who we are and what we'll be.

'Travels in Europe' amounts to an edited version of a research diary: for ten days in October I went off to Vienna, Budapest, and Paris to watch commercials. I chose Europe because what I'll call the Global Narrative represents this continent as one of the great arenas where the 'new' (meaning European unity and the culture of consumption) is overcoming the 'old' (meaning national traditions and the Communist legacy). My research consisted largely of sitting in hotel rooms watching local and satellite TV at all hours of the day to see how commercials were clustered, what styles they took, the images they employed, and the meanings they purveyed. I must emphasize that I have no understanding of either Hungarian or German, little of Italian, and only a limited capacity to handle spoken French. But my focus was on the visual, not the verbal, on what I could see or hear, not on what was said (although, in fact, a lot of what was said was in English). My purpose was to test just how common the visual language of television advertising was at one fleeting moment in time.

Vienna

Among much else, this wealthy and charming city offered the viewer a TV bonanza, including RAI UNO (Italian), Eurosport (English), TV 5 (French), as well as Austrian and German channels. I concentrated almost exclusively on three German-language channels: SAT 1, PRO 7, and RTL Plus. What I found most frustrating was just how difficult it was to locate commercials. North Americans are used to constant interruptions. Not so the Europeans: you could wait an hour or more, especially during a movie, to find a cluster. But when that came, the break might last six or seven minutes: so during a telecast of the movie *Police Academy 2* (in translation) on SAT 1 on Friday night (9 October), the commercial break at 9:15 PM contained nineteen separate commercials. The actual number of ads depended on the time of day, though – a mere three ads on PRO 7 on Saturday morning about 10:40 AM and ten ads on SAT 1 at 2:40 PM.

While the clusters seemed a bit strange, the sponsors and many of their messages didn't. Over the course of three days, I watched ads for both Sega Game Gear and Super Nintendo; Time Life's musical collection 'Spirit of the Sixties'; Toys 'R' Us, Honda Civic, Heinz Ketchup, Pampers, and Silhouettes. The two commercials for Sega and Heinz had English soundtracks, though each contained a German voice-over at the end. Perhaps the most famous ad character of them all, Kellogg's Tony the Tiger, turned up on SAT 1. (Back in Toronto, the *Star* [7 November] told me that this favourite, 'forty years old this year,' had topped a reader's poll of 'advertising spokespeople or spokescritters.') Present also on RTL was Ronald McDonald and even the Hamburglar, the favourite of the younger generation.

Nor would a North American be much surprised by the appeals made to consumers. A whole range of ads, in Budapest and Paris as well as Vienna, used that old staple, the product demonstration. One cluster on SAT 1, for instance, offered an ironic juxtaposition of a Pampers commercial for disposable diapers and a Silhouette ad for sanitary napkins, each of which highlighted (as tastefully as possible) the way their product could retain moisture, or rather a blue liquid. There was an example of the hard sell, this for a collection of sentimental hits, featuring a rapid sequence of pictures, bits of songs, brief flashes of the singers' names, a fast-paced voice-over, and of course the price, though in four different currencies (such are the problems of Euromarketing). Even the romantic style of advertising, little favoured by European judges at ad festivals, turned up in commercials for a cake mix (so easy to prepare the kids could do the job for their absent parents) and a baby milk (where we move from the infant sucking on mother's breast to pictures of contented cows and pure milk).

Those familiar images pointed to something else that was shared, namely the representation of women and children. One late afternoon cluster on RTL on Sunday amounted to a celebration of traditional femininity: commercials for a cooking oil, softening lotion, perfume, detergent, and hair shampoo portrayed women happily doing domestic chores or enthusiastically preparing themselves for public display. Ads aimed at kids involved images of play, featured aggressive children, and embodied a certain disdain for adults. Super Nintendo explained how a group of youngsters took over a TV studio to play their games, which caused consternation and later excitement among the men and women, who naturally got caught up in the frenzied spirit of play. Put another way, the Brat has triumphed not just in North America but in the art of consumer societies elsewhere, and I include Paris as well as Vienna in that comment.

Budapest

Television in Budapest was a study in contrasts. That was like the city itself. I stayed in a downtown hotel on the Vaci utca, which is part of a pedestrian zone (full of visitors and youth, it would seem) where the stores and signs touted brand-name goods from giants like Sony, Benetton, Philip Morris, Nike and Reebok, Coca-Cola, and so on. Compare such emblems of affluence with statistics published in *Budapest Week* (8–14 October), an English-language paper that declared the average monthly wage in twenty large occupations amounted to U.S. $315 or Ft 23,491. I was able to pick up such foreign channels as SAT 1 and RTL, Super Channel (British), Tele 5 (French), and MTV. How available these were to locals wasn't clear, though looking out my tenth floor window I saw a host of television antennae and the occasional satellite receiver. Presumably much more widespread was the reception of two Hungarian channels, TV1 and TV2, then caught up in a time of awkward transition. Viewers were suffering from a two-year moratorium on television development occasioned by political disputes, though both a private foreign consortium and a government-backed venture had just announced plans to launch satellite services in the near future.

'Nothing regional, nothing national.' This was the order given by Clive Pearse, hosting the 'Competition Day' of 'On the Air' (Super Channel, Tuesday, 13 October, 5:40 PM), when he spoke to listeners who wished to win a prize if their phone rang – they were supposed to make a chicken sound! In fact the command suited both the advertising as well as the programming of Super Channel and MTV. I found ads for a French bank, a German-language spot touting Ridley Scott's movie 1492, an Italian ad for Tic Tacs (the candy), a British ad for Terry's Moments (chocolates), even a classic Coke ad with a distinct American accent. MTV carried a Benetton spot that displayed a sequence of young faces, male and female, black and white and Asian, some sad and some happy: nothing was said, though at the end came the slogan 'The United Colours of Benetton.' Super Channel offered a public service announcement for a united Europe, complete with the sounds of children, which ended with an on-screen message in German, then French, and finally English – 'The only future for children is Europe.' MTV aired a Czech ad for world harmony that presented a series of contrasts (live fish swimming/fish skeletons falling or people dancing/people fighting) before ending with an image of the globe united. One language you couldn't find was Hungarian.

Much of the programming on the two local channels seemed primitive, even naïf, by comparison with the flash and glamour of the satellite services. You could find a heavy play, opera, some sports, news, public affairs, a clever bit of satire, but above all lots of talking heads. Apparently a chronic lack of funds meant programmers had bought up ancient American series to fill the schedule. The clusters of ads, each called Reklám, were few and far between. Not only were these clusters labelled on screen, but one daily newspaper actually listed the times in its TV schedule: Tuesday's schedule for TV2 showed a Reklám at 5:20, 5:57, 6:17, 7:00, 7:52, 9:56, and 10:23, all PM.

The off-prime clusters in the morning and afternoon contained only a few spots for local stores selling kitchen knives, rugs, an exercise machine, a record, a kids' game, and so on. The same exercise machine had also been pushed on American TV, and the Hungarian version included the same shot of Suzanne Somers's attractive legs to introduce the spiel. '101 Hits' was a typical hard sell of old American rock from Buddy Holly, Chuck Berry, the Everly Brothers, and others. The exercise machine, by the way, cost Ft 2,999 and the five CD collection Ft 5,990 (or a quarter of the average monthly salary mentioned in Budapest Week).

The most repeated ad sung the praises of Belly Ball, offered at a mere Ft 1,750 by the TV Shop. This device is a belt to which was attached a hoop and a ball, so that vigorous movement of the hips or stomach would drive the ball through the hoop. No wonder one promise was good health and good looks: use the Belly Ball and improve your figure. But the overall message was fun, fun, fun. The spot was full of scenes of frenzy, of excess, of young people happily breaking free from routine – here we see the body in an orgy of movement. Two adults, a male policeman and a female teacher, were first mocked and then later shown indulging in play. Those old techniques of loud music, unusual camera angles, a hyped-up voice-over, and quick cuts were used to hold interest. I imagine this vigorous commercial was made elsewhere, perhaps in the United States, because at one point such words as 'wild,' 'wacky,' 'hips,' 'tummy,' and 'tail' flashed on the screen. Whatever its origin, though, the Belly Ball spot conveyed many of the same messages about youth, fun, play, and frenzy that were so common in the Bessies.

Things changed after 6 PM, when presumably the Hungarian channels managed to capture a much larger audience. Not only were the clusters longer, they featured ads for products familiar to western Europe and North America. So the 7 PM Reklám on Tuesday carried by TV2 was made up of spots for Coke, M&Ms, Wrigley's Gum, Colgate toothpaste, L'Oreal Plenitude, eleven products in all. Sometimes the makers of these and other primetime ads were actually listed on screen, which, by the way, is a common practice in France: the names Grey Advertising, Young & Rubicam, and Ogilvy & Mather, for example, were flashed very quickly at the bottom of the screen in the opening shots of three commercials. The ordinary Hungarian viewer might be deprived of much of the richness of recent foreign programming; but he or she was subjected to translated versions of the kinds of ads produced nowadays for audiences in the affluent world.

Paris

Elsewhere in the world, advertising has often been treated as a debased or bastardized form of expression. (In Canada, for example, it was not included in the so-called culture clauses of the Free Trade Agreement, which were designed to protect the country's legitimate artistic expression against American competition.) Not so in France. Advertising here is widely accepted as a part of popular culture. That Art et Publicité exhibit at the Centre Pompidou was one indication of the attitude in the artistic establishment. Paris now boasts an impressive Centre National des Archives de la Publicité (CNAP), where an enormous range of commercials are housed and catalogued. This institution is funded through the Ministry of Culture, a sign of the official recognition of publicity's worth.

I detected other signs of how enlightened the French were during my research visit. First, the very fact that the commercial clusters are introduced with an on-screen '*Publicité*' and, sometimes, special graphic effects suggests the commercial break is more than just an interruption in the normal flow of programming. The way the originating agency is identified in the more elaborate commercials evokes the notion of the artist's signature on his or her work. One of the French channels, M6, actually offered a late night program on Sundays entitled 'Culture Pub': when I viewed this, on 18 October, the half-hour show looked at advertising that mocked its own form and explored the evolution of the slightly risqué and humorous style of ads for Eminence, a brand of male underwear. The most striking evidence, however, was a two-hour documentary entitled 'La nuit des publivores' on France 2, Sunday morning at 12:30 AM, a repeat brought back by popular demand. This documentary abbreviated the five-hour showing of honoured and loved commercials orga-nized by Jean-Marie Boursicot at the Palais des Congrès back in late February. While the stars of the documentary were the commercials themselves, and these included not only French productions but British, Japanese, American, and even a few from Quebec, the camera occasionally focused upon a very lively audience: people laughed at the jokes, sang along with the music, cheered old favourites, in short, treated the whole evening as a marvellous and engaging spectacle.

I concentrated my viewing on four French channels: TF1, France 2, France 3, and M6 (though other channels like Canal Plus and Arte, as well as a range of cable services, were available to Parisian viewers). Once more, I was struck by how difficult it was to find the commercials. On Thursday night (15 October), during a long police drama on TF1, I came across one cluster of ten commercials at roughly 9:30 and I had to wait until 10:25 for the second cluster of twelve ads. The two clusters conformed to what appears to be a universal design: that is, a hodgepodge of spots for a shampoo, a car, skin cream, clothes, cheese, bananas, detergent, and other mass-marketed goods.

Many more of these commercials than is the case in North America were shaped to entertain the viewer with humour, a particular plot, startling images, or even a puzzle. Consider an ad for Super Nintendo, which I caught twice during my visit. It told the story of a young man who used the video game to triumph over an opponent. The commercial was full of stunning visuals, exemplifying in particular what's called 'morphing,' where a figure is trans-formed into a different shape. Our hero literally fell into a world of fantasy, becoming a mix of wizard and warrior, man and machine, his arms turning into metal weapons as he battled with a monstrous enemy that looked like a swollen spider. The battle was fast-paced, the soundtrack dominated by the heavy beat of hard rock, and the screen filled with coruscating lines of force to denote the waves of destruction the two players exchanged. There were allusions to the genres of both science fiction and horror, and indeed to the whole mythos of High Tech. The spot was full of images of peril and violence, evoking the world of risk that youth supposedly wishes to inhabit. But overriding was the aura of power, personal power, the promise of some extraordinary ability to exercise awesome strength – mind and body were liberated, but they were also enhanced and the pleasures of triumph over the great evil were sublime. Only at the end did the ad mention the name 'Super Nintendo,' spelled out on-screen in thick black letters and repeated by an echoing macho voice. What lingered in the mind was the frenzy of the contest and the seductive promise of power. It was an ad I wanted to see again and again. Super Nintendo had conveyed its message of play by involving the viewer in a minimovie.

A series of three ads for Rodier stores achieved their purpose in a more subtle and gentle fashion by concocting romantic stories of ordinary life. I was treated to the meeting of two beautiful people in a rainstorm, a couple enjoying themselves at a fashionable resort in the mountains, and another couple (or perhaps the same couple – unfortunately I couldn't be sure) buying a home. Running through each was that superhit of years ago by Elvis Presley, 'Love Me Tender.' Here the aura was of love, though very much the love of sophisticated, affluent souls who had both the means and the knowledge to enjoy life to the fullest. The suggestion of class was conveyed through their dress and their manner, both identifying these people as the type who shopped at Rodier.

I found aspects of this campaign, notably the commercial set in the resort, spiced with a hint of sensuality. That brings me to another way in which French commercials differed so markedly from the North American variant. Particularly since the late 1980s, ad-makers in the United States and even more in Canada have come to downplay or even deny that old representation of the feminine body as a sensual object, though there remain many ads (notably America's beer ads) where the sexual appeal of the female body is displayed, often with a vulgar enthusiasm. I ascribe this denial to the rising force of political correctness, more properly to the champions of feminism like Naomi Wolf, who have tried to rule out of bounds the definition of women as the embodiment of sensuality and beauty. I share with Camille Paglia the belief that this is a most unfortunate aspect of the public face of feminism in North America. It is such prudery that provokes an even more unpleasant extreme, the pornographic display of women and men, as in the case of Madonna's best seller, *Sex*.

In France, by contrast, all sorts of commercials assumed the 'natural' affinity of women and sensuality. One might regret that even here the ad-makers rarely treated the male body with the same affection. The very first cluster I observed revealed the French taste for female display: beautiful young women showed off their attractive faces, their lustrous hair, their long shapely legs, even a slim waist (for a diet product). The next cluster brought images of the 'femme fatale' (a mannequin awakened by the smell of Carte Noir, a coffee), the 'natural beauty' (a girl-woman vamping on her bed, who thus by accident presented her legs as objects of desire, all for Wells nylons), and the 'femme naïf' (astonished by the magic of Mir shampoo that so enhanced her charms). An oft-repeated spot for the Schick FX razor, aimed at men, portrayed another 'natural beauty' whose light, white clothes were plastered to her body by a sudden rain, revealing the outline of her breasts and her erect nipples, which caused a man to shave off his stubble to attract her attention – he succeeds, of course. Another ad, this for the shampoo Mixa bébé, put mother and boy in a shower where they shared the sensual pleasures of washing each other, where she even kissed him on the mouth (something I've never seen in a North American ad). I found similar scenes in many other commercials: a brief focus on a mother's legs, their sensuality accentuated by a short skirt and high heels (Opticiens Krys); a close-up of a woman's inviting lips (Sanogyl toothpaste); a lingering glance at swelling breasts (a wool ad); a languid exposé of a woman bathing and lazing in the tub (Fa); a happy soul who displays her long legs and provokes the surrender of everyone else to her charms (Dim Macadam). The presentation may be subtle or blunt, knowing or apparently accidental, sometimes straight, but often humorous. It is the sheer volume of such images of sensuality that is so unusual to the North American eye.

This might suggest that the Global Narrative serves as much to obscure as to explain what's happening across the world. Everywhere I found that commercials regularly drew upon a common repertoire of designs, images, and sounds. I was intrigued by how often the music of American rock 'n' roll informed advertising, be that the Mamas & Papas' 'Dream of Me' (a clothing ad in Budapest) or the Beach Boys' 'Good Vibrations' (Chrysler's Voyageur in Paris). But in Vienna I was struck by the familiar, in Budapest by the contrasts, and in Paris by the differences. Probably had I spent more time in Paris, and for that matter in Vienna, I would have detected other, less obvious signs of diversity. Once I saw an advocacy ad on M6 in Paris which mixed the narratives of Nature (pictures of a green wilderness) and Modernity (pictures of a clean scientific establishment) to argue that electricity generated by nuclear power was a boon to humanity. I can't recall seeing so bold a defence of nuclear power in Canada or the United States for years. Television advertising is the most common form of art these days, and what its character demonstrates is that beneath the surface of an apparent uniformity, there persist all kinds of variety.

Appendix:
How to View Commercials

Appreciating fine art requires more than just a good eye. Commercials are no different. What follows is a brief outline of the final scheme I employed to analyse many of the ads discussed in the book. I have focused on *Global*, a 1990 Cannes winner made for British Airways, to ensure that the discussion remains concrete. One caveat: carrying out this sort of analysis really requires a video copy of the ad plus a VCR to allow repeated viewings. That's the only way to come to grips with all the components of a commercial. Even so, once you organize your perception of ads, you will find it easier to enjoy commercials while watching television.

Summary

Since I cannot supply a copy of the commercial, I will have to explain the progression of pictures and sounds in this ninety-second ad. *Global* was part of a long-running, international campaign that positioned British Airways as a key player in what I have called elsewhere the Global Narrative. It was similar in tone to Coca-Cola's famous *Hilltop*, where the emphasis was upon harmony, friendship, and togetherness. *Global* was divided into six major sequences, largely without any voice-over, but with a musical soundtrack dominated by drums and a women's chant (it was impossible to make out clearly what was being said). The music was taken from Léo Delibes' masterpiece 'Lakmé' (1883), which has been updated by Malcolm McLaren in a track called 'Operaa House!' Only towards the end did it become clear that the commercial was selling British Airways.

The Lips (roughly eighteen seconds long): The commercial opens with a close-up of male and female swimmers, each of them wearing a red cap, and the dominant colours are this red and the blue of the ocean. We get a very brief flash

Figure A.1: The huge lips. (Courtesy of British Airways PLC)

of a woman's lips, slightly open, which segues into an aerial shot of a huge pair of rosy red lips arranged by the team of swimmers. These lips are then shown moving from the sea onto the beach and then inland. The sequence involves seven distinct camera shots.

The preferred meaning of this sequence would likely not be apparent to a first-time viewer. But the unusual image of the huge lips, the bold colours, and the heavy beat of the song were the kind of gimmicks that might capture that person's attention.

The Eye (ten seconds): The camera now positions itself behind what appears to be a large, ancient building topped by giant statues of eagles, once again looking down from the air, to display a second group of blue dots. We get a brief close-up of a real eye (in which the dots are reflected) and then on to a more detailed display of people, wearing either blue or black (representing the iris), who have arranged themselves as a gigantic eye. The camera swings to a medium shot of some of the walkers, revealing a Middle Eastern or Central Asian face of a woman, complete with earrings and a blue scarf covering her hair, the back of her neck, and shoulders. Thereupon the camera gives us

Figure A.2: The eye. (Courtesy of British Airways PLC)

another aerial shot of the fully constituted eye. This sequence involves five shots.

By this time, many viewers would probably have gathered that the ad was showing how a mix of people were creating the features of a human face. But why remained a puzzle, which of course would better serve to keep the individual interested.

The Ear (eight seconds): Now that the viewer is attuned to what's going on, the next sequence involves a mere two shots, both aerial pans, that display people in white making an ear in a large open field.

The Face (thirteen seconds): The camera initially focuses on the line of red, then on the red lips, and moves out and up to reveal an outline of a face with two eyes, a nose (shown as a green, L-shaped line), and lips, all on a very large white plain. The four shots here involve both pans (that is, the camera moves to reveal more of the image) and fades (one image is allowed to fade into another).

The Display of Harmony (twenty-five seconds): This sequence opens with an establishing shot, a focus on a handshake between two males, one arm clothed in blue and the other in red, which amounts to a metaphor for friendship. (One

Figure A.3: A joyful meeting. (Courtesy of British Airways PLC)

might ponder why the close-up was of female lips in the first sequence and a male handshake here, which suggests conformity to the gender code that prevails in affluent societies.) The screen then displays two different kinds of pictures, each of which has been slowed slightly to enable a viewer to understand better and to give the scenes depicted a stylized quality. The first kind involves scenes of coming together: hugs and kisses from people of both sexes, all ages, and an assortment of races. This gives off an aura of harmony, since these folk are so obviously happy, welcoming each other, however different, as members of one big family. Sometimes in the background are bits of a huge British flag, once resting on the ground where all the action is taking place. This sign of the sponsor is linked to the second kind of picture, where we see female and then male flight personnel, the woman looking like a flight attendant and the males like pilots, who are apparently welcoming and guiding people. At times the background becomes almost luminous and some heads seem wrapped in a halo. This, the longest and most complicated sequence, includes eleven distinct shots.

Even if the viewer missed the hints about who was the sponsor, an English-accented voice-over explains in measured tones, his words emphasized because

Figure A.4: The happy face of humanity. (Courtesy of British Airways PLC)

they are separated into sound bites: 'Every year the world's favourite airline brings twenty-four million people together.' That 'together' carries over into the last sequence. Furthermore, the theme song changes slightly to include what seem to be the sounds of a plane.

The Happy Face/Globe (seventeen seconds): This sequence commences with an aerial shot of red lips in a sea of white dots, some of which then shift to push the lips into a smile. The camera moves up to reveal a huge happy face of neatly arranged dots, and one eye winks at the audience. As the camera slowly moves higher and higher to show how the image rests in a huge, dun-coloured plain, the happy face changes into a map of the world, complete with white polar caps, the sea in blue, and the continents in red. The words 'British Airways' finally appear on screen, underneath the globe, just before the close of the commercial. Also at the end, there's a loud swoosh, the sound of a jet engine that signifies both flight and the company. This sequence requires only two distinct shots.

Discussion

The following analysis and explanation identify the key ingredients of *Global*,

Subject: British Airways *Global* (ID: #C90024)

Readings
Preferred: British Airways is the world leader in air travel, bringing people together as one happy family.
Alternate: Evokes images of an imperial past, when many peoples marched under the British flag.

Aesthetics

length: ninety seconds	spacing: medium	verbal/visual balance: visual+
voice-over: male	singer(s): female	direct address: none
orientation: user	humour: none	comparative: no
sounds: airplane noises		music: exotic (rock and opera)
awe: yes	cast: positive	excess: yes

gimmicks: aerial photographs; panorama/close-up; bold colours.
commentary: unusual and effective, changing perspectives, scenes of joy.

Structure

design: drama	quest: harmony	school: romantic (& mannerist)
strategy: emotion	narrator: God	listener: human being

commentary: illusion of the all-seeing eye. Encourages awe and sentimentality.

Metaphors and images
1. colour = races   2. handshake = friendship 3. happy face = togetherness
commentary: both the handshake and the happy face are striking images. The different colours and styles of dress become metaphors for the variety of peoples.

Binary Logic

1. diversity/unity	2. humanity/British Airways	3. harmony/acrimony
peoples/humanity	clients/friends	cooperation/conflict
individual/mass	happiness/efficiency	peace/war

commentary: the way different peoples can unite for a common purpose. Note this ideal works against the unspoken reality of racial/national acrimony.

Cultural References

1. the global narrative	2. the team spirit	3. travel
Specifics: the union of peoples	organized sport	homecoming

commentary: reference to the team spirit evokes memories of organized sports, spectators at football games (in the U.S.A.), marches by parading soldiers, etc.

Representations

number of persons: many	person kind: ordinary
group(s): teams	lifestyle(s): unspecified
gender: masculine and feminine	class: unspecified
race: mixed	age: mixed

commentary: a suggestion of white leadership, given the prominence of white faces and the fact that the flight personnel are white.

Ideology
wants: 1. togetherness   2. n/a   3. n/a
motifs: one world, the friendly corporation.
commentary: ad presents British Airways as a key force in building bridges among peoples, thus establishing it as in the vanguard of human progress.

admittedly at some expense to its aesthetic integrity. It might seem that some of the questions and answers overlap – the reason is to ensure that the critic will do justice to the character of the commercial. This is a case of 'one scheme fits all,' which requires an approach suitable to a range of different types of ads. Personally, I've found that the most useful way to unlock the mysteries of the ad is to identify the contrasts, since these are normally basic to the argument.

Readings: 'Preferred' – what is the overt purpose and meaning of the commercial? 'Alternate' – what other reading(s) is/are possible? Part of the pleasure in watching commercials is to try to discover what may be plausible alternate readings.

Aesthetics: This is a grab-bag category of assorted attributes of the commercial that make it pleasing or effective. 'Pacing' refers to the number of different shots, in this case thirty-one, thus neither fast (at least one shot for each second) nor slow (less than one shot for each five seconds). 'Verbal/visual balance' registers whether the commercial operates more through words or through pictures. 'Direct address' refers to a conscious effort to speak to the viewer, either by invoking the word 'you,' by commanding her/him to do something, or through eye-contact. A commercial may be oriented towards the user, the product, and/or a lifestyle. Consumer commercials usually have a positive cast, while the infamous attack ads of American election campaigns boast a negative cast. The signs of excess, whether sad or happy, physical or emotional, whatever, have become a very common way of attracting the viewer's eye.

Structure: What are the leading characteristics of the commercial? 'Design': a drama (rather than vignette, display, a testimonial/interview), meaning it follows through a progression of events to a conclusion. 'Quest': harmony. What does the commercial seek to gain? Answers here could range from satisfaction to justice, perhaps love, occasionally revenge. 'School': romantic, though with an element of the mannerist because the pictures are so stylized. The music works with the pictures to create a mood of celebration, if not awe. Elsewhere in the book I have identified the other schools – naturalist, essentialist, absurdist, mannerist, and surreal. 'Strategy': emotion, rather than reason-why or irony, meaning an appeal to 'the heart.' 'Narrator': who is speaking to us in this commercial, a friend, an expert, etc.? In the case of *Global*, the fact that the camera uses so many aerial shots and the screen displays so many panoramic scenes, plus the vaguely sacred quality of the music, creates the illusion of the all-seeing eye, which is a representation of God. 'Listener': what is the definition of the ideal viewer – citizen, consumer, voyeur, parent, etc.? Viewers of *Global* are being addressed as members of humanity, irrespective of their age, class, race, gender, whatever.

Metaphors and Images: Usually I try to identify the three most crucial metaphors. In fact there are many more metaphors at work in *Global*. The flight personnel stand for British Airways itself, the brief picture of a Chinese baby suggests vulnerability, the assorted people represent the diversity of nations, and so on.

Binary Logic: My concern here is to discover the series of contrasts or oppositions that are used to organize the argument. I try to arrange these contrasts in chains, since that is how the preferred meaning is both presented and repeated. I search for up to three series, ranked in order of significance, though in the case of *Global* there were only two main series. I should add that you can find in *Global* hints of a very common contrast, between the feminine and the masculine, though this is submerged by comparison with the other series.

These contrasts may be implicit as well as explicit. The last contrast in *Global* (commencing harmony/acrimony) is implicit, because there are no verbal, audio, or visual stimuli that would directly suggest acrimony. Nonetheless such a contrast fits the binary logic of the commercial and demonstrates how the most trivial of artworks can comment on the most significant of issues. Recognize, however, that this swiftly becomes an exercise in reductionism. *Global* is not about peace versus war, though it may evoke such a contrast.

Cultural References: Up to three resources (plus their specific elements) the commercial draws upon to make its claims. The presumption is that viewers will use knowledge of these resources to understand the preferred meaning. It is here that ad-makers can run into serious difficulty. For example, if a viewer draws upon a knowledge of Britain's imperial past or the structure of racism in the First World then, unintentionally, the commercial apparently embodies a vision of a future dominated by whites and Anglos. It is particularly difficult for the ad-maker to prevent this kind of reading when the commercial is meant to be aired in a wide range of different communities. Even when the commercial is shown only in one place, different resources, such as feminism, the cult of domesticity, neo-conservatism, or a working-class consciousness make it hard for the ad-maker to exercise closure on the minds of prospective viewers.

Representations: How are people presented in the commercial? What biases or preferences are embedded in the visuals or the text? In *Global* the people are supposed to be ordinary, though in other commercials they may be beautiful, imaginary, and/or celebrities, each of which conveys distinct meanings. Other possible groups are couples, buddies, families, crowds, or mobs. Among the most commonly represented lifestyles are normal, upscale, youth, child, though occasionally you will find traditional or exotic, working class, even outdoors/athletic.

Ideology: What are the 'deeper meanings' of the commercial? 'Wants': I look for up to three wants and needs a commercial may promise to satisfy. These wants may range from security, comfort, good health, or social esteem to excitement or adventure, sensuality, or even personal power. In the case of *Global*, the focus is almost always on togetherness. 'Motifs': one world. That's the most obvious motif, here a visible demonstration of the happy side of the persistent narrative of globalization. All the world's problems are washed away in a moment of common joy. Riding on top of this, however, is the motif of the friendly corporation that positions British Airways as the friend of humanity.

Listing of Commercials

These listings do not include all the commercials consulted, merely those cited briefly in the text. An explanation of the identification scheme will be found at the end of the introduction. I have supplied as much data as will conveniently fit on one line.

A. The Diamant Collection of Classic Clios (1948–58)

The first two digits indicate the year in which the commercial was first aired.

ID	Title	Product	Client	Agency
D4801	*Barn Dance*	Lucky Strike	American Tobacco	N.W. Ayer
D5103	*Sexy Cigar*	Murial Cigars	P. Lorillard	Lennen & Newell
D5215	*The Great A & B Race*	Bufferin	Bristol-Myers	Young & Rubicam
D5219	*How 'R Ya Fixed*	Razor	Gillette	Maxon Inc.
D5242	*Bear Beer*	Hamms Beer	Theo. Hamm	Campbell-Mithun
D5316	*Speedy*	Alka-Seltzer	Miles Laboratories	Wade Advertising
D5350	*Dragnet?*	Bardahl Oil	Bardahl	Miller, Mackay, Hoeck & Hartung
D5426	*Chicken Zoop*	Soups	Lipton	Young & Rubicam
D5427	*Hey, Hey, Hey!*	Ritz Crackers	National Biscuit	McCann-Erickson
D5428	*$%&()**	Worcestershire Sauce	H.J. Heinz	Maxon Advertising
D5442	*Dry Bones*	Gasoline	Speedway Petroleum	W.B. Doner
D5443	*Hey, Mabel*	Black Label Beer	Carling	Lang, Fisher & Stashower
D5459	*Ladder Drop*	Portable radio	RCA	Kenyon & Eckhardt
D5461	*<u>Can</u> You Be Sure ...?*	Refrigerator	Westinghouse	McCann-Erickson
D5505	*Smoker*	Marlboro	Philip Morris	Leo Burnett
D5510	*Soap Opera*	S.O.S. Pads	S.O.S	McCann-Erickson
D5521	*Sporting Shaves*	Razor	Gillette	Maxon

ID	Title	Product	Client	Agency
D5530	*Bop Corn*	E - Z Pop	Top Pop Products	W.B. Doner
D5531	*Busy Day*	Jell-O Puddings	General Foods	Young & Rubicam
D5533	*Life of a Baby*	Evaporated Milk	Pet	Gardner Advertising
D5536	*I Built Me a Dodge*	Dodge	Chrysler	Grant Advertising
D5544	*Bert & Harry*	Piel's Beer	Piel Bros.	Young & Rubicam
D5545	*Was It Paris?*	Tonic Water	Schweppes U.S.A	Ogilvy & Mather
D5554	*Instant Money*	Consumer loans	Bank of America	Johnson & Lewis
D5555	*Chalk Talk*	Yellow Pages	New York Telephone	BBDO
D5560	*Over the Falls*	Watches	Bulova Watches	N/A
D5607	*Winston Tastes Good*	Winston	R.J. Reynolds	William Esty
D5611	*Killer Raid*	Raid	S.C. Johnson	Foote, Cone & Belding
D5617	*Boil an Egg*	Band-Aid	Johnson & Johnson	Young & Rubicam
D5634	*John & Marsha*	Snowdrift	Hunt Foods	Fitzgerald
D5635	*Battlin' Danny*	Quik	Nestlé	McCann-Erickson
D5636	*I Want My Maypo*	Maypo Cereal	Heublein	Fletcher Richards, Calkins & Holden
D5639	*Flavor Buds*	Maxwell House	General Foods	Benton & Bowles
D5640	*Take Tea*	Tea	National Tea Council	Leo Burnett
D5662	*Dirty Sand Test*	Washer	Westinghouse	McCann-Erickson
D5664	*Alcan Champs*	Chevrolet trucks	General Motors	Campbell-Ewald
D5708	*Smoking Cowboy*	Chesterfield	Liggett & Myers	McCann-Erickson
D5712	*Good Manners*	Kleenex Napkins	Kimberly-Clark	Foote, Cone & Belding
D5718	*Funny Bandages*	Band-Aid	Johnson & Johnson	Young & Rubicam
D5724	*Does She ... Or Doesn't She?*	Miss Colour	Clairol	Foote, Cone & Belding
D5737	*Soup Twins*	Andersen Soups	Heublein	Fletcher Richards, Calkin's & Holden
D5747	*There's Bud*	Budweiser	Anheuser-Busch	D'Arcy
D5751	*Plane in Fog*	Delco batteries	General Motors	Campbell-Ewald
D5766	*Chinese Baby*	Jell-O	General Foods	Young & Rubicam
D5813	*Meet Mr. Clean*	Mr. Clean	Procter & Gamble	Tatham-Laird
D5814	*Cleanest Clean*	Tide	Procter & Gamble	Benton & Bowles
D5825	*Look, Ma*	Crest toothpaste	Procter & Gamble	Benton & Bowles
D5849	*Pour, Pour the Rosé*	Wine	E. & J. Gallo	Doyle Dane Bernbach
D5853	*They Oughta' Advertise*	Chevron Supreme	Standard Oil	BBDO
D5858	*A Lady Isn't Dressed*	Nylons	Chemstrand	Doyle Dane Bernbach
D5866	*Somewhat Subliminal*	Chevrolet	General Motors	Campbell-Ewald
D5867	*Brand New Door*	Chevrolet	General Motors	Campbell-Ewald
D5868	*Boy Meets Impala*	Chevrolet	General Motors	Campbell-Ewald

B. The Young & Rubicam Collection (1963–87)

The identification scheme differs here. The first two digits indicate the year of broadcast, normally taken from the catalogue, though since some commercials on the tapes are not listed, I have had to guess at the year in these instances – such a guess is indicated by the single quotation marks around the 'title' I have given the commercial. The last digits indicate the run order of the commercial within a particular decade of spots, commencing with the year 1980, 1970, and 1963.

ID	Title	Product	Advertiser	Length
Y63077	Jack Benny	Jell-O	General Foods	:60
Y65078	Birds	Travel	Eastern Airlines	2:00
Y65088	Foggy Road	Double Eagle Tires	Goodyear Tire	:60
Y66084	Clapping Hamburgers	Hunt's Ketchup	Hunt-Wesson Foods	:60
Y67086	Devil	Lay's Potato Chips	Frito-Lay	:40
Y67087	'Acapulco'	Travel	Eastern Airlines	:60
Y67089	Shoe Store	Excedrin	Bristol-Myers	:45
Y67092	Deaf Child	Corporate	Union Carbide	2:00
Y67093	9 Months	Watches	Bulova Watches	:60
Y67094	Tax Audit	Excedrin	Bristol-Myers	:45
Y67095	Wrestling	Beautyrest Mattress	Simmons	:60
Y67098	'Lady Shopper'	Trademark	Sanforized	:60
Y67101	Insulation	Corporate	Union Carbide	2:00
Y68102	Custodian	Spic and Span	Procter & Gamble	:60
Y68105	Slumlord	'Give a Damn'	New York Urban Co.	:60
Y69109	Dots	Modess	Johnson & Johnson	:60
Y70042	Montreal	Tourism	Eastern Airlines	:60
Y72056	Torture Test	Double Eagle Tires	Goodyear Tire	:60
Y72073	Karen	Antidrugs	Narcotics Control	:60
Y73047	Front Porch	Dr Pepper	Dr Pepper	:30
Y73048	Silent Movie	Dr Pepper	Dr Pepper	:60
Y73050	Jogger	Travel	Eastern Airlines	:60
Y73052	Gatsby	Arrow casual wear	Cluett, Peabody	:60
Y74055	Partnership	Life insurance	Metropolitan Life	:60
Y74057	Cookie Monster	Good eating habits	Advertising Council	:60
Y75061	School Bus	Life insurance	Metropolitan Life	:60
Y76063	Diver	Lay's Potato Chips	Frito-Lay	:30
Y76065	Venice	Birds Eye Vegetables	General Foods	:30
Y77059	Auto Loan	Automobile loan	Manufacturers Hanover	:60
Y77066	Celebrities	Zip codes	U.S. Postal Service	:60
Y77067	Lunar Mountain	Tang	General Foods	:60
Y78049	Vacation Island	Travel	Eastern Airlines	:60
Y78069	Heads Are Turning	Vitalis	Bristol-Myers	:30

ID	Title	Product	Advertiser	Length
Y78071	*New Babies*	Baby products	Johnson & Johnson	:60
Y80001	*Capri Magic*	Capri	Lincoln-Mercury Ford	1:40
Y80002	*China Shop*	Investment service	Merrill Lynch	:30
Y81003	*Come Back to Gentility*	Jamaica travel	Jamaican Tourist Board	:60
Y82004	*Music Professor*	Cards	Hallmark	1:30
Y82005	*Christmas Wish*	Cards	Hallmark	2:00
Y82006	*'Sister & Brother'*	Cards	Hallmark	:60
Y84008	*'Man in Desert'*	Irish Spring soap	N/A	:45
Y84009	*Leontyne Price*	Donations	United Negro College Fund	:60
Y84011	*Tyrell Biggs*	Corporate: 7-Eleven	Southland Corp.	:60
Y84012	*Crying Babies*	Anbesol	Whitehall Lab.	:30
Y84013	*Godzilla*	Dr Pepper	Dr Pepper	:60
Y84014	*Born to Be Wild*	Mercury Cougar	Lincoln-Mercury Ford	:60
Y84015	*Snorkel*	Seltzer	Canada Dry	:30
Y84016	*Space Cowboy*	Dr Pepper	Dr Pepper	:60
Y84017	*Billy Olson*	Corporate: 7-Eleven	Southland Corp.	:60
Y84026	*Proud Mary*	Mercury Cougar	Lincoln-Mercury Ford	:60
Y85021	*One Potato*	7-Eleven	Southland Corp.	:30
Y85022	*Godfather*	Jell-O Pudding	General Foods	:30
Y85023	*'Red Dress'*	Fresh Start	Colgate-Palmolive	:30
Y85025	*Help*	Mercury Full Line	Lincoln-Mercury Ford	:60
Y85027	*'The What's Up Call'*	Nynex	New York Telephone	:30
Y86028	*Corporate Exec*	Sugar Free Dr Pepper	Dr Pepper	:30
Y86031	*'Body-Builder'*	Sugar Free Dr Pepper	Dr Pepper	:30
Y86032	*'Upscale Eating'*	Birds Eye Vegetables	General Foods	:30
Y86034	*'Jamaican Fun'*	Jamaica travel	Jamaican Tourist Board	:60
Y86035	*'Writer'*	Jamaica travel	Jamaican Tourist Board	:60
Y86038	*'Singer'*	Sugar Free Dr Pepper	Dr Pepper	:30
Y86039	*Creation*	Unisys Office Systems	Unisys	:60
Y87030	*'Goodbye/Hello'*	Long distance	AT&T	:60

C. Bessies (1973–92)

ID	Title	Product	Client	Agency
B7301	*Cutaway Car*	Pinto	Ford Canada	J. Walter Thompson
B7302	*Income Tax*	Toyota	Canadian Motors	Ronalds/Reynolds
B7303	*Bottle Maker*	Black Label Beer	Canadian Breweries	F.H. Hayhurst
B7304	*Raise a Glass*	Canadian Beer	Molson	MacLaren
B7305	*Drayman*	Black Label Beer	Canadian Breweries	F.H. Hayhurst
B7306	*Softball*	Export Ale	Molson	Cockfield, Brown
B7307	*Church*	Salada Tea	Salada Foods	Leo Burnett
B7310	*Pool Hall*	Resdan	Whitehall Lab.	Young & Rubicam

ID	Title	Product	Client	Agency
B7311	*Convenience Foods*	Jell-O Puddings	General Foods	MacLaren
B7312	*Children's Choir*	Xmas shopping	Simpson's	Foote, Cone & Belding
B7315	*Yachts*	Banking	Bank of Montreal	Spitzer, Mills & Bates
B7316	*Home*	Banking	CIBC	McKim/Benton & Bowles
B7321	*Talking Water Heater*	Oil-fired water heater	Imperial Oil	Cockfield, Brown
B7322	*Pizza*	Mufflers	Speedy Muffler King	Goodis Goldberg Soren
B7323	*Jack-in-Basement*	Home heating	Gulf Oil Canada	Vickers & Benson
B7328	*Laughing Windows*	Windex	Bristol-Myers	MacLaren
B7341	*Torture Test*	Telephones	Bell Canada	Cockfield, Brown
B7342	*Connections*	Telephones	Bell Canada	Cockfield, Brown
B7345	*Roller Coaster*	Skiddoo	Moto-Ski	Young & Rubicam
B7347	*Gypsy Caravan*	Europe tour	Air Canada	Foster
B7348	*Friendly Invasion*	Hotels	Canadian Pacific	Corporad
B7349	*England & Wales*	British travel	B.O.A.C.	Freeman, Milne, Bozell & Jacobs
B7404	*Winter Theme*	Volkswagen	Volkswagen Canada	Doyle Dane Bernbach
B7405	*Exotic Bird*	Pontiac Firebird	GM Canada	Foster
B7410	*Fishing Camp*	Export Ale	Molson	Cockfield, Brown
B7411	*Winter Home-coming*	'50'	Labatt	J. Walter Thompson
B7413/4/5	*'Odd Couple'*	Coffee	Nescafé	Spitzer, Mills & Bates
B7416	*3M Duel*	3M copier	3M Canada	Vickers & Benson
B7420	*Boy and Dog*	Candies	Kraft	Foote Cone & Belding
B7421/2/3	*'Nature Campaign'*	Corporate	MacMillan Bloedel	Cockfield, Brown
B7427	*Hot Springs*	Banking	Bank of Montreal	Spitzer, Mills & Bates
B7428	*First Account*	Banking	CIBC	McKim/Benton & Bowles
B7429	*Birth*	London Life	London Life	Goodis, Goldberg, Soren
B7432	*Winter Day*	Habitant Soups	Catelli	MacLaren
B7441	*Grannie*	Long distance	Trans-Canada Tel.	McKim
B7449	*Yorkshire*	European holidays	Air Canada	Foster
B7601	*Durability*	Toyota	Canadian Motor	Ronalds-Reynolds
B7603	*Men's Club*	Service	Gulf Oil Canada	Vickers & Benson
B7604	*Dangerfield*	Mufflers	Speedy Muffler King	Goodis Goldberg, Soren
B7605	*Party Tricks*	O'Keefe Ale	Carling O'Keefe	Caledon Advertising
B7607	*Milk Moustache/ Hats*	Milk	Ontario Milk	Ogilvy & Mather
B7612	*Fruitified*	Adams Fruit Gums	Warner Lambert	Spitzer, Mills & Bates
B7613	*The General*	Smarties	Rowntree Mackintosh	Ogilvy & Mather
B7614	*Spoon*	Corporate	Gulf Oil Canada	Vickers & Benson
B7615	*Employment Agency*	Corporate	Canadian Pacific	Corporad

ID	Title	Product	Client	Agency
B7616	*Fly Away Home*	Lady Bug Shaver	Philips Electronics	McCann-Erickson
B7617	*Handwriting*	Cachet	Chesebrough-Pond	McCann-Erickson
B7623	*Chef*	Real Lemon	Borden Company	F.H. Hayhurst
B7630	*Inflation*	Telephone service	Bell Canada	Vickers & Benson
B7632	*Number One*	Eaton's fashions	Eaton's	None
B7633	*Shetland Sweaters*	Sweaters	The Bay	Cancom Advertising
B7636	*Buick Flying Machines*	Buick cars	GM Canada	Foster
B7640	*Spread*	Life Savers	Life Savers Ltd.	Baker Lovick
B7642	*Woman*	Investments	Royal Trust	F.H. Hayhurst
B7643	*Reunion*	Insurance	London Life	Goodis, Goldberg,Soren
B7701	*Lion*	Hair dryer	Philips Electronics	McCann-Erickson
B7704	*Winter Tough*	Toyota	Canadian Motors	Ronalds-Reynolds
B7715	*Big Guy – Little Guy*	Corporate	Union Gas	McKim
B7716	*Squirrel*	Union Gas	Union Gas	McKim
B7721	*Frenchman*	Pork	Ontario Pork Prod.	McCann-Erickson
B7722	*Party*	Onion Soup	Lipton	Young & Rubicam
B7733	*Clam Shell*	Beauty set	Philips Electronics	McCann-Erickson
B7735	*Souperb*	Milk	Ontario Milk	Richmond Advertising
B7736	*Shuffleboard*	Export Ale	Molson	Cockfield, Brown
B7740	*Family*	Crackerbarrel	Kraft	J. Walter Thompson
B7744	*Jugglers*	Business long distance	Trans-Canada Tel.	McKim
B7802	*Bursting Bubbles*	Bubbilicious Gum	Warner Lambert	Spitzer, Mills & Bates
B7809	*Grandma's Pies*	Tenderflake	Canada Packers	Cockfield, Brown
B7812	*Restaurant*	Canned Spaghetti	Libby's	J. Walter Thompson
B7816	*Family*	Bath soap	Andrew Jergens	Vickers & Benson
B7821	*Big Fish*	Export Ale	Molson	Cockfield, Brown
B7823	*Brother John*	Self-service	Gulf Oil Canada	Vickers & Benson
B7824	*Everybody*	Popcornplus	William Neilson	Baker Lovick
B7828	*Intruders*	Lysol Spray	Sterling Products	SSC&B: Lintas
B7840	*Tub*	Camay	Procter & Gamble	Leo Burnett
B7847	*Wedding*	Insurance	London Life	Goodis, Goldberg, Soren
B7905	*Snow White*	Corningware	Corning Canada	Ogilvy & Mather
B7909	*Soft & Dri*	Deodorant	Gillette	McKim
B7912	*Train*	Electric Shaver	Philips Electronics	McCann-Erickson
B7915	*For a Few Dollars More*	Datsun Sport-truck	Nissan	Leo Burnett
B7916	*Guarantees*	Mufflers	Speedy Muffler King	Goodis, Goldberg, Soren
B7917	*Hiring*	Midas Muffler	International Parts	J. Walter Thompson
B7922	*Logging*	Magnum Ale	Carling O'Keefe	Ogilvy & Mather
B7925	*Tastes So Wow*	Milk	Ontario Milk	Ogilvy & Mather
B7935	*Chicken*	Service	Bell Canada	McKim
B7938	*Harper*	Listerine	Warner Lambert	J. Walter Thompson
B7940	*Working Man*	Insurance	London Life	Goodis, Goldberg, Soren

ID	Title	Product	Client	Agency
B7941	*Honey Bee*	Sealtest Yoghurt	Dominion Dairies	Enterprise Advertising
B7942	*Montage*	Macaroni dinner	Kraft	J. Walter Thompson
B7943	*Art Class*	Cookies	Christie Brown	McCann-Erickson
B7946	*Food Critic*	Cheese	Holland Cheese	McCann-Erickson
B7947	*Power Eruption*	Ray-O-Vac	ESB Canada	Anderson Advertising
B7949	*Flight*	STP Repellant	STP of Canada	J. Walter Thompson
B7957	*Cricket*	British travel	British Airways	Ogilvey & Mather
B8001	*Blast Off*	SuperSteam II	Proctor-Silex	J. Walter Thompson
B8008	*Demonstration*	Fram Oil Filter	Fram Oil	Ambrose, Carr, DeForest, & Linton
B8009	*New Business*	Carlsberg Beer	Carling O'Keefe	Ogilvy & Mather
B8013	*Saddle*	Milk	Ontario Milk	McKim Advertising
B8037	*For Beautiful Skin*	Nivea	Smith & Nephew	J. Walter Thompson
B8051	*80's Ladies*	Eaton's fashions	Eaton's	Foster
B8055	*Progress*	French's Mustard	Beckett & Coleman	SSC&B: Quadrant
B8059	*Coming Back*	India Beer	Molson Nfdl.	MacLaren
B8062	*Bake a Little Love*	Flour	Robin Hood	F.H. Hayhurst
B8063	*Gentlemen First*	Men's Fashions	Eaton's	Hunter Daniels
B8116	*Essence*	Palmolive Soap	Colgate-Palmolive	Norma, Craig & Kummel
B8117	*Ocean Duel*	Special Light	Labatt Ontario	Enterprise Advertising
B8120	*Cycle/Kayak/Arab*	Milk	Ontario Milk	McKim
B8121	*Chunky Situation*	Chunky Soup	Campbell Soup	McKim
B8122	*Electric Orange*	Fanta	Coca-Cola	McCann-Erickson
B8128	*Best of Both Worlds*	Agree Shampoo	S.C. Johnson & Son	Foote Cone & Belding
B8135	*Freighter*	Labatt's '50'	Labatt's Ontario	Enterprise Advertising
B8137	*Hockey*	Quik	Nestlé	Ronalds-Reynolds
B8147	*Supersoft Panty-Hose*	Danskin	Caprice	Krohn
B8202	*Talking Food*	Microwave	Litton Products	Ted Bates
B8206	*Brake Specialist*	Midas service	Midas Canada	JWT Direct
B8217	*April Showers*	Banking	Bank of Nova Scotia	Jerry Goodis Agency
B8225	*Smart Move Robbie*	Home Insulation	Fiberglas Canada	Cockfield Brown
B8230	*Dorlinger*	Business long distance	Trans-Canada Tel.	McKim
B8240	*Energy Efficiency*	Corporate	Imperial Oil	Cockfield, Brown
B8244	*Youth*	Corporate	Royal Bank	Foster
B8247	*After Hours*	Undergarments	Playtex	Grey
B8301	*Swim*	Corporate	Imperial Oil	MacLaren
B8307	*Video Games*	Potato chips	Hostess	McKim
B8308	*Jungle Fighter*	Ultraban	Clairol Canada	Scali, McCabe, Sloves
B8309	*Midnight Rider*	Midnight	Yamaha Canada	SMW Advertising
B8310	*Magna - Disappear*	Motorcycle	Honda Canada	Ambrose, Carr, DeForest & Linton
B8312	*Close Encounters*	Accord	Honda Canada	Needham, Harper & Steers

ID	Title	Product	Client	Agency
B8314	*Moose II*	Midas service	Midas Canada	JWT Direct
B8319	*Toboggan*	Milk	Ontario Milk	Watt Burt/McKim
B8320	*Porch*	Alpine Beer	Moosehead	Ogilvy & Mather
B8323	*Griswald*	Business long distance	Trans-Canada Tel.	McKim
B8325	*Red Tab*	Jeans	Levi Strauss	McCann-Erickson
B8326	*Bear*	Kodiak Boots	Greb Industries	J. Walter Thompson
B8333	*Broken Telephone*	Banking	Bank of Nova Scotia	Jerry Goodis Agency
B8346	*Guess Whose Mamma*	Oxydol	Procter & Gamble	Young & Rubicam
B8347	*Keeps Right On*	Spic and Span	Procter & Gamble	Young & Rubicam
B8348	*Uncle Edgar*	Water Pik	Teledyne Canada	J. Walter Thompson
B8357	*Junkanoo*	Bahamas travel	Bahamas Tourism	PIR Advertising
B8359	*Charlie*	Purina Dog Chow	Ralston Purina	Scali, McCabe, Sloves
B8360	*Danny-Boy*	Purina Dog Chow	Ralston Purina	Scali, McCabe, Sloves
B8401	*Electronics*	GM cars	GM Canada	MacLaren
B8405	*Jet*	Accord	Honda Canada	Needham, Harper & Steers
B8412	*Modern Lunch II*	Milk	Ontario Milk	Watt Burt/McKim
B8413	*Shake It Up – Teenager*	Tang	General Foods	Ogilvy & Mather
B8414	*Workout*	Tab	Coca-Cola	McCann-Erickson
B8431	*It Blows My Mind*	Crunchie Bar	Cadbury Schweppes Powell	Scali, McCabe, Sloves
B8438	*Crunchier*	Glosette Peanuts	Nabisco/Lowney	Carder Gray
B8453	*Goodbye*	Slim-Fast	Stella Pharmaceutical	Campbell-Ewald
B8455	*Boardroom*	Ice cream	Swensen's	McCann-Erickson
B8459	*Steel Worker*	Corn Flakes	Kellogg Salada	Leo Burnett
B8465	*Daycare*	Lestoil	Noxzema	SSC&B: Lintas
B8466	*A Day in the Life of Daniel*	Pine Sol	Shulton Canada	Doyle Dane Bernbach
B8470	*1/2 Price Steak Sale*	Ponderosa	Ponderosa Restaurant	Goodis-Wolf
B8471	*Big Family Part Two*	Swiss Chalet	Swiss Chalet	Ambrose, Carr, DeForest & Linton
B8472	*Rose*	Q-tips	Chesebrough-Pond's	Hayhurst Advertising
B8477	*Hats Off*	L'Image	Clairol Canada	The Gloucester Group
B8478	*Experience*	Hair-dryer	Braun	Benton & Bowles
B8479	*White Water*	Ultrabrite	Colgate-Palmolive	Foote, Cone & Belding
B8480	*Maritime Morning*	Old Spice	Shulton Canada	Foote, Cone & Belding
B8481	*Dance*	Close-Up	Lever Detergents	J. Walter Thompson
B8482	*Kids*	Electric Heating	Ontario Hydro	Foster
B8498	*Hard Work*	Real Estate Service	Royal Trust	Ogilvy & Mather
B8499	*Ballet*	Kodak Film	Kodak Canada	McCann-Erickson
B84102	*Neighbours II*	Canon Copier	Canon Canada	Ian Roberts Inc.
B84103	*Eight Ball*	PuroLetter	Purolater	Grant & Denike

ID	Title	Product	Client	Agency
B84109	*Sears Baby Week*	Sale	Sears	In House (Sears)
B84116	*Holiday Feet*	Eastern Airlines	Eastern Airlines	Campbell-Ewald
B84122	*Umbrellas*	Mattel Barbies	Mattel Canada	Ogilvy & Mather
B8501	*Wait For It*	Coffeemaker	Moulinex Canada	Ronalds Reynolds
B8507	*Dream Weaver*	Nissan 85 300ZX	Nissan Canada	Ted Bates
B8509	*Amusement Park*	Honda ATC	Honda Canada	Ambrose, Carr, DeForest & Linton
B8510	*Dangerous Journey*	Speedy	Speedy Muffler	Grant Tandy
B8516	*Rebecca*	Milk	Ontario Milk	Watt Burt/McKim
B8518	*Lili*	Milk	Ontario Milk	Watt Burt/McKim
B8519	*Harriet*	Milk	Ontario Milk	Watt Burt/McKim
B8522	*Margaret Springs*	Labatt's Select	Labatt	Scali, McCabe, Sloves
B8523	*Dance to the Music*	Canadian	Molson Ontario	MacLaren
B8525	*Dancing in the Street*	Canadian	Molson Ontario	MacLaren
B8532	*Zap*	Coffee Crisp	Rowntree Mackintosh	Ogilvy & Mather
B8535	*Scotford*	Corporate	Shell Canada	Carder Gray
B8538	*CN Group of Companies*	Corporate	Canadian National	MacLaren
B8544	*The Longer Lunch*	McDonald's	McDonald's Rest.	Vickers & Benson
B8548	*Pit Stop (Girl)*	Velveeta Slices	Kraft	J. Walter Thompson
B8557	*It's Okay to Play with an Oreo*	Oreo Cookies	Christie Brown	McCann-Erickson
B8564	*Space*	Rice Krispies	Kellogg Salada	Leo Burnett
B8566	*Traffic Jam*	Impulse Spray	Lever Detergents	J. Walter Thompson
B8572	*Day In, Day Out*	Ultrabalance	Johnson & Johnson	Ogilvy & Mather
B8575	*Softer Kittens*	Toilet paper	Facelle Company	Hayhurst Advertising
B8579	*Flamingoes: How You Can Save*	Home insulation	Fiberglas Canada	Campbell-Ewald
B8585	*Bla Bla*	Montreal Gazette	Montreal Gazette	Kitching Advertising
B8594	*My Dad*	Public service	Canadian National Institute for the Blind	Vickers & Benson
B85101	*Bait & Switch*	Retail	Factory Carpet	Gray O'Rourke Sussman
B85105	*Samples*	Retail	Factory Carpet	Gray O'Rourke Sussman
B85115	*Magic of the Rainbow*	Rainbow Bright	Mattel Canada	Ogilvy & Mather
B85121	*Sea Cruise*	Canadian	Molson Ontario	MacLaren
B8602	*Little Sucker*	The Arm	Panasonic	Cossette C.-M.
B8604	*McDonald's Farm*	ATVs	Honda Canada	Ambrose, Carr, DeForest, & Linton
B8607	*Car Wash Ride*	Gulf car wash	Gulf Canada	Vickers & Benson
B8608	*Space Chase*	Esso	Imperial Oil	MacLaren
B8610	*Nobody Knows*	Esso Service	Imperial Oil	MacLaren
B8612	*Overload*	Diet Pepsi	Pepsi-Cola Canada	J. Walter Thompson

ID	Title	Product	Client	Agency
B8614	*Max Collage 1*	Maxwell House	General Foods	Ogilvy & Mather
B8615	*Max Collage 2*	Maxwell House	General Foods	Ogilvy & Mather
B8616	*Beach*	Canadian Beer	Molson	MacLaren
B8618	*Bear Trap/Grin*	Grizzly Beer	Amstel Brewery	Doyle Dane Bernbach
B8619	*Storm*	Priority Post	Canada Post	McKim
B8621	*Chewy Bar Feelin'*	Chewy Bar	Quaker Oats Canada	Doyle Dane Bernbach
B8622	*Breathless*	Certs	Warner Lambert	Ted Bates
B8624	*Sweet Marie*	Sweet Marie	William Neilson	Campbell-Ewald
B8627	*Families*	Corporate	Catelli	Miller Myers Bruce DallaCosta Harrod Mirlin
B8628	*75th Anniversary*	Corporate	Shell Canada	Carder Gray
B8630	*Mum's Night Out*	Soup	Campbell Soup	Ogilvy & Mather
B8636	*Airship*	Energizer battery	Union Carbide	Ted Bates
B8637	*Rookie (Burp)*	Whisk	Lever Detergents	J. Walter Thompson
B8639	*Edna*	Home insulation	Fiberglas Canada	Campbell-Ewald
B8646	*Family*	Long distance	Bell Canada	McKim
B8653	*Systems*	Retail	IKEA	McCann-Erickson
B8654	*Colour Yellow*	Vacations	Air Canada	Foster
B8655	*Colour Blue*	Vacations	Air Canada	Foster
B8701	*Nice Car*	Diet 7-Up	Pepsico Canada	Leo Burnett
B8702	*Hand of Max 1*	Maxwell House	General Foods	Ogilvy & Mather
B8705	*The Italian*	McNuggets	McDonald's Rest.	Cossette C.-M.
B8715	*Spot Light*	Alpine Beer	Moosehead	Ogilvy & Mather
B8718	*Hard Day's Night Twist*	Canadian Beer	Molson	MacLaren
B8720	*Creative Impulse*	Amiga	Commodore	Ted Bates
B8722	*Mountain*	Silkience	Gillette	McKim
B8723	*Rock*	Dial soap	Canada Packers	Miller Myers Bruce DallaCosta
B8727	*Pool Party*	Home insulation	Fiberglas Canada	Lowe, Marschalk, Goodgoll
B8730	*Zip - Farmer & Wife*	Homes and Bargains sale	Canadian Tire	W.B. Doner (Canada)
B8733	*Sophisticates*	Furnishings	IKEA Canada	McCann-Erickson
B8735	*Portrait*	Panasonic	Matsushita Canada	Carder Gray
B8737	*Growing Up – Jimmy*	Kraft Cheese	Kraft	J. Walter Thompson
B8738	*Corn Girl*	Butter	Dairy Bureau	Vickers & Benson
B8741	*Kids*	Rice Krispies	Kellogg Salada	Leo Burnett
B8745	*Burt & Betty*	Auto service	Speedy Muffler King	SSC&B: Lintas
B8748	*New World*	Canada travel	Tourism Canada	Camp Associates
B8749	*Old World*	Canada travel	Tourism Canada	Camp Associates
B8750	*Chuck & I*	Chiclets	Adams Brands	J. Walter Thompson
B8752	*U.S. & Them*	Chiclets	Adams Brands	J. Walter Thompson
B8760	*Sign Language*	Corn Flakes	Kellogg Salada	Leo Burnett

ID	Title	Product	Client	Agency
B8761	*Wild World*	Canada travel	Tourism Canada	Camp Associates
B8806	*Gill Flakes*	Shreddies	Nabisco	Saatchi & Saatchi Compton Hayhurst
B8808	*Chunky Challenge*	Chunky Soup	Campbell Soup	McKim
B8809	*Exposé*	Meow Mix	Ralston Purina	Scali, McCabe, Sloves
B8811	*When the Magic Happens*	Corporate	Fiberglas Canada	Lowe, Goodgoll
B8812	*Louise Bonneau*	Corporate	Eaton's	Deane Advertising
B8813	*Christmas Pageant*	Corporate	Kraft	Leo Burnett
B8816	*Mirror, Mirror*	Telephones	Northern Telecom	J. Walter Thompson
B8817	*Old Friends*	Bell Long Distance	Telecom Canada	Miller Myers Bruce DallaCosta
B8818	*Bowser*	EnerMark	Ontario Hydro	Foster
B8819	*Milton*	Cougar Rangers	Susan Shoes	Harrod & Mirlin
B8820	*Heart of Fire – The Heat Is On*	Pontiac Grand Prix SE	GM of Canada	Foster
B8825	*The Bellman*	Headstart	CIBA Geigy Canada	MacLaren
B8831	*All That Snow*	Alberta Summer	Alberta Govt./Travel Alberta	Multicom
B8833	*Gilles/Kim in Water*	Club Med	Club Med Sales	Nathan Fraser Agency
B8841	*Robot*	Catalogue	IKEA Canada	McCann-Erickson
B8842	*Dancing*	Maxwell House	General Foods	Ogilvy & Mather
B8845	*Rise N Shine*	Maxwell House	General Foods	Ogilvy & Mather
B8849	*Grandpa's Computer*	Public service	Ontario Ministry for Senior Citizens' Affairs	Anderson Advertising
B8852/72/3	*'Magic Moments'*	Canadian Beer	Molson	MacLaren
B8854	*Incredible Journey*	Kokanee Beer	Columbia Brewing	Scali, McCabe, Sloves
B8857	*The Conversation*	Easy-Off Cleaner	Boyle-Midway	Leo Burnett
B8901/4/5	*'Makes the Ordinary Extraordinary'*	Hellmann's Mayonnaise	Best Foods Canada	MacLaren
B8907	*The Brass Ring*	Digital Equipment	Digital Canada	DDB Needham
B8908	*Egg*	Spillbuster	Black & Decker Can.	Baker Lovick
B8909	*Cord*	Dustbuster Upright	Black & Decker Can.	Baker Lovick
B8910	*Static Free*	Cordless phones	Sanyo Canada	Schur Peppler
B8911	*Blue Moon*	Services	Volkswagen Canada	DDB Needham
B8916	*Captions Kid*	Country Fibre Cookies	Christie Brown	Foster/McCann-Erickson
B8923	*A Day in the Life*	1989 Sentra	Nissan Canada	Chiat/Day
B8924	*Hairdryer*	Pulsar	Nissan Canada	Chiat/Day
B8927	*9B-Kids*	TV series	CBC	CBC
B8929	*6/36 God's Gift*	Lottery	W. Canada Lottery	Hayhurst
B8930	*Rexy*	Milk	Ontario Milk	Watt Burt/McKim

ID	Title	Product	Client	Agency
B8932	Cops	7-Up	Pepsi-Cola Canada	Leo Burnett
B8933	Skier – Time Out – Stages 29	Milk	Ontario Milk	Watt Burt/McKim
B8934	Train Adventure	Milk	Ontario Milk	Watt Burt/McKim
B8938	Percussion	Shower Massage	Teledyne Canada	J. Walter Thompson
B8950	The Human Body	Gold's Gym	Super Gym	None
B8951	Wild Times	Uno	Canada Games	Kornblum International
B8953	Advantage	Schick Razor	Warner Lambert – Parke Davis	J. Walter Thompson
B8942	Son	Sunlight	Lever Brothers	MacLaren
B8944	Backyard	Sunlight	Lever Brothers	MacLaren
B8955	Touching Shower	Noxzema	Noxell Canada	MacLaren: Lintas
B8956	When I Get a Cold	Tempra Cold Care	Mead Johnson	Harrod & Mirlin
B8964	Flying Office	Executive Class	Air Canada	Cossette Communication
B8967	Wedding	Canadian Beer	Molson	MacLaren
B8968	Images	Black Label Beer	Carling O'Keefe	Palmer Bonner BCP
B8971	Common Man's Anthem	Foster's Light Beer	Carling O'Keefe	Baker Spielvogel Bates Canada
B8977	Daughter in Black	Sunlight	Lever Brothers	MacLaren
B8981/2/3	'G.E. Talking Cool'	Personal Stereos	Thomson Electronics	Leo Burnett
B9001	Feed the Cats	Football	Hamilton Ti-Cats	Thornley/Interchange
B9003	Fresh Meat	Football	Hamilton Ti-Cats	Thornley/Interchange
B9006	Workshop Blues	Workspace System	Rubbermaid	Carder Gray DDB Needham
B9008	Jump	Armed Forces Recruitment	Dept. of National Defence	McLaughlin, Mohr, Massey
B9012	Wolves	Long distance	Bell Canada	McKim
B9016	Honda's Show room	Accord	Honda Canada	Doner Schur Peppler
B9019	Playing With Fire	Blue brand	Labatt	Scali, McCabe, Sloves
B9023	Hack Woman	Delsym Cough Remedy	Fisons Consumer Health	Brydon Harris Davidson
B9024	Hack Man	Delsym Cough Remedy	Fisons Consumer Health	Brydon Harris Davidson
B9025	Aaaaah Si	Correctol	School Plough Can.	Palmer Bonner
B9028	Wrist	Corporate	Noranda	Ambrose Carr Linton Kelly
B9029	A Bike Story	Corporate	Canadian Tire	Doner Schur Peppler
B9037	Dock	Crispix	Kellogg	J. Walter Thompson
B9040	Two Speeds	Crunchie Bar	William Neilson	Scali, McCabe, Sloves
B9050	Cool Guy	Punto Lottery	B.C. Lottery	Baker Lovick
B9053	Loons	Corporate	Bell Canada	McKim
B9101	Bad Day	Lawnmower	John Deere	Baker Lovick
B9102	Eagle	Handycam	Sony of Canada	Miller Myers Bruce DallaCosta

ID	Title	Product	Client	Agency
B9107	*Mandrill*	Handycam	Sony of Canada	Miller Myers Bruce DallaCosta
B9108	*Subdivision*	Burger Buddies	Burger King Canada	J. Walter Thompson
B9109	*Sensual*	Swiss Chalet	Cara Operations	Ambrose Carr Linton Kelly
B9121	*Restaurant*	Choclairs	Dalin	J. Walter Thompson
B9122	*Teddy Grahams*	Cookies	Christie Brown	Harrod & Mirlin
B9123	*Why Does Bob Eat Doritos*	Doritos	Hostess Frito-Lay	Young & Rubicam
B9124	*Dirty Ducts*	Duct cleaning	Ontario Duct Cleaning	Paul, Phelan & Perry
B9126	*Man's Day*	Milk	Ontario Milk	Watt Burt/McKim
B8127	*Young Woman*	Milk	Ontario Milk	Watt Burt/McKim
B9130	*The Kid*	Coca-Cola Classic	Coca-Cola	McCann-Erickson
B9139	*Point of No Returns*	Telecommuni- cations	Telecom Canada	Leo Burnett
B9140	*Spaghetti*	Lea & Perrins	E.D. Smith	Bozell Palmer Bonner
B9144	*Chrismas Corn*	Corn Flakes	Kellogg Canada	Leo Burnett
B9145	*Bread Dance*	Butter	Dairy Bureau of Canada	Watt Burt/Vickers & Benson
B9158	*Chaplain*	Anglican ministry	Anglican Church	None
B9168	*Self-Towing*	Road service	BC Auto Association	McKim
B9180	*Dejeuner Sur L'Herbe*	Seldane	Merrell Dow Pharmaceuticals	Carder Gray DDB Needham
B9181	*Sub-Silence*	Novahistex Cough Syrup	Merrell Dow Pharmaceuticals	Carder Gray DDB Needham
B9182	*Dream*	Tourism	Tourism Canada	Camp Associates
B9185	*Man Smiling Sun- glasses/Emerging Girl Horizontal*		Club Med Sales	Robert Kyle Agency
B9186	*Deux Cafés*	Canada Travel	Tourism Canada	Camp Associates
B9187	*Raven*	Canada Travel	Tourism Canada	Camp Associates
B9188	*Football Game*	Company Jeans	Great Western Garment Co.	Harrod & Mirlin
B9190	*Good Old Days*	Jetta	Volkswagen Canada	Carder Grey DDB Needham
B9192	*Engineers Think Alike*	Honda Accord	Honda Canada	Doner Schur Peppler
B9194	*Diner*	Passat	Volkswagen Canada	Carder Gray DDB Needham
B9201	*Short Story*	Mr. Big Bar	William Neilson	Leo Burnett
B9203	*Pool Hall*	Doritos	Hostess Frito-Lay	Young & Rubicam
B9209	*Skier*	Labatt .5 Beer	Labatt	Chiat/Day/Mojo
B9210	*Dr. Ballards*	Dog food	Nestlé	MacLaren: Lintas
B9214	*Strawberries*	Ziploc Bags	DowBrands Canada	Baker Lovick/BBDO
B9218	*Daughters*	Soup	Campbell Soup	Ogilvy & Mather

ID	Title	Product	Client	Agency
B9221	*Ignore It*	Tires	Goodyear Canada	McCann-Erickson
B9225	*One Voice*	Telephone services	Bell Canada	McKim
B9228	*Old Friends*	McDonald's	McDonald's Rest.	Cossette Communication
B9230	*Airport*	Teleconferencing	Bell Canada	Leo Burnett
B9231	*Zen Master*	Business long distance	B.C. Tel	Baker Lovick/BBDO
B9232	*Manifesto*	Cars	Nissan Canada	Chiat/Day/Mojo
B9236	*So Much Land*	Pathfinder	Nissan Canada	Chiat/Day/Mojo
B9241	*Violins*	Dental Floss	Colgate-Palmolive	Young & Rubicam
B9245	*Coming Down*	AntiDrug	Concerned Children's Advertisers	FCB/Ronalds-Reynolds
B9252	*Roger & Anita*	Amstel Beer	Amstel Canada	Vickers & Benson
B9253	*Mark Stafford*	Amstel Beer	Amstel Canada	Vickers & Benson
B9256	*Ken Wong/ National*	Business travel	Canadian Airlines	Chiat/Day/Mojo
B9259	*The Dream*	Travel	Club Med Sales	Robert Kyle Agency
B9260	*Inconnu*	Canada travel	Tourism Canada	Camp Associates
B9264	*Runaround*	Banking	National Trust	Baker Lovick/BBDO
B9265	*Silver Balls*	Banking	National Trust	Baker Lovick/BBDO
B9266	*Mrs. McIlquham*	Banking	Bank of Montreal	Vickers & Benson
B9268	*Club House*	Sears Club	Sears Canada	Franklin Dallas

D. Cannes Lions (1984–91)

ID	Title	Product/Advertiser	Country	Award
C84005	*More Taste*	Woodpecker Beer	Great Britain	Runner-up
C84007	*Gone Fishin'*	McEwan's	Great Britain	Runner-up
C84012	*Mama's*	Promordo	Brazil	Runner-up
C84024	*Secret Agent*	Peugeot	France	Runner-up
C84027	*Dreams*	Ricard	Spain	Runner-up
C84028	*Vita Vita*	Sangenini	Italy	Runner-up
C84032	*Palace*	Barilla	France	Runner-up
C84036	*Behind the Scene*	Malt 90	Brazil	Runner-up
C84037	*Waiting*	Yoplait Yoghurt	Great Britain	Runner-up
C84038	*007*	Kangaroo	Germany	Runner-up
C84039	*In the Mood*	Hering	Brazil	Runner-up
C84041	*Ballad*	Dim Nylons	France	Runner-up
C84042	*Restaurant*	BarclayCard	Great Britain	Runner-up
C84044	*Tourist*	Amro Bank	Holland	Runner-up
C84051	*Tootsie*	TAM	Brazil	Runner-up
C84054	*Reunion*	Kodak	United States	Runner-up
C84055	*Cocoa*	Sony	Great Britain	Runner-up

ID	Title	Product/Advertiser	Country	Award
C84079	*Roof*	Volvo	Australia	Bronze
C84080	*Busy Day*	Lee Jeans	Argentina	Bronze
C84082	*Prisoner of Zenda*	Grandee Cigars	Great Britain	Bronze
C84083	*Eagle*	Winston	Great Britain	Bronze
C84084	*Hotel Lift*	Clairol's Glints	Great Britain	Bronze
C84085	*Images*	Cacharel	France	Bronze
C84088	*Zestless*	Robertson's Marmalade	Great Britain	Bronze
C84095	*Flamenco*	Orangina	France	Bronze
C84102	*Girls*	British Caledonia	Great Britain	Silver
C84103	*Cabin*	British Caledonia	Great Britain	Silver
C84104	*Animal Trail*	Olympus Cameras	Japan	Silver
C84105	*The Vultures*	Hertz	France	Silver
C84115	*Flying Doctor*	Castelmaine XXXX	Great Britain	Silver
C84116	*Wayne*	Holsten Pils	Great Britain	Silver
C84117	*Bogart*	Holsten Pils	Great Britain	Silver
C84118	*Cagney*	Holsten Pils	Great Britain	Silver
C84119	*Baby Seals*	Antifur	United States	Gold
C84120	Unlisted	Graphite Technology	Japan	Gold
C84124	*Family Travels*	Kodak	France	Gold
C84126	*Questions*	Avis car rental	United States	Gold
C84129	*Life's Too Short*	Jacques Jaune Clothing	France	Gold
C84131	*The Boogie Man*	Pioneer Electronics	France	Gold
C84134	*Shakin' All Over*	Rowntree	Great Britain	Gold
C84138	*Tigers Head*	Cinzano	Great Britain	Gold
C85007	*Changes 'Makeup'*	The Boots Co.	Great Britain	Gold
C85008	*Skincare*	The Boots Co.	Great Britain	Gold
C85010	*Pink Shiny Dome*	Hamlet Cigars	Great Britain	Gold
C85011	*Le Clemenceau*	Citroën	France	Gold
C85012	*La 2CV*	Durex Contraceptives	Belgium	Gold
C85016	*Conference Room*	Alaska Airlines	United States	Gold
C85021	*Sunny Side Up*	Matsushita Robots	Japan	Gold
C85026	*Robots*	Pepsi	United States	Silver
C85030	*Interview*	Sadia Turkey Pieces	Brazil	Silver
C85036	*White Make-Up*	Shiseido	Japan	Silver
C85044	*Wild Horses*	Citroën	France	Silver
C85045	*Wendy's Fashion Show*	Wendy's	United States	Silver
C85061	*Surfen*	Langnese	Germany	Bronze
C85066	*Sounding the Gong*	Cemedine	Japan	Bronze
C85070	*Battle*	Check-Up	United States	Bronze
C85071	*Darts*	Appliances	Creda	Bronze
C85072	*Wet Monday*	Appliances	Creda	Bronze
C85073	*Baby*	Appliances	Creda	Bronze
C85076	*Men Aeroplane*	Men cigarettes	Austria	Bronze
C85079	*Pump Hose*	Fiat Uno	Brazil	Bronze
C85081	*Perpetual Motion*	Cosifits	Great Britain	Bronze

ID	Title	Product/Advertiser	Country	Award
C85092/3	Parrot & Dummy	Businessland	United States	Bronze
C85094	La Cave	Freetime	France	Bronze
C85097-9	Ship I, II, III	Book Club	Norway	Bronze
C85107	The Television Man	Suntory Whiskey	Japan	Diploma
C85108	Blooming Light Bulbs	Matsushita	Japan	Diploma
C85109	White Car in the Garden	Toyota MR-2	Japan	Diploma
C85112	Le Tube	Radio station	France	Diploma
C86008	Cat	Pretty Polly	Great Britain	Runner-up
C86009	[Unlisted]	Suntory	Japan	Runner-up
C86010	Vultures	Hertz	France	Runner-up
C86014	The Pick-Up	Berlitz	France	Runner-up
C86016	Fun & Games	Cidil-Milk	France	Runner-up
C86019	Waves	Coca-Cola	United States	Runner-up
C86020	[Unlisted]	Holsten Pils	Great Britain	Runner-up
C86031	Juliette	Lesieur Oil	France	Runner-up
C86034	Mischief	Daikin	Japan	Runner-up
C86045	Yellow Box	La Jaunie	France	Diploma
C86046	Casino	Volkswagen	Great Britain	Diploma
C86048	Parrot	VG	Norway	Diploma
C86049	Weed Killer	Atochem	France	Diploma
C86050	The Dream	Perrier	France	Bronze
C86051	Embraceable	Dulopillo	France	Bronze
C86053	400' Cliff	Tonka Toys	Great Britain	Bronze
C86056	[Unlisted]	Carling Black Label	Great Britain	Bronze
C86058	Surprise	News Cosmetics	Germany	Bronze
C86059	[Unlisted]	Vauxhall Nova	Great Britain	Bronze
C86070	The Screwdriver	Radio Rentals	Great Britain	Silver
C86080	AC/DC	Hamlet Cigars	Great Britain	Silver
C86084	The Couch	Lottery	Sweden	Silver
C86090	Grace Jones	Citroën CX2	France	Silver
C86092	Naughty Boy	Delco	Great Britain	Silver
C86098	Sea of Wrinkles	Matsushita	Japan	Gold
C86101	Nap	Swedish Rail	Sweden	Gold
C86102	Submarine	Gallaher	Great Britain	Gold
C86110	Any One Out There	The Samaritans	Great Britain	Gold
C86114	[Unlisted]	Shiseido	Japan	Gold
C86117	Laundrette	Levi Strauss	Great Britain	Gold
C87002	The Pyramid	Studio magazine	France	Bronze
C87005	Two Strangers	Campari	Belgium	Bronze
C87016	Cuckoo Clock	Glad Garbage Bags	Australia	Bronze
C87022	Don't Cry Baby	Helena Rubinstein	Israel	Bronze
C87023	Crystal Statue	Nivea	France	Bronze
C87025	Elite	BMW	Great Britain	Bronze
C87026	Dam Rover	Land Rover	Great Britain	Bronze

ID	Title	Product/Advertiser	Country	Award
C87030	*The Film*	Wrangler Jeans	Brazil	Bronze
C87035	*Different Strokes*	Thomson Holidays	Great Britain	Bronze
C87041	*Barsebäck*	Antinuclear	Denmark	Bronze
C87046	*Train Driver*	Lottery	Sweden	Bronze
C87049	*One Is No One*	Antidrugs	Argentina	Bronze
C87050	*Night Moves*	Michelob	United States	Silver
C87064	*The Dog*	Loctite	France	Silver
C87065	*Nocturne*	Italtel	Italy	Silver
C87067	*Boatmen*	Matsushita	Japan	Silver
C87069	*Monument*	Chanel No. 5	France	Silver
C87070	*Night Blue*	Shiseido	Japan	Silver
C87073	*Ice*	Peugeot	France	Silver
C87074	*Pleasure*	Yamaha	Germany	Silver
C87076	*Rituals*	Lee Jeans	United States	Silver
C87078	*The Dog*	Nokia	Sweden	Silver
C87088	*Sauna*	Ekstrabladet	Denmark	Silver
C87094	*People*	*The Independent*	Great Britain	Silver
C87097	*La Traviata*	Takara Shuzo	Japan	Gold
C87098	*Apartment 10E*	Diet Pepsi	United States	Gold
C87101	*Let Me Try Again*	Danone	Spain	Gold
C87105	*Lou Lou*	Cacharel	France	Gold
C87106	*Mother*	Isuzu	United States	Gold
C87107	*First Brassiere*	Valisère	Brazil	Gold
C87108	*Parting*	Levi Strauss	Great Britain	Gold
C87112	*Dodgy Duo*	Radio Rentals	Great Britain	Gold
C88002	*Higher & Higher*	Arrow Shirts	United States	Bronze
C88003	*Marilyn Monroe*	Holsten Pils	Great Britain	Bronze
C88011	*Turning Bertie*	Geo. Bassett	Great Britain	Bronze
C88016	*Heavy Traffic*	Volvo	United States	Bronze
C88019	*Questions*	Honda Cycle	United States	Bronze
C88020	*Climate*	Levi Strauss	Great Britain	Bronze
C88039	*Secrets*	Cacharel	France	Bronze
C88040	*Furie*	Antiabuse	Canada	Bronze
C88041	*Soccer*	DeMillus Bras	Brazil	Bronze
C88042	*Spin the Disc*	Durex Contraceptives	Belgium	Bronze
C88061	*Identikit*	Rimmel Make-Up	Great Britain	Silver
C88063	*Changes*	Volkswagen	Great Britain	Silver
C88067	*Creaks*	K Shoes	Great Britain	Silver
C88078	*Lynchburg*	Suntory	Japan	Silver
C88079	*Compressed Car*	Four Roses Whiskey	France	Silver
C88085	*Ugly Woman*	Max Factor	Brazil	Silver
C88086	*Bullet*	Isuzu	United States	Silver
C88089	*School*	Independent Life	United States	Silver
C88093	*Eddie Cochran*	Levi Strauss	Great Britain	Silver
C88098	*In the Dog House*	Heineken	Great Britain	Gold
C88119	*Mother & Daughter*	Phebo	Brazil	Gold

ID	Title	Product/Advertiser	Country	Award
C88120	*Love*	Anti-AIDS	Italy	Gold
C89001	*Satellite*	Dommelsche Beer	Holland	Bronze
C89002	*My Own Breakfast*	Quaker Cruesli	Holland	Bronze
C89005	*Gossip*	Insurance	Norway	Bronze
C89006	*Like Father*	Renault	Spain	Bronze
C89007	*Missing the Train*	Railway system	Spain	Bronze
C89014	*Sueno*	Freixenet	Spain	Silver
C89015	*A Way of Life*	Evian	Spain	Silver
C89019	*Prickar*	Fazer	Sweden	Silver
C89028	*Old Masters*	Tesa Adhesive	Germany	Silver
C89032	*Sumo-No-No*	Henkel	Germany	Silver
C89039	*Perspective*	Shiseido	Japan	Silver
C89041	*Surveillance*	Isuzu	United States	Silver
C89045	*Great Idea*	K Shoes	Great Britain	Silver
C89046	*War Dance*	Bata	Zimbabwe	Silver
C89053	*Conference Call*	U.S. Sprint	United States	Silver
C89060	*Electricity*	Siemens	Germany	Silver
C89061	*La Dame*	PDM Videocassettes	France	Silver
C89066	*Slaughter*	Animal rights	United States	Silver
C89083	*Cans*	Araldite Glue	Brazil	Gold
C89085	*Wherever You Go*	Hitachi	Japan	Gold
C89090	*La Femme*	Scandale	France	Gold
C89092	*Pick-Up*	Levi Strauss	Great Britain	Gold
C89095	*Qaddafi*	Beneficial	United States	Gold
C89097	[Unlisted]	Oslo bus service	Norway	Gold
C89106	*The Day It Came*	National Answer Phone	Japan	Gold
C89112	*Lunch Is Ready*	Famine Relief	France	Gold
C90003	*Blimp I*	E & J. Gallo Winery	United States	Bronze
C90004	*Gratuitous Violence*	Schweppes	Great Britain	Bronze
C90005	*Umbrella*	Pepsico	United States	Bronze
C90009	*The Thief*	Dairies Association	Norway	Bronze
C90012	*Angry Bees*	Glad-Lock Zipper Bags	United States	Bronze
C90014	*Twist*	Colgate-Palmolive	Brazil	Bronze
C90024	*Global*	British Airways	Great Britain	Bronze
C90033	*Hit the Road, Mac*	Apple's Portable Mac	United States	Bronze
C90036	*Little Old Lady*	Road Safety Council	Denmark	Bronze
C90053	*Darts*	TOA Gosei Superset	Japan	Silver
C90055	*Feet*	Boehringer Mannheim	Spain	Silver
C90059	*Independence*	Porsche	United States	Silver
C90061	*Bollé Protection*	Bill Blass Optical	Australia	Silver
C90062	*La Soirée*	Eram Shoes	France	Silver
C90063	*Bo Diddley*	Nike Shoes	United States	Silver
C90068	*The Wall*	Red Roof Inns	United States	Silver
C90077	*Dambusters*	Carling Black Label	Great Britain	Gold
C90078	*Ray Charles*	Diet Pepsi	United States	Gold
C90079	*That's Life*	Calbee Foods Co.	Japan	Gold

ID	Title	Product/Advertiser	Country	Award
C90084	*Rocking Chair*	Loctite	Chile	Gold
C90086	*Egoïste*	Chanel	France	Gold
C90087	*Chapmans Peak*	Mercedes-Benz	South Africa	Gold
C90098	*Concentration Camp*	Third World Assistance	Great Britain	Gold
C91001	*Bridge*	Castlemaine XXXX	Great Britain	Bronze
C91002	*Flies*	Castlemaine XXXX	Great Britain	Bronze
C91003/4	*Bar & Club*	Red Rock Cider	Great Britain	Bronze
C91012	*Horse Play*	Nobby's Nuts	Australia	Bronze
C91014	*Just Moo It*	Milk	Australia	Bronze
C91020	*Blue Velvet*	Nivea Lotion	Great Britain	Bronze
C91021	*Hitchcock*	Johnson's Handcream	Spain	Bronze
C91022	*Relax*	Peugeot 605	Great Britain	Bronze
C91024	*Surfer's/Coltrane* [*sic*]	Nike Shoes	United States	Bronze
C91025	*Surfer's/Coltrane* [*sic*]	Nike Shoes	United States	Bronze
C91030	*The Stove*	Storebrand Insurance	Norway	Bronze
C91037	*Bye Bye Love*	Dunkin Donuts	Brazil	Bronze
C91044	*Flower*	Pixel Dio colour copier	Japan	Bronze
C91045	*Operators*	Southern Bell	United States	Bronze
C91050	*Rain Forest Burn*	Save the Amazon	Brazil	Bronze
C91054	*Voice Recognition*	Toshiba Corporation	Japan	Bronze
C91057	*Up the Irns*	Irn Bru	Great Britain	Silver
C91062	*Japan Demonstration*	Domopak Oven Paper	Italy	Silver
C91063	*Dance With Your Feet*	Energizer batteries	United States	Silver
C91064	*Phone Company*	Energizer batteries	United States	Silver
C91065	*Hips*	Energizer batteries	United States	Silver
C91066	*Head for Heights*	Reebok Sports Shoes	United States	Silver
C91067	*Lassie*	Maidenform Lingerie	United States	Silver
C91068	*Images*	Maidenform Lingerie	United States	Silver
C91077	*Speeding Photo-copier*	Toshiba	Japan	Silver
C91081	*M.C Hammer: Switch*	Pepsi	United States	Gold
C91082	*Spots*	Purina	United States	Gold
C91086	*Safety Car Crash*	Mercedes-Benz	Australia	Gold
C91091	*Don Juan*	Hawaiian Tourism	United States	Gold
C91092	*Bob & Ellen*	Hawaiian Tourism	United States	Gold
C91094/5	*Movers &Salesmen*	IKEA U.S.A.	United States	Gold
C91104	*The Lion & Lioness*	Perrier	France	Grand Prix

E. International Showcase (1987–92)

The initial two digits indicate the annual tape, not the actual date of the commercial.

ID	Title	Product	Advertiser	Length
IS8702	*Waltz*	Isuzu	Japan	:30
IS8704	*Grace Jones*	Citroën	France	:45
IS8714	*Escher*	McEwan's	Great Britain	1:20
IS8719	*Chain Reaction*	Del Monte	United States	:60
IS8726	*Picture Show*	Guess Jeans	Great Britain	:60
IS8758	*Indian*	Firestone Tires	Chile	:60
IS8761	*Human Train*	Tuborg Lager	Great Britain	:60
IS8763	*Night Moves*	Michelob	United States	:60
IS8769	*Rush*	Lee Cooper Jeans	France	:30
IS8772	*Hospital*	General Accident Ins.	Great Britain	:30
IS8809	*9 1/2 Weeks*	French's	Venezuela	:40
IS8811	*Chocostar*	Bahlsen	France	:30
IS8812	*Image 87*	Langnese	Germany	:55
IS8826	*Insects*	Antifur	Great Britain	1:30
IS8832	*Sisters*	Nationwide Anglia	Great Britain	:42
IS8847	*Good Friends*	Smirnoff Vodka	Jamaica	:60
IS8857	*VW*	Heineken	Great Britain	:20
IS8861	*Laundromat*	Carling Black Label	Great Britain	:40
IS8869	*Sleeping Beauty*	Pruf	Ecuador	:30
IS8874	*On the Rocks*	Serkova Vodka	Greece	:15
IS8908	*Iron Man*	Kellogg's Nutri Grain	Australia	:60
IS8916	*Snow White*	Ajax Window Cleaner	Germany	:20
IS8927	*Grim Reaper*	Anti-AIDS	Australia	:30
IS8931	*Bathroom*	Page toilet paper	Holland	:30
IS8953	*Manniquin* [sic]	Sheer Indulgence	United States	:60
IS8955	*Car Park*	Montego 1.6	Great Britain	:60
IS8961	*Street Urchin*	Krizia Perfume	Italy	:60
IS8968	*Rocking Sikh*	Poppadums Chips	Great Britain	:30
IS9002	*Don't Wrap It*	Australia Post	Australia	:30
IS9021	*Ka-Cho-Fu-Getsu*	Gekkeikan Sake	Japan	:30
IS9024	*Twiggy*	Austin Mini	Great Britain	:30
IS9029	*Dirty Words*	Boka Loka	Brazil	:30
IS9034	*Complan*	Vitamins	Great Britain	:30
IS9039	*Spot the Lizard*	FM 105	Australia	:60
IS9054	*Desnudos*	Moda de Espana	Spain	:45
IS9082	*Still More Dancing Cars*	Isuzu	Japan	:30
IS9087	*Pink Rabbits*	Slice Soda	United States	:30
IS9088	*Hard Sell*	Slice Soda	United States	:30
IS9109	*Balloon*	Metro/Rover Cars	Great Britain	:40

ID	Title	Product	Advertiser	Length
IS9111	*God Bless the Child*	Volkswagen	Great Britain	:60
IS9125	*Flasher*	West cigarettes	Germany	:50
IS9126	*Rhino*	Animal rights	Great Britain	:40
IS9202	*Stiff Chedder*	*Cleo* magazine	Australia	:30
IS9210	*Nonsense*	Absolut Vodka	Great Britain	:30
IS9215	*Transformations*	Flour	Japan	:30
IS9226	*Darwin Camels*	Toyota	Australia	:30
IS9237	*Der Reigen*	Kattus Sparkling	Spain	:30
IS9243	*The Girlfriend*	Accident prevention	Australia	:60
IS9263	*Uncivilized*	Swedish Rail	Sweden	:15
IS9265	*Red Woman Rendezvous*	Nestlé chocolate bar	Holland	:30
IS9275	*Miles*	TDK cassettes	Japan	:30
IS9276	*Mah-Jong*	Alinamin	Japan	:30

Sources

A. Bibliographical Essay

Some sources have provided information or opinions used throughout the book. Others I have listed here because of their value to anyone who wishes to investigate further advertising and culture.

A good place to start is Daniel Pope's *The Making of Modern Advertising* (New York: Basic Books, 1983), which is useful for a general overview of what happened. The well-regarded textbook by William Leiss, Stephen Kline, and Sut Jhally, *Social Communication in Advertising: Persons, Products, & Images of Well-Being*, 2nd ed. (Scarborough: Nelson Canada, 1990), contains a brief historical overview of the industry as well as the evolution of ad styles. John Sinclair's *Images Incorporated: Advertising as Industry and Ideology* (London and New York: Croom Helm, 1987) deserves special mention: it is a thoughtful survey of the theory and practice of advertising in the First and Third Worlds. Eric Clark's *The Want Makers* (London: Hodder & Stoughton, 1988) is a grab-bag of fascinating stories about the industry and the craft throughout the world; by contrast, Armand Mattelart's *Advertising International: The Privatisation of Public Space*, translated by Michael Chanan (London: Routledge, 1991), is a scholarly treatment of the globalization of advertising. The best account I've found of ad-making is Michael J. Arlen's witty book, *Thirty Seconds* (Markham, Ont.: Penguin, 1981), where he tracks the creation and the production of an AT&T commercial.

There are some excellent works on various aspects of the American story. Stephen Fox's *The Mirror Makers: A History of American Advertising and Its Creators* (New York: Vintage Books, 1985) offers a superb account of the history of the industry in the United States. In *Advertising, the Uneasy Persuasion: Its Dubious Impact on American Society* (New York: Basic Books,

1984), Michael Schudson explores the nature of recent and past American advertising to demonstrate how limited he believes are the effects of advertising. He labels advertising a species of 'Capitalist Realism.' The more specialized book by Roland Marchand, *Advertising the American Dream: Making Way for Modernity 1920–1940* (Berkeley: University of California Press, 1985) is an outstanding model for the cultural analysis of advertising – indeed, Marchand's work is one of those 'modern classics' in the history of popular culture. Martin Davidson's *The Consumerist Manifesto: Advertising in Postmodern Times* (London: Comedia, 1992) offers some intriguing insights into the development of British advertising during the 1980s.

My view of popular culture owes much to John Fiske's two books, *Understanding Popular Culture* and *Reading the Popular* (Boston: Unwin Hyman, 1989), which outline how people rework mass culture to suit their purposes. Readers may also detect my debt to cultural anthropologists who have explored the meaning of commodities and of consumption, notably Mary Douglas and Baron Isherwood, *The World of Goods: Towards an Anthropology of Consumption* (London: Allen Lane, 1973) and Grant McCracken's *Culture and Consumption: New Approaches to the Symbolic Character of Consumer Goods and Activities* (Bloomington: Indiana University Press, 1988).

I have drawn extensively upon theories current in what is called the school of Cultural Studies, though I cannot share their enthusiasm for a strategy of intervention and confrontation. A good introduction to the virtues and absurdities of Cultural Studies is an edited collection by Lawrence Grossberg, Gary Nelson, and Paula Treichler, entitled *Cultural Studies* (New York: Routledge, 1992), which includes papers from a conference held in 1990 that attracted scholars and others from the United States and elsewhere. I recommend a work by Raymond Williams, one of that school's gurus, as a broad introduction to the analysis of advertising: 'Advertising: The Magic System,' in his *Problems in Materialism and Culture: Selected Essays* (London: Verso, 1980), 170–95. Here Williams calls advertising 'the official art of modern capitalist society.'

Introduction: Ads as Art

The exhibit Art et Publicité, 1890–1990 has been catalogued in a collection of essays entitled *Art & Pub*, Nicole Ouvrard, coordinator (Paris: Éditions du Centre Pompidou, 1990). There is a much more accessible and very imaginative discussion of advertising and art in another exhibition catalogue: Kirk Varnedoe and Adam Gopnik, *High & Low: Modern Art & Popular Culture* (New York: Museum of Modern Art, 1990). My comments on the analogy of the medieval icon come from viewing Christian painting in galleries across Europe, especially in London, Barcelona, Athens, and Moscow.

A number of earlier writers have been intrigued by this question. John Berger was one of the first to discern the link between centuries of fine art and modern advertising in *Ways of Seeing* (London: BBC and Penguin, 1972). Bruce Kurtz wrote *Spots: The Popular Art of American Television Commercials* (New York: Arts Communication, 1977) to draw attention to how a small group of directors of commercials employed the same sort of techniques and approaches valued by art historians. In 'Television Commercials: The "Unpopular Art,"' *Journal of Advertising* 13, no. 1 (1984): 4–10, Florence Feasely dealt more briefly with a wider range of television advertising.

There have been various attempts to analyse both advertising and commercials. Varda Langholz Leymore first elaborated the binary logic implicit in advertising, employing the techniques of structural anthropology in her *Hidden Myth: Structure & Symbolism in Advertising* (New York: Basic Books, 1975), a study that suffers from the sins of extreme reductionism common to that school. Sut Jhally's *The Codes of Advertising: Fetishism and the Political Economy of Meaning in the Consumer Society* (London: Frances Pinter, 1987) includes a chapter devoted to a content analysis of primetime and sports-time commercials aired in the TV year 1980–1, though his account generates so many categories that it becomes difficult to comprehend the character of the advertising. The most elaborate analysis of advertising, and an essential primer for anyone bent on studying the phenomenon, is Gillian Dyer's *Advertising as Communication* (London: Routledge, 1988), where you'll learn more than enough about 'how to do it.'

Also well worth consulting is Mark Crispin Miller's *Boxed In: The Culture of TV* (Evanston, Il.: Northwestern University Press, 1988). Miller includes a variety of neatly crafted readings of particular commercials as part of his general diatribe against the commercialism of television. Andrew Wernick's provocative study *Promotional Culture: Advertising, Ideology and Symbolic Expression* (London: Sage, 1991) treats some of the same questions raised here, though from a different perspective, since Wernick argues that advertising is really a species of rhetoric, 'combining elements of information and art.' (Wernick has an especially fascinating discussion of the changing images of the car in *Promotional Culture*.) Finally, there is Guy Cook's *The Discourse of Advertising* (London and New York: Routledge, 1992). Cook, a linguist, draws upon a wide range of print and television ads from Great Britain to explain his comparison between advertising and literature. The result is a readable and informative introduction to the particular characteristics of advertising, which he regards as an especially 'parasitic' form of discourse that borrows its styles and techniques from many different kinds of texts.

1. The First Clios (1948–58)

The two main sources are Lincoln Diamant, *Television's Classic Commercials: The Golden Years 1948–58* (New York: Hastings House, 1971) and the tape of the ads available from the Television Center of Brooklyn College, City University of New York. The collection supposedly included sixty-nine examples, though one (a Canadian commercial made in New York for Imperial Esso gasoline) does not appear on the tape.

The section 'In the Beginning' draws upon a variety of published accounts. The history of television in America has been dealt with in Eric Barnouw's classic, *Tube of Plenty: The Evolution of American Television* (New York: Oxford, 1975), as well as in his investigation of the influence of advertisers, *The Sponsor: Notes on a Modern Potentate* (New York: Oxford, 1978). There is also a much more recent account of the evolution of the TV industry in the 1950s: William Boddy, *Fifties Television: The Industry and Its Critics* (Urbana and Chicago: University of Illinois Press, 1990). Kenneth Hey's article, '*Marty*: Aesthetics vs. Medium in Early Television Drama,' in *American History American Television: Interpreting the Video Past*, edited by John E. O'Connor (New York: Frederick Unger, 1983), 95–133, contains a discussion of the way commercials structured the teleplay. I have also used Cobbett Steinberg's *TV Facts* (New York: Facts on File Inc., 1980) for a variety of basic statistics on the American industry and O.J. Firestone's *Broadcast Advertising in Canada: Past and Future Growth* (Ottawa: University of Ottawa Press, 1966), which, despite its title, includes information on the American advertising scene received from government agencies.

There are excellent discussions of American life and culture during the postwar years in Lary May, ed., *Recasting America: Culture and Politics in the Age of the Cold War* (Chicago: University of Chicago Press, 1989), 1–16, and Roland Marchand, 'Visions of Classlessness, Quests for Dominion: American Popular Culture, 1945–1960,' *Reshaping America: Society and Institutions 1945–1960*, edited by Robert H. Brenner and Gary W. Reichard (Columbus: Ohio State University Press, 1982), 163–90. An important contemporary source, first published in 1950, is David Riesman with Nathan Glazier and Reuel Denney, *The Lonely Crowd: A Study of the Changing American Character*, abridged ed. (New Haven and London: Yale University Press, 1969), which delves into the social personalities of Americans.

On the contrast between mass and segmented marketing and the issue of 'universal' goods, see Richard S. Tedlow, *New and Improved: The Story of Mass Marketing in America* (New York: Basic Books, 1990), especially 4–12. Tedlow's work is a fascinating study of four important stories in the history of American marketing (the Cola Wars, Ford versus General Motors, A&P, and Sears), in which advertising was only one method of winning sales.

For a discussion of the mass culture debate, see Andrew Ross, *No Respect: Intellectuals & Popular Culture* (New York and London: Routledge, 1989), 42–64. In retrospect, while Packard's *The Hidden Persuaders* (New York: Pocket Books, 1958) seems to be a very mild critique of advertising, Galbraith's *The Affluent Society*, 2nd ed. (New York: The New American Library, 1970) is a frighteningly accurate appraisal of what happens when people value private goods over public goods. For an update of the Packard critique, see Wilson Bryan Key's *Media Sexploitation* (Englewood Cliffs: Prentice-Hall Inc., 1976) and *The Age of Manipulation* (New York: Henry Holt & Company, 1989). Stuart Ewen has written a number of books on advertising, including *All Consuming Images: The Politics of Style in Contemporary Culture* (New York: Basic Books, 1988). David Ogilvy's *Confessions of an Advertising Man* (New York: Atheneum, 1963) remains an entertaining account of what it was like to work in adland during the 1950s. Gary Steiner's *The People Look at Television: A Study of Audience Attitudes* (New York: Knopf, 1963) was one of the first major surveys of the audience response to television.

2. Studies in American Excellence

The story of the three campaigns is based upon records at the Coca-Cola Archives in Atlanta and the 'Marlboro Country' and the Pepsi-Cola Advertising collections housed at the Centre for Advertising History, National Museum of American History, Smithsonian Institution, Washington, D.C.

The Coca-Cola Archives contains a 'Coca-Cola Historical Composite Tape of Commercials' of about forty samples covering the years 1951 through 1988, plus a wide assortment of special tapes of domestic and international commercials, especially those made in the 1980s. These holdings, by the way, cover campaigns for Diet Coke, Fanta, and Coca-Cola-owned beverages in other parts of the world. In addition, the archives has company documents and press clippings pertinent to any study of Coca-Cola advertising.

The 'Marlboro Country' collection includes tapes of American ads made in the 1950s and 1960s; a huge number of interviews carried out by Scott Ellsworth with people employed by the Leo Burnett agency, Philip Morris, and its allies in other parts of the world; plus some documentary information about the campaign and the industry. The Pepsi-Cola Advertising Collection has two tapes of commercials covering the years 1946 to 1984, a series of interviews with BBDO and Pepsi-Cola personnel (also carried out by Scott Ellsworth), and a lot of paper records about advertising. I have also made use of award-winning Pepsi ads in the tapes of the Cannes Lions, 1984–6. The interviews in the two oral history collections have been summarized in detailed abstracts, which makes it very easy to survey opinions and track down comments.

I have supplemented the 'Marlboro Country' collection with information from James Overton's excellent account of the industry, 'Diversification and International Expansion: The Future of the American Tobacco Manufacturing Industry with Corporate Profiles of the "Big Six,"' in *The Tobacco Industry in Transition: Policies for the 1980s, edited by William R. Finger* (Lexington: Lexington Books, 1981), 159–95; Robert Sobel's interesting history, *They Satisfy: The Cigarette in American Life* (Garden City, N.Y.: Anchor Books, 1978); Robert H. Miles, *Coffin Nails and Corporate Strategies* (Englewood Cliffs, N.J.: Prentice-Hall, 1982); and Susan Wagner, *Cigarette Country: Tobacco in American History and Politics* (New York: Praeger, 1971). There are also two articles in the *Journal of Popular Culture* on the ad campaign: Bruce Lohof's 'The Higher Meaning of Marlboro Cigarettes,' 3 (Winter 1969): 441–50 and Michael E. Starr's 'The Marlboro Man: Cigarette Smoking and Masculinity in America,' 17 (Spring 1984): 45–57, though that essay deals with the whole history of smoking and borrows heavily from Sobel's book.

The study of Coke and Pepsi advertising draws upon facts and views found in two academic studies: Richard S. Tedlow, 'The Great Cola Wars: Coke vs. Pepsi' in his *New and Improved: The Story of Mass Marketing* (New York: Basic Books, 1990), 22–111, and Robert D. Tollison, David P. Kaplan, and Richard S. Higgins, *Competition and Concentration: The Economics of the Carbonated Soft Drink Industry* (Lexington: Lexington Books, 1991). Particularly useful regarding Pepsi-Cola are two books co-written by businessmen, John Sculley with John A. Byrne, *Odyssey* (New York: Harper & Row, 1987) and Roger Enrico with Jesse Kornbluth, *The Other Guy Blinked: How Pepsi Won the Cola Wars* (New York: Bantam, 1986). There are other popular accounts on what happened in Douglas K. Ramsay, 'Clash of the Colas: Coke vs. Pepsi' in his *The Corporate Warriors: Six Classic Cases in American Business* (Boston: Houghton Mifflin, 1987), 54–95, where he probes the Diet Coke launch in particular, and in Steve Blount and Lisa Walker, *The Best of Ad Campaigns!* (Cranbury, N.J.: Rockport, 1988), which carries chapters, complete with pictures, devoted to the Diet Coke and the 'New Generation' campaigns. Coca-Cola's own centennial history, *Coca-Cola: The First Hundred Years*, text by Anne Hoy (Atlanta: Coca-Cola Company, 1986), contains some interesting anecdotes and marvellous reproductions of advertisements over the years.

3. Art in the Service of Commerce

The discussion of the 'creative revolution' draws from material in two popular histories: Larry Dobrow's *When Advertising Tried Harder: The Sixties: The Golden Age of American Advertising* (New York: Friendly Press, 1984), which covers some of the best campaigns of the decade, and Bob Levinson's *Bill Bernbach's Book: A History of the Advertising That Changed the History of Advertising* (New York: Villard Books, 1987), which includes bits from Bernbach's own writings and speeches. I found especially useful two reminiscences: Jerry Della Femina's delightful *From Those Wonderful Folks Who Gave You Pearl Harbor*, edited by Charles Sopkin (Richmond Hill, Ont.: Simon & Schuster of Canada, 1971) and Jerry Goodis's *Have I Ever Lied to You Before?* (Toronto and Montreal: McClelland and Stewart, 1972), which is a refreshing survey of Canadian advertising in the 1960s and early 1970s. Steinberg's *TV Facts* contains a breakdown of the Clio awards for the 1960s and 1970s. On Pop Art, I recommend Christin J. Mamiya's *Pop Art and Consumer Culture* (Austin: University of Texas Press, 1992), which explores the way the movement embodied what she feels was the dominant ideology and styles of the times.

Some of the information about the views of participants is drawn from abstracts of interviews available from the Centre for Advertising History – in particular Tom Anderson, Phil Dusenberry, and Rick Levine in the 'Pepsi Generation' collection and Marvin Honig, Roy Grace, and Gene Case in the Alka-Seltzer collection. The Alka-Seltzer collection contains some insights into the way a campaign of the fifties changed to suit the sixties.

The description of Doyle Dane Bernbach's Volkswagen campaign rests in large part on the television reel in *Volkswagen Advertising: A Case History for College Lecture Use II*, 2nd ed. (initially published in 1972). This package also contains an interesting discussion of print and television advertising, though the latter can be misleading – it suggests VW didn't really start on TV until 1965, when in fact DDB won a campaign Clio in 1961 for its Volkswagen ads.

The Young & Rubicam collection is located in New York's Museum of Television and Radio, and is readily available to researchers and the public. I have also made use of the catalogue, entitled *Y&R and Broadcasting: Radio and Television Advertising: Growing Up Together* (New York: Museum of Broadcasting, 1988), which contains the excellent article by William A. Henry III, reflections by Joan Hafey and Stan Freberg, and brief descriptions of many of the commercials.

The discussion of the malaise in New York's creative circles in the first half of the 1980s is based on press clippings in the Federal Express collection at the

Center for Advertising History. I have made use of the extensive holdings of the Independent Television Association Film Library in London. The library had historical tapes such as 'Moments to Remember' ('50s and '60s ads), a 'Fairy Snow Historical Reel,' and a 'Heineken Show Reel' (1974–83), plus a host of cassettes on categories of advertising aired during the late 1970s and throughout the 1980s. These holdings have since been transferred to the National Museum of Photography, Film, and Television in Bradford, West Yorkshire. The ads analysed towards the end of the section are derived from tapes of Cannes award winners.

Very little has been written about the Canadian advertising industry. There is a special section on advertising in the late 1960s in Hopkins, Hedlin Limited, *Words, Music, and Dollars*, vol. 2 of the *Report* of the Special Senate Committee on Mass Media. Kristian S. Palda has produced an analysis of the industry in the 1970s and early 1980s: *The Role of Advertising Agencies in Canada's Service Sector* (Vancouver: The Fraser Institute, 1988). Those readers interested in the life of an ad-maker would be well advised to view the documentary on Jerry Goodis by the National Film Board of Canada, entitled *Have I Ever Lied To You Before?* (1976). In addition, there is Goodis's more recent work, *Goodis: Shaking the Canadian Advertising Tree*, with Gene O'Keefe (Toronto: Fitzhenry & Whiteside, 1991). This is full of informative stories about his career and profession.

The main Bessie Collection was sold to me for research purposes by the Television Bureau of Canada, based in Toronto. The TvB also markets a tape of the annual Bessie award winners (plus an International Showcase collection), as well as a 'Solid Gold' tape of all the gold Bessies since 1963 and, more recently, Campaign Firsts. The National Archives of Canada has both the main collection and the Bessie contenders of the late 1960s and early 1970s.

I will only cite a couple of works on postmodernism that have contributed to my observations here, though readers need only go to the catalogue of any decent university library to discover just how much of an industry the study of this phenomenon became. A good place to start is with the brief exploration by Todd Gitlin, 'Hip-Deep in Post-Modernism,' *New York Times Book Review*, 6 September 1988, 1, 35–6. Then there is the initial work of the critic Frederic Jameson, too full of theory for my taste, which launched the great excitement: 'Postmodernism, or the Cultural Logic of Late Capitalism,' *New Left Review*, no. 146 (July-August 1984): 53–92. In the light of such arguments, it is interesting to reread Marshall McLuhan's work of genius, *Understanding Media: The Extensions of Man* (New York: New American Library 1964), especially his brief section on ads (201–7). Among the most outlandish of the books that found favour was Jean Baudrillard's *Simulations* (New York:

Semiotext[e], Inc., 1983), where he virtually announced the death of reality. One of the most informed treatments of literary postmodernism is by Linda Hutcheon, *A Poetics of Postmodernism: History, Theory, Fiction* (New York and London: Routledge, 1988), which explores such issues as parody, irony, decentredness, and the like. Finally, there is a slightly later work by Mike Featherstone, *Consumer Culture & Postmodernism* (London: Sage, 1991) that is useful because it appeared after the first wave of enthusiasm and makes the link between the phenomenon and the self-interest of culture critics.

4. Reading the Bessies

I have been guided by some of the observations of Roland Marchand in his advertising history, by Judith Williamson's reading of (mostly) magazine ads in *Decoding Advertisements* (London: Marion Boyars, 1978), and by John Fiske's reflections on excess in his two books. It was E. Goffman's *Gender Advertisements* (London: Macmillan, 1979) that first alerted me to the signal importance of the different ways men and women were portrayed. The thoughts on youth were suggested by reading John Hartley, 'Television and the Power of Dirt,' in *Tele-ology: Studies in Television* (London and New York: Routledge, 1992): 21–42.

5. The Cannes Lions, Etc. (1984–92)

The debate over the existence and nature of a global culture is going hot and heavy in the early 1990s, though not with much result. Reading a recent collection of essays edited by Mike Featherstone, *Global Culture: Nationalism, Globalization and Modernity* (London: Sage, 1990), for example, leaves one confused by a welter of conflicting theories. I've found much more insightful Pico Iyer's marvellous *Video Night in Kathmandu* (New York: Knopf, 1988), although his reports are already a bit dated because of the speed with which the Superculture seems to alter shape and tone.

I have used tapes of the Cannes award winners purchased from AdFilms in Toronto, which also supplies a run sheet that identifies each winner. In fact, some of these tapes include a few commercials that are not identified on the run sheets. The Aquarius and Georgia commercials mentioned near the beginning of the chapter were acquired from the Coca-Cola Archives in Atlanta. The International Showcase tapes are marketed by the Television Bureau of Canada, and are drawn from a variety of different sources – the 1992 tape, for example, included commercials from Lurzers 4/91 (meaning the fourth tape from a special archive of international commercials), Australia's Facts 1991 (awards),

British 1991 (awards), MacLaren 1991 and McCann 1992 (presumably named after ad agencies), and something called Eurasia 1991 and Creative 1991 & O 1992.

6. The Captivated Viewer and Other Tales

This chapter uses a wide range of material from archives, surveys of public behaviour, student questionnaires, popular and academic literature, newspapers, and magazines. The opening paragraph draws on a number of the sources cited below in the 'Brief Listing,' plus a collection of press clippings. The highly critical *Adbusters Quarterly*, a Vancouver-based periodical, waged war against all forms of commercial advertising in the early 1990s and attempted to sponsor a counter or Green advertising.

It is a difficult task to find much material prepared for or by advertising agencies on the way people respond to commercials. Fortunately, I was able to locate some data in the Federal Express collection (which also includes the Video Storyboard Tests of the early 1980s) and the Campbell Soup Oral History and Documentation Project. Both collections are available at the Center for Advertising History. I have also used documents on advertising regulations, advertising practices, and consumer responses in Britain that were supplied to me by the Independent Television Association Film Library. Although neither of the authors are cited in the text, I have learned a lot of ad lore about people and their responses from two textbooks: Winston Mahatoo's *The Dynamics of Consumer Behaviour* (Toronto: John Wiley & Sons, 1985) and Keith Tuckwell's *Canadian Advertising in Action* (Scarborough, Ont.: Prentice-Hall Canada, 1988). I have also made use of material found in these popular works: 'Sex, Buys & Advertising,' an NBC special documentary, broadcast 31 July 1990, which contains some fascinating interviews with industry personnel; Martin Mayer's *Whatever Happened to Madison Avenue? Advertising in the '90s* (Boston: Little, Brown, 1991), an incisive account of a now troubled industry; and Tony Schwartz's *The Responsive Chord* (New York: Anchor Press/Doubleday, 1973), which deserves more attention than it usually receives in academic circles.

Information on popular attitudes or viewing habits comes from the Canadian Radio-television and Telecommunications Commission, Research Branch, *Attitudes of Canadians toward Advertising on Television*, prepared by Avrim Lazar and Associates Ltd. (Ottawa: Ministry of Supply and Services, 1978); Gary Steiner's *The People Look at Television*; and Martin Goldfarb Consultants' 'The Media and the People.' Two especially useful academic investigations on viewing are Patrick Barwise and Andrew Ehrenberg's *Television and Its*

Audience (London: Sage 1988) and Robert Kubey and Mihaly Csikszentmihalyi's *Television and the Quality of Life: How Viewing Shapes Everyday Experience* (Hillsdale, New Jersey: Lawrence Erlbaum Associates, 1990). W. Russell Neuman's *The Future of the Mass Audience* (Cambridge: Cambridge University Press, 1991) is a corrective to claims that the mass audience is fragmenting in the era of new electronic media.

The discussion of the aesthetic experience utilizes arguments in Mihaly Csikszentmihalyi and Rick E. Robinson's *The Art of Seeing: An Interpretation of the Aesthetic Encounter* (Malibu, Ca: J. Paul Getty Museum, 1990), which probes the ways in which museum professionals respond to art. Roger Chartier's work, 'Texts, Printing, Readings,' in *The New Cultural History*, edited by Lynn Hunt (Berkeley: University of California Press, 1989) is an account of the many attributes of any document that can affect its meanings. Mark Roskill and David Carrier in *Truth and Falsehood in Visual Images* (Amherst: University of Massachusetts Press, 1983) make a series of intriguing observations about the special characteristics of pictures as a source of information. Ellen Handler Spitz applies the lessons of psychological research to the understanding of art in *Art and Psyche: A Study in Psychoanalysis and Aesthetics* (New Haven: Yale University Press, 1985).

Afterword: Travels in Europe

The books referred to here are a mixed lot of best sellers. Naomi Wolf's *The Beauty Myth* (Toronto: Vintage, 1991) purports to show how American women are enslaved by the pursuit of beauty. Camille Paglia takes on contemporary feminism, among much else, in her collection of essays *Sex, Art, and American Culture* (New York: Vintage, 1992). Madonna's *Sex* (New York: Warner, 1992) is a compilation of what used to be called dirty pictures and smutty talk that embodies her own representation of the carefree and empowered woman.

B. Brief Listing

Adair, Gilbert. 1986. *Myths & Memories* (London: Fontana).
Auletta, Ken. 1991. *Three Blind Mice: How the TV Networks Lost Their Way* (New York: Random House).
Bauer, Raymond, and Stephen Greyser. 1968. *Advertising in America* (Boston: Harvard).
Berger, Warren. 1990. 'They Know Bo,' *New York Times Magazine*, 11 November.

Brown, Les. 1992. *Encyclopedia of Television*, 3rd ed. (Detroit: Visible Ink Press).

Collins, Richard. 1990. *Culture, Communication & National Identity: The Case of Canadian Television* (Toronto: University of Toronto Press).

Comstock, George. 1980. *Television in America* (Beverly Hills: Sage).

Dissanayake, Ellen. 1988. *What Is Art For?* (Seattle: University of Washington Press).

Dizard, Wilson P. 1966. *Television: A World View* (Syracuse: Syracuse University Press).

Dunnett, Peter. 1990. *The World Television Industry: An Economic Analysis* (London: Routledge).

Eco, Umberto. 1986. *Travels in Hyperreality* (London: Picador).

Ehrenreich, Barbara. 1989. *Fear of Falling: The Inner Life of the Middle Class* (New York: Pantheon).

Emery, Walter B. 1969. *National and International Systems of Broadcasting: Their History, Operation and Control* (East Lansing: Michigan State University Press).

Fallon, Ivan. 1988. *The Brothers: The Rise & Rise of Saatchi & Saatchi* (London: Hutchinson).

Frye, Northrop. 1967. *The Modern Century: The Whidden Lectures 1967* (Toronto: Oxford University Press).

Kleinfeld, N.R. 1991. 'What Is Chris Whittle Teaching Our Children?' *New York Times Magazine*, 19 May.

Kruger, Barbara. 1990. *Love for Sale: The Words and Pictures of Barbara Kruger*. Text by Kate Linker (New York: Harry N. Abrams).

Krugman, Herbert. 1965. 'The Impact of Television Advertising: Learning without Involvement,' *Public Opinion Quarterly* xxix, no. 3 (Fall): 349–56.

Lewis, Justin. 1991. *The Ideological Octopus: An Exploration of Television & Its Audience* (New York: Routledge).

Martin Goldfarb Consultants. 1970. 'The Media and the People', in Special Senate Committee on Mass Media, *Report*, vol. 3: *Good, Bad, or Simply Inevitable?* (Ottawa: Queen's Printer).

Miller, Mary Jane. 1987. *Turn Up the Contrast: CBC Television Drama since 1952* (Vancouver: University of British Columbia Press/CBC Enterprises).

Morrison, Roger. 1988. 'How Many Cameras Will That Commercial Sell?' in *People Meters: An Assessment Plus a Look at the Future* (Advertising Research Foundation).

Paulu, Burton. 1961. *British Broadcasting in Transition* (Minneapolis: University of Minnesota Press).

Postman, Neil. 1986. *Amusing Ourselves to Death: Public Discourse in the Age of Show Business* (New York: Penguin).

Riordan, Steve, ed. 1989. *Clio Awards: Part I: A Tribute to 30 Years of Advertising Excellence 1960–1989* (New York: CLIO Enterprises).

Rutherford, Paul. 1990. *When Television Was Young: Primetime Canada 1952–1967* (Toronto: University of Toronto Press).

Stewart, David, and David Furse. 1986. *Effective Television Advertising: A Study of 1000 Commercials* (Lexington: Lexington Books).

Van Den Haag, Ernest. 1957. 'Of Happiness and of Despair We Have No Measure' in *Mass Culture: The Popular Arts in America,* edited by Bernard Rosenberg and David Manning White (New York: Free Press).

Wilson, H.H. 1961. *Pressure Group: The Campaign for Commercial Television* (London: Secker & Warburg).

Wolfe, Morris. 1985. *Jolts: The TV Wasteland and the Canadian Oasis* (Toronto: James Lorimer & Company).

Index